Quality of Service in ATM Networks

ISBN 0-13-095387-3

9 780130 953872

90000

Quality of Service in ATM Networks:
State-of-the-Art Traffic Management

Natalie Giroux

Newbridge Networks Corporation

Sudhakar Ganti

Newbridge Networks Corporation

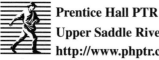

Prentice Hall PTR
Upper Saddle River, NJ 07458
http://www.phptr.com/

Library of Congress Cataloging-in-Publication Data

Giroux, Natalie.

    Quality of service in ATM networks : state-of-the-art traffic
management / Natalie Giroux, Sudhakar Ganti.

      p. cm.

    Includes bibliographical references and index.

    ISBN 0-13-095387-3

    1. Asynchronous transfer mode.   2. Telecommunication--Traffic.
I. Ganti, Sudhakar. II. Title.

TK5105.35.G58   1998

004.6'6--dc21   98-40883

                                         CIP

Editorial/Production Supervision: *Precision Graphics*
Acquisitions Editor: *Mary Franz*
Marketing Manager: *Miles Williams*
Cover Design: *Design Source*
Cover Design Direction: *Jerry Votta*
Manufacturing Manager: *Alexis R. Heydt*

 © 1999 Prentice Hall PTR
Prentice-Hall, Inc.
A Simon & Schuster Company
Upper Saddle River, NJ 07458

Prentice Hall books are widely used by corporations and government agencies
for training, marketing, and resale.

The publisher offers discounts on this book when ordered in bulk quantities.
For more information, contact Corporate Sales Department, phone: 800-382-3419;
fax: 201-236-7141; e-mail: corpsales@prenhall.com or write:
Prentice Hall PTR
Corporate Sales Department
One Lake Street
Upper Saddle River, NJ 07458

Printed in the United States of America
10 9 8 7 6 5 4 3 2 1

ISBN 0-13-095387-3

Prentice-Hall International (UK) Limited, **London**
Prentice-Hall of Australia Pty. Limited, **Sydney**
Prentice-Hall Canada Inc., **Toronto**
Prentice-Hall Hispanoamericana, S.A., **Mexico**
Prentice-Hall of India Private Limited, **New Delhi**
Prentice-Hall of Japan, Inc., **Tokyo**
Simon & Schuster Asia Pte. Ltd., **Singapore**
Editora Prentice-Hall do Brasil, Ltda., **Rio de Janeiro**

A mon père et ma mère (NG)
To Amma and Nanna (SG)

CONTENTS

4   Connection Admission Control   62

5   Queuing and Scheduling   85

6   ABR Flow Control   122

Appendices

Over the past decade there has been tremendous momentum in the development and standardization of the Asynchronous Transfer Mode (ATM) technology with a very strong focus on its traffic management (TM) capability. ATM has become a networking technology capable of integrating different types of networks into a single, consolidated, broadband network.

The objective of this book is to demystify the ATM traffic management strategy. The book provides a structured, detailed description of all the TM functions needed to efficiently support a wide range of services in a single network. Although this book focuses specifically on ATM traffic management strategy, the general concepts also apply to any networking technology that attempts to support multiple services with varying quality-of-service objectives.

The book describes and explains the content of the ATM Forum and ITU-T* traffic management specifications and standards. It also covers in detail the elements that are not subject for standardization. Thorough literature review and analysis provide insight into possible implementation of the TM concepts. Specifically, conformance, admission control, scheduling, flow control, and congestion control are discussed in detail. The book also discusses how other networking technologies such as Frame Relay and the Internet Protocol (IP) can be carried efficiently on an ATM network.

The book also provides highly technical and mathematical material useful for readers familiar with the subject.

Acknowledgments

Natalie Giroux would like to thank Alan Bryenton for continuous support, encouragement, and insightful comments. Sudhakar Ganti would like to thank Sridevi and Pranav Ganti for their support and encouragement during the course of this work.

*ITU-T—International Telecommunication Union–Telecommunication Standardization Sector

The authors would like to express their gratitude to Newbridge Networks Corporation for allowing them to accomplish this project. The authors would also like to acknowledge the contribution of the following individuals: Louis Wojnarowski, Emmanuel Desmet, Vijay Samalam, Shawn McAllister, Subha Ramanan, Tom Davis, Mustapha Aissaoui, Bryan Morris, Steve Rosenberg, Marie-Claude Bonneau, and other members of the Newbridge Performance Engineering group; Scott Brim, Mike Gassewitz, and Keith Galway. Finally, the authors would like to thank the reviewers of the book for their thorough reviews.

This book represents the views of the authors, and cannot be attributed to their employer, Newbridge Networks Corporation.

Natalie Giroux
Sudhakar Ganti

Quality of Service
in ATM Networks

The Challenges of Managing ATM Traffic

Internet, World Wide Web, telephony, desktop video conferencing, video on demand, telemedicine, and many other popular networking applications impose an ever increasing demand for bandwidth and simultaneous support of different types of service on the same telecommunication network. To meet these demands, a new generation of high-performance networks is being deployed. A technology of choice used to deploy the next generation networks is Asynchronous Transfer Mode (ATM). It has been designed to meet the end users' and the network providers' sophisticated set of requirements[ADA97].

Network users want access to large amount of bandwidth as soon as needed and as cheaply as possible. Many require the capability of routing traffic generated by legacy protocols (e.g., IP or Frame Relay) over high-speed links. The transmission links accessing the network have a wide variety of data rates (e.g., 1.5 Mbps to 622 Mbps). Some of the applications require very low latency, while other applications cannot tolerate loss of information but can support reasonable delays. Users also want a *predictable and consistent* level of quality when using a service.

Quality of service (QoS) becomes a key factor in the deployment of the next generation networks. QoS differentiates the services from one and another. A service is advertised to be of a certain quality if it can consistently meet the same level of quality for a given set of measurable parameters. In plain old telephone systems (POTS), for example, QoS is measured in terms of delay to obtain dial tone, delay to set up the connection, trunk availability, quality of sound (e.g., noise, echo), and reliability of the connection. On the other hand, the internet was designed as a "best-effort" network, and did not originally intend to make any QoS commitments. The Internet is, however, rapidly evolving toward support of QoS to handle the diverse mixture of application requirements. The current Internet best-effort philosophy is quickly becoming unacceptable because the quality degrades rapidly as the network grows. Simply deploying larger bandwidth links or extremely large buffers cannot provide QoS guarantees.

The network providers are, in turn, faced with a set of conflicting requirements when deploying the next generation networks. Worldwide deregulation of the networking services

means offering competitive, creative, and flexible pricing while satisfying the end users' requirements. In order to be competitive, network providers will have to maximize network efficiency
while meeting the specific QoS needs of the applications. The networks must also be capable of
sharing bandwidth fairly among users and need to ensure that any given user traffic cannot affect
the QoS of other users. In addition, the networks have to be capable of converting traffic coming
from various networking protocols and must carry them efficiently on a single network infrastructure. Network operators also want to deploy the network using products from multiple vendors, which therefore have to interoperate seamlessly. The networks have to support permanent
connections as well as switched connections, which have very different holding-time and utilization characteristics. Permanent connections are not set up and torn down frequently, but the
link bandwidth may not be utilized at all times. In contrast, switched connections are set up and
torn down frequently and the link bandwidth is generally highly utilized during the lifetime of
the connection. Because of the diversity in the link speeds both in the access to the network and
in the trunks, large speed mismatches need to be handled efficiently.

   The inherent conflict created by the need to optimize bandwidth while ensuring different
QoS can be resolved by using a combination of traffic control or *traffic management* techniques.
The ATM technology, with its sophisticated *traffic management* capabilities, is the key to meeting these conflicting objectives. Furthermore, ATM can handle diverse access speeds and adapt
easily to non-native ATM traffic while consolidating traffic from various protocols over a single
network infrastructure.

   Other technologies, such as Time Division Multiplexing (TDM), do not require such complex traffic control functions. Since users are assigned fixed time slots, quality of service is
deterministic and predictable (except for transmission errors and call blocking) and one user
cannot affect the QoS of another user. There is no contention for bandwidth or resources, other
than the access to time slots that could impact the capability of setting up a connection. However, the TDM technology does not allow a network operator to meet the important goal of maximizing bandwidth usage. Many applications (e.g., file transfer, WWW, email) require variable
amount of bandwidth for the duration of their data transmission. Such applications are referred
to as *bursty*. The TDM technology requires static allocation of the highest possible bandwidth
requirement for the duration of the call. Such over-allocation of bandwidth leads to severe inef-
ficiencies, because the bandwidth unused by idle or slower connections could be used by other
users who would benefit from an increased transmission rate. That is, in TDM the time slots are
allocated to a connection even if the user is not sending any data. The time slots cannot be
reused until the connection is torn down. Because of the static allocation of time slots, the TDM
technology is not efficient for carrying bursty data traffic. However it is very efficient for carrying voice traffic [FLA91].

   Another technology, designed to carry data, is generally called *packet switching*. Packet
switching carries data without setting up a connection (e.g., Internet Protocol - IP). Packets are
routed on a hop-by-hop basis, and no bandwidth is preallocated for a given connection. This
technology has the capability to maximize the bandwidth usage but cannot guarantee specific

quality to a given connection since the path is not known and the bandwidth required is not allocated.

ATM combines the connection-oriented approach of TDM enhanced with flexible traffic management functions to maximize bandwidth utilization while supporting a flexible set of services offering different QoS. ATM also allows connections to specify their bandwidth requirement with a fine granularity. The complexity of managing traffic in an ATM network arises because of the attempt to maximize efficiency by statistical multiplexing of bursty traffic generated from several sources and services types.

ATM traffic management (TM) functions are designed to prevent the network and the end system from becoming overloaded, but if overload does occur, the TM functions can react to the congestion so as to maintain QoS objectives while maximizing the use of network resources. TM functions can be implemented in a more or less complex way to achieve higher or lower levels of network efficiency, respectively: Increased complexity allows more efficient use of the bandwidth and increased fairness in the bandwidth allocation among connections of various types.

It should be noted that the complexity of managing ATM traffic is not inherent to ATM technology. The complexity arises from trying to resolve the conflicting goals of guaranteeing QoS and maximizing network utilization. Other data technologies, such as IP and frame relay, do not currently require such a high level of sophistication, but as those technologies aspire to support and consistently provide different levels of service quality, they will have to develop the technology to handle a similar set of traffic management functions. IP is already developing concepts of a reservation protocol, DIFFerentiated SERVices and others, in order to support QoS. In order to differentiate services, IP will eventually need to support a set of traffic management components similar to the set currently defined for ATM. Because of the fixed cell size, the implementation of these TM functions is simpler for ATM than for other technologies which deal with variable size data units; furthermore, the standardization of the basic TM functionality of ATM is completed.

This book provides a detailed description of the traffic management capability of ATM and explores various techniques that can be used to implement the traffic control functions. It is assumed that the reader has a basic understanding of ATM technology. This chapter provides a basic overview of the technology, focusing on the concepts related to traffic management. The reader is referred to [MCD94, ADA97] for an introduction to the ATM technology.

Standardization of ATM Traffic Management

In order for equipment from multiple vendors to co-exist in a single network, some of the traffic management functions and procedures need to be defined in such a way as to allow interoperability. Two major organizations are responsible for ensuring interoperability of the traffic management aspects of ATM: the ITU-T Study Group XIII/ working party 2 and the ATM Forum Traffic Management working group. The ITU-T sets formal standards. The ATM Forum is an organization created by a group of companies (vendors, network/service providers, users) to develop *interoperability specifications*.

These two organizations work in parallel and consult each other in order to define the proper set of functionality required to achieve TM interoperability. In April 1996 the ATM Forum ratified its first standalone traffic management specification [TM4.0], which included the elements previously documented as part of the User-Network Interface specification [UNI3.1, Sec. 3.6]. In May 1996 the ITU-T approved an updated version of the traffic management standard for ATM [I.371]. In June 1997 the ITU-T released [I.371.1], an extension of [I.371]. The next release of [I.371] will merge both documents. The ITU-T developed recommendation [I.356], covering the QoS aspects, in parallel to [I.371]. The [I.371] combined with the [I.356] align with [TM4.0] on a common set of functions, although each document also covers specific functions not recognized by the other organization. The terminology adopted by the two organizations also differs in some cases.

This book uses the ATM Forum terminology unless otherwise specified. Appendix A provides a comparison between the contents of [I.371], [I.356], and [TM4.0].

Components of Traffic Management

ATM traffic management (TM) can be divided into layers of functions and procedures. Figure 1.1 depicts the relationship of the ATM layer traffic management components. The objective of this book is to describe each component in detail and how it relates to the others.

An application negotiates a traffic contract with the network for each virtual connection. The *traffic contract* is an agreement on the behavior of the traffic and the level of service that is required for the connection. One key element of the traffic contract is the service category. Any application using an ATM network maps virtual connections into an appropriate ATM layer *service category*. A service category defines the expected quality of service (QoS) class and also specifies the expected behavior of the traffic generated by the application (*traffic descriptors*). The traffic contract is discussed in detail in Chap. 2. Once the traffic contract is defined for a connection, the network applies a *connection admission* algorithm to evaluate whether the connection can be admitted and achieve the expected QoS but without jeopardizing the QoS of previously established connections. Connection admission control (CAC), discussed in detail in Chap. 4, is a complex function that has direct impact on network efficiency. If the connection is accepted, then the cells can start to flow in the network. In order to guarantee that QoS is maintained for both new connection and existing ones, the network has to ensure that the connection's traffic follows the traffic contract. Therefore the network can apply to the traffic flow *conformance monitoring* functions (Chap. 3) to ensure that a misbehaving user cannot affect the QoS of other users. Conformance monitoring is presented before the connection admission control chapter because it introduces many useful concepts.

The traffic that successfully passes through the conformance monitoring function enters the network and is multiplexed at different points. In order to achieve statistical multiplexing gains (see Chap. 4), the traffic may be *queued or buffered* before being transmitted on intermediate links. The queues are serviced according to a *scheduling algorithm* specifically designed to meet the QoS of the different types of connections. Queuing and scheduling functions are

Figure 1.1.   Relationship of traffic management functions.

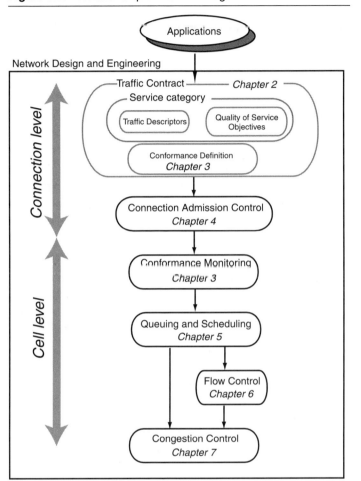

described in Chap. 5. Although connection admission is performed at connection setup, congestion in network elements (overflowing of the buffers) can still occur. Congestion is caused by statistical overlap of traffic bursts at a contention point. *Congestion control* deals with the handling of traffic arriving at a contention point to ensure that cells are discarded in a fair manner and that QoS is guaranteed. Congestion control functions are described in Chap. 7. Scheduling deals with cells departing from a contention point by arbitrating between a number of queues in order to provide the required QoS and to allocate bandwidth fairly according to specific policies. For some services the network and the end systems implement a *flow control* procedure (Chap. 6). Flow control allows the network to prevent congestion by conveying information to the end systems that react appropriately.

Network design and engineering is performed prior to commissioning the network and is refined periodically to adapt to network evolution. Network design includes capacity planning, reliability, and survivability issues. Network engineering considers, among other things, how to tune the different traffic management parameters (e.g., CAC) based on measured utilization so that better use of the resources can be achieved. Network design and engineering is not, however, within the scope of this book.

The traffic management functions act in different time scales to achieve the objectives stated above. The CAC is applied per connection when the connection is set up, while the conformance monitoring, queuing/scheduling, and congestion/flow control are applied on a cell-by-cell basis. The CAC, conformance monitoring, queuing/scheduling, and flow control are referred to as *preventive* controls or *congestion avoidance*, and are designed to prevent congestion from happening. The congestion control techniques are referred to as *reactive* control mechanisms, which are applied when congestion cannot be avoided [WOO88, WOO90, ECK92].

Basic ATM Principles

This section reviews basic principles of the ATM technology. This description provides the reader with enough elements to understand the traffic management concepts presented in this book. The reader should refer to [MCD94] for more details on the ATM technology.

ATM uses fixed-size transfer units called *cells* as the basic transfer unit. ATM users establish virtual connections (VC) to carry cells from a given source to a given destination. Multiple VCs can be bundled together into a virtual path (VP) to simplify the management of the networks by reducing the number of elements to manage. Each connection has a unique identifier, of local significance, obtained by combining the VC identification and the VP identification. Connections can be set up as permanent virtual connection (PVC) via a network management system. Alternatively, connections that can be dynamically set up and torn down are referred to as switched virtual connections (SVC) [SIG4.0]. Routes can be determined, for example, using the private network–network interface (PNNI) routing protocol [PNNI1.0] or via static routing tables.

Some switches support VCs and VPs, while a VP switch supports only VPs and is not aware of the VCs that are using the VP. Such switches do not perform the call processing of the VCs and do not maintain any VC information.

Applications generally access the ATM transport layer via an *ATM adaptation layer* (AAL). The most commonly used adaptation layers are AAL1 and AAL5. AAL1 is used for traffic that requires timing synchronization (e.g., to emulate voice circuits). The AAL5 is used to carry data that has no timing requirements.

An ATM cell has a fixed size of 53 bytes. The cell has 48 bytes of payload and 5 bytes for the header. The ATM cell header uses

- 24 bits for the connection identifier (VP/VC identification),
- 4 bits for generic flow control (GFC),
- 3 bits to identify the payload type (PT),

• 1 bit to indicate the cell loss priority (CLP),
• 8 bits for cyclic redundancy check (CRC) code.

   Figure 1.2 depicts the format of an ATM cell.

   The VCI/VPI field is used to identify the connection. It contains a virtual connection identifier (VCI) and a virtual path identifier (VPI).

   The GFC field is designed to control the rate of a terminal using a stop-and-go flow control scheme [I.371]. The GFC rate control capability is not used by the ATM Forum specifications.

   The CRC is used to detect errors in the header to prevent sending a cell to the wrong destination (cell misinsertion). In case of single-bit errors, the CRC may be used to correct the error [UNI3.1].

   The payload is not protected by the CRC located in the header. The payload type (PT) identifies whether the payload contains user data, signaling, or maintenance information. A user data cell has the first bit of the PT set to zero; the second bit is the *explicit forward congestion indication* (EFCI), which when enabled indicates that congestion is impending in the path. This bit can be used for flow control (Chap. 6). The last bit is enabled when using AAL5 to indicate that the cell is the last cell of a higher-layer protocol data unit (PDU). This information is useful to implement frame-level discard schemes (Chap. 7).

   The CLP bit is enabled (e.g., set to a one) to indicate that a cell has a lower discard priority than a cell with the bit set to zero. Generally, lower discard priority cells are not guaranteed to receive the agreed QoS and are discarded first when congestion is impending (Chap. 7), although under some exceptions the CLP bit is ignored (see Chap. 3 for CLP transparency).

   An application can *mark* or *tag* specific cells as lower discard priority cells, if their nondelivery does not degrade the quality below an acceptable level [FOR77] and if the nondelivered

Figure 1.2. ATM cell format. Source: [UNI3.1] The ATM Forum Technical Committee. *User-Network Interface Specification,* version 3.1, 1994. Copyright © 1994 The ATM Forum. Used with permission.

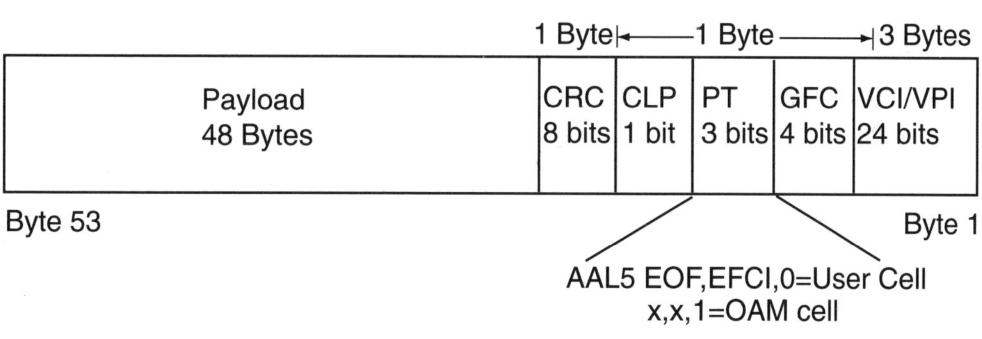

			1 Byte	←——1 Byte——→	3 Bytes
Payload 48 Bytes	CRC 8 bits	CLP 1 bit	PT 3 bits	GFC 4 bits	VCI/VPI 24 bits

Byte 53   Byte 1

AAL5 EOF,EFCI,0=User Cell
x,x,1=OAM cell

cells do not get retransmitted by the application. If the connection does not conform to the contracted traffic descriptors, the network may also lower the priority of a cell (Chap. 3) by setting the CLP bit to one. This action is referred to as *tagging* a cell.

Special cells, referred to as operation administration and maintenance (OAM) cells, can be inserted by the user or the network among the user's data cells. These cells are used, for example, to measure performance of the connection or to test connectivity.

Some protocols use other special cells, referred to as resource management (RM) cells to control the flow of the traffic (Chap. 7) or to reserve bandwidth (App. A).

Figure 1.3 describes some of the terminology used in the rest of this book. The user-to-network interface (UNI) is the interface between a user or private network and a public network. The broadband intercarrier interface (BICI) is the interface between two public networks, and the ATM Internetwork interface (AINI) is the interface between two networks (private or public) implementing the PNNI protocol [PNNI1.0]. A network-to-network interface (NNI) is the generic name of an interface between two networks.

In this book, unless otherwise specified, the following terminology and conventions are used:

- Switch A is said to be located *upstream* from switch B, and conversely, switch B is located *downstream* from switch A (see Fig. 1.3).

Figure 1.3.   Network interfaces and terminology.

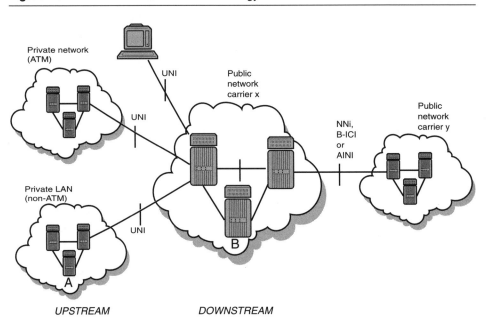

- In the graphical network examples, for simplification the traffic is unidirectional and flows from left to right. For example, in Fig. 1.3, traffic flows from switch A to switch B.
- Examples are expressed in *time units* that can be translated to any line speeds.

Review

The ATM technology is unique in that it supports on a single network multiple applications requiring a wide range of different qualities of service (QoS). In order to support QoS guarantees and allow for efficient use of resources, the network needs to support a rich set of traffic management capabilities. This book offers a comprehensive description of the traffic management capability defined for ATM. It covers functionality described in the standards [I.356, I.371] and interoperability specifications [TM4.0], along with other proprietary functions that can be implemented in order to provide increased control, flexibility, fairness, and resource optimization.

References

[ADA97] Adams, J. *ATM for Service Providers.* London: Chapman & Hall, 1997.

[ECK92] Eckberg, A.E. "B-ISDN/ATM Traffic and Congestion Control." *IEEE Network,* September 1992.

[FOR77] Forgie, J., and Nemeth, A.G. *An Efficient Packetized Voice Data Network Using Statistical Flow Control.* ICC, June 1977.

[FLA91] Flanagan, W. *Frames, Packets and Cells in Broadband Networks.* New York: Telecom Library, 1991.

[I.356] ITU-Telecommunication Standardization Sector. *B-ATM Layer Cell Transfer Performance,* recommendation I.356. October 1996.

[I.371.1] ITU-Telecommunication Standardization Sector. *Traffic Control and Congestion Control in B-ISDN-ABR and ABT Conformance Definitions,* recommendation I.371.1, June 1997.

[I.371] ITU-Telecommunication Standardization Sector. *Traffic Control and Congestion Control in B-ISDN,* recommendation I.371, May 1996.

[MCD94] McDysan, D.E., and Spohn, D.L. *ATM, Theory and Application,* McGraw-Hill Series on Computer Communications, 1994.

[PNNI1.0] The ATM Forum Technical Committee. *Private Network-Network Interface Specification,* version 1.0, 1996.

[SIG4.0] The ATM Forum Technical Committee. *User-Network Interface Signaling Specification,* version 4.0, 1996.

[TM4.0] The ATM Forum Technical Committee. *Traffic Management Specification,* version 4.0, af-tm-0056.000, April 1996.

[UNI3.1] The ATM Forum Technical Committee. *User-Network Interface Specification,* version 3.1, 1994.

[WOO88] Woodroff, G.M., Rogers, R., and Richards, P. "A Congestion Control Framework for High Speed Integrated Packetized Networks." *Proceedings of IEEE Globecom* (1988), 203–207.

[WOO90] Woodruff, G., and Kositpaiboon, R. "Multimedia Traffic Management Principles for Guaranteed ATM Network Performance." *IEEE Journal on Selected Areas in Telecommunications,* vol. 8, no. 3 (April 1990).

The Traffic Contract

The increasing need for efficient communication has led to the creation of a large number of applications. The Internet, World Wide Web browsing, telemedicine, and teleconferencing are only a small subset of the rapidly growing set of applications. These applications have varying bandwidth needs, traffic characteristics, and *end-to-end* performance requirements. *End-to-end* comprises all elements of the network(s) between the source of the traffic and the recipient(s). Previous generations of networks evolved by handling different types of applications using separate network infrastructures or overlays (e.g., telephony, leased lines, frame relay, etc). Each network is separately managed and uses different switching equipment and transmission links. Significant infrastructure, management, and real estate cost savings can be achieved by consolidating all of the services offered onto one network. ATM allows implementation of such a consolidated network, since it can simultaneously support the quality of service required by any existing applications as well as any foreseeable new applications—through the selection of an appropriate *service category*.

An application using an ATM network conveys its bandwidth and performance requirements (via signaling for SVC or via the network management system for PVC) by means of the traffic contract. The traffic contract includes the following components:

- the service category,
- the required quality of service (QoS),
- the traffic characteristics of the connection,
- the definition of how the traffic should behave (conformance definition).

This chapter describes the first three components of the traffic contract, how they are negotiated within the network, and how the quality of the service is measured. The conformance definition is discussed in Chap. 3.

Service Categories

In order to efficiently support this multi-application environment in a potentially multivendor network, a set of predefined ATM layer service categories has been standardized. The ATM service categories are defined to cover the spectrum of current and potential future applications using the ATM network. Services offer different QoS commitments in terms of delay and loss tolerance. The services also differ in how the network allocates bandwidth and applies different traffic management functions. The service categories are:

- constant bit rate (CBR) service,
- variable bit rate (VBR) service,
- available bit rate (ABR) service,
- guaranteed frame rate (GFR) service,
- unspecified bit rate (UBR) service.

For CBR and VBR services, bandwidth is allocated by the connection admission control (CAC) for the duration of the connection, even though the connection may not use it all the time. In order to build cost-effective networks, there is a need to maximize the utilization of the bandwidth, which becomes dynamically available as connections go idle. The ABR, GFR, and UBR services target the dynamically available bandwidth for use, although in the case of ABR and GFR some minimum amount of bandwidth can also be statically allocated. These services are referred to as *bandwidth-on-demand* services. The goal of bandwidth-on-demand services is to acquire as fast as possible a fair share of the bandwidth that is dynamically available in the network. Unlike UBR, the ABR and GFR services can guarantee that the network carries a minimal amount of bandwidth. The ABR service includes a well-defined closed-loop flow control protocol that aims at minimizing the cell loss within the network. The GFR and UBR services do not control the flow of traffic but rely on higher-layer protocols (e.g., transmission control protocol—TCP) to perform the flow control (Chap. 9).

CBR Service

Real-time applications are predominantly those that contain video or audio information. These applications have stringent delay requirements and the end systems may be sensitive to variations in the end-to-end transmission delay. The application may be bursty in nature, but the peak bandwidth is statically allocated for the duration of the connection even though it may not be needed constantly.

The constant bit rate (CBR) service is designed to support real-time applications. It provides the connection with dedicated bandwidth providing extremely low probability of cell loss, as well as low and predictable delay. The inter-arrival time between two cells is constant and can be characterized as a minimum cell inter-arrival, which corresponds to a known peak emission rate, referred to as the peak cell rate (PCR). The CBR connection may not use the allocated bandwidth constantly, but when needed it is made available instantly in order to meet the delay/jitter requirements. Generally, the peak bandwidth of the connection is allocated statically and no statistical gains are achieved within this service. However, some level of statistical gains can be achieved by overbooking the resources (Chap. 4).

VBR Service

The VBR service category is mainly intended for more efficient support of video applications and frame relay traffic or any other applications that have known or predictable bursty traffic characteristics. VBR traffic can be characterized by a sustained cell rate (SCR), and a peak cell rate (PCR). The SCR is measured over a defined period and represents the average transmission rate. The PCR represents the minimum spacing of the cells, which represents the peak bandwidth required. Generally, the average transmission rate allows the realization of some statistical gain by statically allocating an amount of bandwidth lower than the peak bandwidth and higher or equal to the average bandwidth (Chap. 4). The VBR service is further divided into two subcategories based on the delay requirements of the applications. The subcategories are referred to as real-time VBR (rt-VBR) and non-real–time VBR (nrt-VBR). The rt-VBR traffic has strict end-to-end delay requirements and therefore cannot be extensively buffered in the network. The nrt-VBR traffic does not guarantee any delay bounds and therefore can be buffered more extensively. The difference in buffer size impacts the amount of bandwidth that is allocated (Chap. 4).

A data application using a nrt-VBR service can be modeled as an ON/OFF source. During the ON period, called the *burst*, cells are generated with a constant inter-arrival time based on a peak emission rate. No cells are generated during the OFF period. The average and peak emission rate requirements can therefore be characterized. The ON period could represent the transmission of a higher-layer protocol data unit (PDU). Figure 2.1 depicts an example of an ON/OFF source transmission rate over time. In this example, the source sends frames at a peak emission rate that is lower than the physical media rate (e.g., due to software limitations or traffic shaping—see Chap. 3). The source is then silent for a period of time before transmitting the next frame.

Video is a typical application for the rt-VBR service. It demonstrates a variable transmission rate without the ON/OFF nature of a data application. In this case, the source rate fluctuates dynamically without exceeding a known peak rate and a predetermined average emission rate. In this example, increases in transmission rate can be caused by increases in the action in the video scene [TAN92]. Figure 2.2 demonstrates this behavior.

Since the average emission rate is known with the VBR service, statistical gains can be achieved by allocating an amount of resources lower than the peak emission rate and using buffers to handle potential overlap of bursts. The CAC (Chap. 4) attempts to minimize the amount of bandwidth allocated while meeting the committed QoS objectives.

Figure 2.1.   Example of ON/OFF behavior.

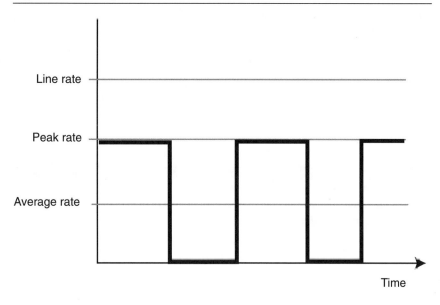

Figure 2.2.   Example of dynamic rate behavior.

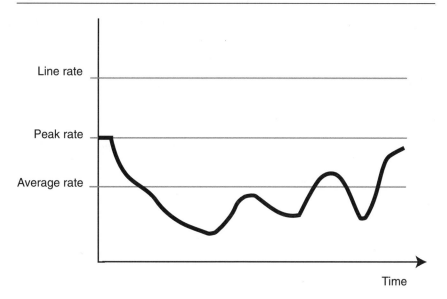

Bandwidth-on-Demand Services

Some data applications do not have a priori knowledge of the required traffic characteristics (other than possibly a peak emission rate) prior to setting up the connection. They do not have real-time delay constraints, and are moderately sensitive to loss. Such applications are good candidates for using one of the bandwidth-on-demand services (ABR, GFR or UBR). End-to-end protocols, such as TCP, regulate the flow of traffic based on packet loss above the ATM layer. Applications making use of such protocols can benefit from the the bandwidth-on-demand services (Chap. 8).

ABR Service

The ABR service can guarantee a minimum amount of bandwidth and may be limited to a specified peak emission rate. The ABR traffic source (e.g., end system or ATM interworking unit) participates actively in a well-defined flow control protocol in order to minimize the potential for cell or frame loss in the network. Using the ABR service, the congestion is pushed from the network to its edges [BON95a, BON95b]. The bandwidth adjustment is done via a specified rate-based flow control mechanism (Chap. 6), and all connections need to follow the protocol in order to minimize the cell loss.

GFR Service

The GFR service does not require adherence to a flow control protocol. The service does guarantee a minimum amount of bandwidth but does not make any commitment regarding the amount of loss when the application exceeds the minimum guaranteed. The GFR service is designed to deal with protocol data units (PDU) from layers above the AAL (e.g., AAL-5). The network aims at discarding complete PDUs instead of dropping cells randomly under congestion (Chap. 7). The GFR service is not part of [TM4.0] and is still being developed by the ATM Forum and the ITU-T. The description contained in this book may change as the specification and the standard reach completion.

UBR Service

The UBR service is very simple in terms of traffic management functionality. That is, UBR connections share the remaining bandwidth without using any specific feedback mechanism. With this service, the application accesses as much bandwidth as the network can provide but it is willing to tolerate an unspecified level of cell loss. This service is often referred to as a "best-effort" service.

The simple UBR service can be enhanced with more sophisticated traffic management features, such as frame discard (Chap. 7), to significantly increase the network capability to carry good packets of data or *goodput*.

The effective QoS of the UBR service can be managed via engineering rules, for example, by limiting the number of connections sharing the remaining bandwidth.

Quality-of-Service Parameters

The ATM layer quality of service (QoS) is defined by a set of parameters characterizing the performance requirements of a connection. These QoS parameters quantify end-to-end network performance requirements at the ATM layer. End-to-end performance combines the performance of all the elements in the network. Figure 2.3 depicts a reference network model showing how QoS applies to the nodal, network, and end-to-end level. The traffic contract defines QoS in terms of end-to-end objectives, that is, between the limits of the ATM network but excluding the end systems.

Figure 2.3. Reference network model.

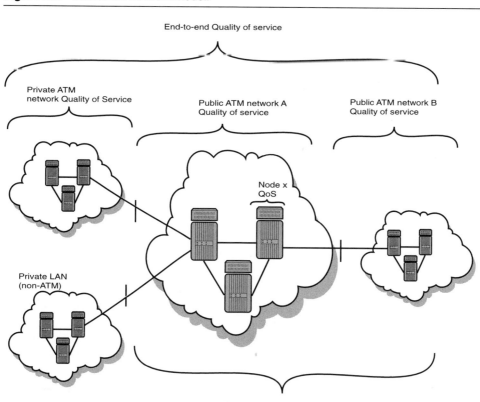

Six QoS parameters are used to measure the performance of the network for a given connection. Three of these may be negotiated between the end-systems and the networks as part of the traffic contract:

- cell loss ratio (CLR)
- maximum cell transfer delay (Max-CTD)
- peak-to-peak cell delay variation (P2P-CDV)

Three other QoS parameters are not negotiable as part of the traffic contract:

- cell error ratio (CER)
- severely errored cell block ratio (SECBR)
- cell misinsertion rate (CMR)

Cell Loss Ratio (CLR)

Cell loss occurs because of overrun of buffering resources due to simultaneous arrivals of bursts from different connections. CAC scheduling and queuing strategies can have an effect on the amount of cell loss. Cell loss may also occur during failure of components and protection switching (e.g., switching over to redundant links during failure). The cell loss ratio is defined on a per connection basis as

$$CLR = \frac{\text{Lost cells}}{\text{Total transmitted cells}} \qquad (2.1)$$

where lost cells include

- the number of cells that did not reach the destination
- the number of cells that were received with an invalid header
- the number of cells for which the content has been corrupted by errors

The total-transmitted-cells is the total number of *conforming* cells transmitted over a time period. The CLR does not account for the cells that are not conforming to the traffic descriptors (Chap. 3) [I.356, Sec. 7].

The measuring period is not standardized but is generally understood as representing the lifetime of the connection. For PVCs, the measuring period is defined by the network operator and is usually large enough to account for short transient congestion periods.

The CLR can be measured for either the (CLP = 0) cells or the aggregate of the cells (with CLP = 0 and CLP = 1), as determined by the applicable conformance definition (Chap. 3).

Delay Parameters

The measured cell transfer delay (CTD) is defined as the time elapsed between the departure time of a cell from the generating end-system and the arrival time at the destination. Figure 2.4 depicts the components of the CTD on a generic node with input and output queuing (refer to Chap. 5 for a discussion of different switching architectures).

The cell transfer delay (CTD) through a network is the accumulation of the cell transfer delays at each node in the path. The CTD encountered at a node includes *internal delays* (due to one or more internal queuing points, switching, processing, and internal transmission link) and *external queuing and transmission delays* encountered prior to exiting the node. Other *processing delays* may be added to these. Once on the link, *propagation delay* also adds to the CTD.

- The *internal queuing and transmission delay* is the time required to queue and transmit the bits on the internal links of the node. The distribution of the queuing delay varies as a function of the load and the type of scheduling algorithm used (Chap. 5). The switch architecture may require zero or many internal queuing stages, with potentially different internal link rates.

Figure 2.4.   Components of cell transfer delay.

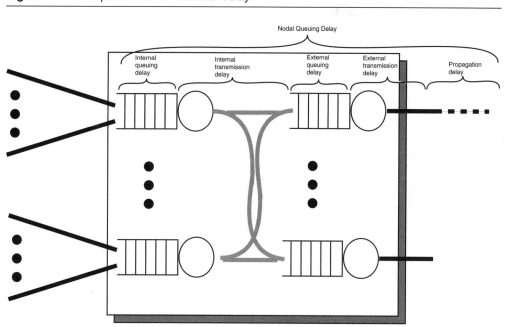

- The *external queuing and transmission delay* is the time required to queue and transmit the bits on the external interface (or output link). The distribution of the queuing delay varies as a function of the load and the scheduling algorithm used at the queuing point (Chap. 5).
- The *propagation delay* is the time required for the bits to propagate on the physical media. A key factor of the propagation delay is the time it takes for a signal to travel between two nodes. Depending on the medium used, electromagnetic signals typically propagate at 0.2 to 0.6 of the speed of light. This factor can become significant over long distances. The propagation delay is calculated as distance/(propagation factor × speed of light), where 0.2 < propagation factor < 0.6.
- *Processing delay* represents non-negligible delays required to process the cell (e.g., to analyze the header).

The minimum CTD is composed of the nonvariable elements of the CTD, that is, the CTD encountered by a single cell traversing the node without being queued. The minimum CTD can be calculated as the sum of the internal, external, processing, and propagation delays over all the links of a node.

Because of the statistical nature of ATM, the queuing delay varies from one cell to another, thus creating variation in the cell delay measure. This variation is referred to as *cell delay variation* (CDV). Because of the CDV, a constantly spaced stream of cells entering a queuing point may result in a bursty (or clumped) stream of cells. This phenomenon affects, for example, the size of the buffers in video receivers and can impact the quality of the image by starving or overflowing the receiver. It can also affect the quality of voice carried over ATM. Different switching architectures and scheduling algorithms impact the variability of the queuing delay.

Figure 2.5 depicts the impact of queuing on the traffic characteristics. In this example, VC1 is multiplexed with six other VCs with different contracted PCR. In this example the input and output links are all of the same speed. The arrival of the first cell of the other six VCs are synchronized, causing queuing to occur, which disturbs the cell flow of VC1.

CDV is a phenomenon that arises at any queuing point partly as a function of the queue size but mainly as a function of the queue scheduling strategy (Chap. 5) employed.

The CDV QoS parameter is easily confused with the cell delay variation tolerance (CDVT), which is a connection traffic descriptor. The CDVT is the maximum tolerated amount of CDV for a given connection beyond which the traffic is judged as non-conforming. The CDVT is discussed in detail in Chap. 3.

To capture these potential impairments in terms of meaningful achievable QoS objectives, two end-to-end QoS parameters are defined:

- maximum cell transfer delay (Max-CTD)
- peak-to-peak cell delay variation (P2P-CDV)

Figure 2.5. CDV illustration.

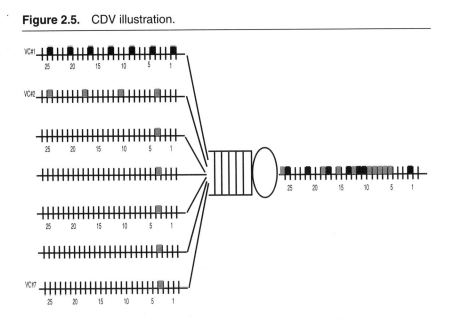

Figure 2.6 on page 20 provides an example of the probability density function of the CTD and relates the two parameters. The probability density function in Fig. 2.6 applies to the peak rate of the real-time traffic, and may not be representative of delay encountered by non–real-time traffic.

Maximum Cell Transfer Delay (Max-CTD)

The maximum cell transfer delay (Max-CTD) represents the $(1 - \alpha)$ quantile of the CTD probability density function, where the cells with delays exceeding this maximum are assumed lost or unusable. The Max-CTD includes the fixed-delay components.

The setting of the α parameter is network specific but can be done with the following procedure. Assume $maxCTD_q$ represents the delay budget allocated to a queue in the path. In order to meet this budget, the queue can be limited to a buffer size B, where

$$B = \frac{maxCTD_q}{\text{Queue Service Rate}} \qquad (2.2)$$

and where the Queue Service Rate represents the rate at which the queue is served. The CAC function uses this queue size to allocate sufficient bandwidth to ensure that the probability of exceeding this queue (e.g., dropping a cell) does not exceed the CLR. The probability of exceeding the

Figure 2.6. Cell transfer delay probability density model.

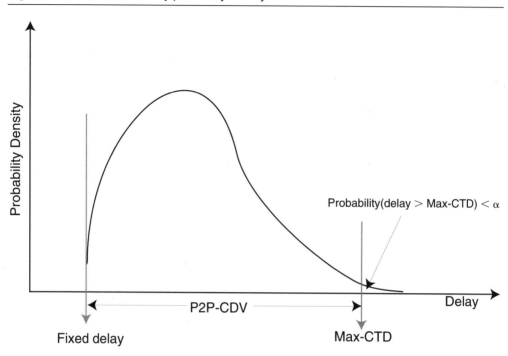

$maxCTD_q$ cannot exceed the CLR, since the cells are dropped when the queue size exceeds B. Therefore, a conservative setting for the α parameter is the CLR. It is likely that over some measurement period the queue is not loaded such that the CLR is reached, and the Max-CTD can be achieved with a lower quantile than the CLR or a lower Max-CTD can be achieved with $\alpha = $ CLR.

Peak-To-Peak Cell Delay Variation (P2P-CDV)

The P2P-CDV represents the difference between the maximum CTD and the minimum CTD (that is, the Max-CTD minus the fixed-delay components). This metric allows the evaluation of the maximum possible delay between two consecutive cells that were deterministically spaced. It also allows estimation of the worst possible amount of clumping due to queuing.

Severely Errored Cell Block Ratio

The severely errored cell block ratio (SECBR) is defined as follows for a connection:

$$\text{SECBR} = \frac{\text{Severely errored cell blocks}}{\text{Total transmitted cell blocks}} \qquad (2.3)$$

A cell block is a sequence of N cells transmitted consecutively on a given connection. A severely errored cell block occurs when more than M errored cells, lost cells, or misinserted cells are observed in a received cell block. For practical measurement purposes, a cell block normally corresponds to the number of user information cells transmitted between successive OAM cells [I.610]. Lost and transmitted cells included in the severely errored cell blocks are excluded from the CLR computation.

Cell Misinsertion Rate

The cell misinsertion rate (CMR) is defined as follows for a connection:

$$\text{CMR} = \frac{\text{Misinserted cells}}{\text{Time interval}} \qquad (2.4)$$

A misinserted cell is a cell that is carried over a VC to which it does not belong. Cell misinsertion on a particular connection is most often due to an undetected error in the header, which causes a cell to be transmitted on the wrong connection. This performance parameter is defined as a rate (rather than the ratio in Eq. 2.3) since the mechanism that produced misinserted cells is independent of the number of transmitted cells received on the corresponding connection.

The cell misinsertion rate is expected to be primarily influenced by undetected or miscorrected errors in the cell header, which in turn is influenced by the transmission error rate. The likelihood that an undetected or miscorrected error in the cell header maps into a valid VPI/VCI also depends on the number of VPI/VCI values that are assigned and are being actively used. The severely errored cell blocks are excluded from the population count when calculating the cell misinsertion rate.

Cell Error Ratio

The cell error ratio (CER) is defined as follows for a connection:

$$\text{CER} = \frac{\text{Errored cells}}{\text{Successfully transferred cells} + \text{Errored cells}} \qquad (2.5)$$

An errored cell is a cell that has had some of its content (header or payload) modified erroneously and which cannot be recovered by error correction techniques. The CER is influenced by the error characteristics of the physical media, the physical distance, and the characteristics of the media.

Traffic Descriptors

An ATM connection characterizes its traffic by using source traffic descriptors. The descriptors attempt to capture the cell inter-arrival pattern for resource allocation (Chap. 4). The source traffic descriptors for an ATM connection include one or more of the following:

- peak cell rate (PCR)
- sustainable cell rate (SCR) and maximum burst size (MBS)
- minimum cell rate (MCR)
- maximum frame size (MFS)

Each connection has two sets of connection traffic descriptors to describe the bidirectional (backward and forward) traffic characteristics. The set of traffic descriptors, which are conveyed at connection setup, varies depending on the connection service category. All source traffic descriptors can be specified only for the cells with CLP = 0, or for the aggregate of the cells of the connection irrespective of the CLP bit (CLP = 0+1). However, *conformance definitions* are specified in [TM4.0], defining a specific subset as of the possible combinations to be implemented to ensure interoperability. Conformance definitions are discussed in Chap. 3.

During the connection setup phase, a cell delay variation tolerance (CDVT) parameter is added to the source traffic descriptors. The *connection traffic descriptors* include the source traffic descriptors and the CDVT. The CDVT is used to verify the conformance of the traffic to the source traffic descriptors and is discussed in Chap. 3.

Peak Cell Rate

The peak cell rate (PCR) represents the peak emission rate of the source. The inverse of the PCR represents the theoretical minimum inter-arrival time of cells for a given connection. PCR can be limited by the physical speed (or link rate) of the source or via shaping the ingress traffic (see Chap. 3). The PCR is expressed in cell/seconds. Figure 2.7 depicts the traffic characteristics of a connection that has contracted a PCR of one-third the line rate. Each time slot rep-

Figure 2.7.   Peak cell rate.

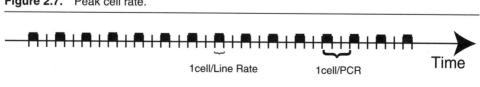

1cell/Line Rate   1cell/PCR   Time

resents the time to transmit one cell at the line rate, so a connection that contracts a PCR at one-third the line rate can send one cell every three time slots.

Except for ABR, the PCR is always defined for the aggregate (CLP = 0 and CLP = 1) cell flow. That is, the cells in Fig. 2.7, are either CLP = 0 or CLP = 1. A connection cannot exceed the PCR by sending lower priority (CLP = 1) cells. In the case of ABR, the PCR is defined only on the CLP = 0 cell flow.

Sustained Cell Rate

The sustainable cell rate (SCR) is an upper bound on the average transmission rate of the conforming cells of an ATM connection over time scales that are long relative to those for which the PCR is defined.

Connections using the VBR service can specify a SCR. The inverse of the SCR represents an upper bound on the theoretical long-term average inter-arrival time of the cells with respect to the link speed. The SCR is always specified along with a corresponding maximum burst size (MBS). The MBS parameter represents the *burstiness* factor of the connection. It specifies the maximum number of cells that can be transmitted by the source at PCR while still complying with the negotiated SCR.

Figure 2.8 provides an example of a connection that has contracted a PCR of one-half the line rate and a SCR of one-fourth the line rate with an MBS of five cells. The connection can send five cells over ten time slots, but it then remains silent for ten time slots in order to meet the average rate of one-fourth the line rate. Alternatively, the connection can send one cell every four time slots, but in this case it would not be taking advantage of the bursting capability.

The SCR can be defined for either the aggregate (CLP = 0 and CLP = 1) cell flow or for only CLP = 0. When defined for the aggregate of all the cells, the cells in Fig. 2.8 can be either CLP = 0 or CLP = 1. In this case, a connection cannot exceed the SCR by sending lower-priority (CLP = 1) cells. When the SCR is defined on the CLP = 0 flow, the connection can exceed the SCR by sending lower-priority (CLP = 1) cells, up to the PCR. Figure 2.9 demonstrates this capability.

Figure 2.8.   Sustained cell rate and maximum burst size.

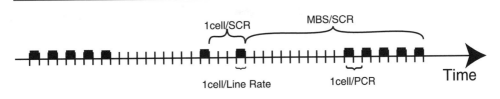

Figure 2.9. Sustained cell rate and maximum burst size.

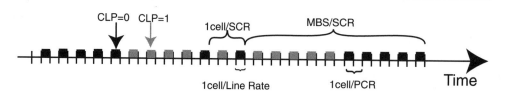

Minimum Cell Rate

The minimum cell rate (MCR) is classified as a traffic descriptor even though it represents a minimum allocated bandwidth for a connection. It does not literally describe the behavior of the traffic; that is, connections can send traffic at a much higher rate than MCR. It is used for the bandwidth-on-demand services (ABR and GFR) to ensure that a connection does not starve when there is no more available bandwidth. Since it also represents a guaranteed minimum throughput, the MCR can also be regarded as a QoS parameter.

Maximum Frame Size

The maximum frame size (MFS) defines the maximum size of an AAL protocol data unit that can be sent on a GFR connection. AAL frames exceeding this size are not eligible to receive the GFR QoS objectives.

Service Classes

In order to limit the amount of possible combinations of QoS parameters and traffic descriptors to be supported by the ATM networks, a set of predefined combinations have been standardized for each service category. Table 2.1, adapted from [TM4.0], describes the combinations. A *specified* parameter is one that is conveyed to the network at connection setup. *Not applicable (N/A)* means that the parameter is not part of the traffic contract for that service category. An *optional* parameter may be included as part of the traffic contract. Default values may be used if the parameter is not included. A *committed* QoS parameter means that the objective is conveyed at connection setup and that the network commits to meeting the objective if the connection is admitted. If the QoS parameter has *no target*, the parameter is not considered in the decision to accept the connection; the network makes no quantitative/measurable commitments regarding this parameter and only commits to deliver the cell as fast as possible (CTD and CDV) or if it is possible (CLR).

For a given service category, a network can offer one or more *classes of service*. A class of service offers a given set of QoS targets and may limit the range of some of the traffic descriptors. For example, a network may offer two QoS classes of CBR service, a premium service with a CLR target of 10^{-10} and a normal service with CLR of 10^{-7}. The lower-quality class may

Table 2.1. QoS and traffic descriptors per service categories.

Attributes	CBR	Real-time VBR	Non–real time VBR	ABR	GFR	UBR
PCR	Specified	Specified	Specified	Specified	Specified	Specified
SCR, MBS	N/A	Specified	Specified	N/A	N/A	N/A
MCR	N/A	N/A	N/A	Optional	N/A	N/A
MCR, MBS, MFS	N/A	N/A	N/A	N/A	Specified	N/A
CLR	Committed	Committed	Committed	No target[1]	No target[1]	No target
Max-CTD	Committed	Committed	No target	No target	No target	No target
P2P-CDV	Committed	Committed	No target	No target	No target	No target

[1]For ABR and GFR, the CLR should be extremely low when a connection transmits below the guaranteed MCR. Above the MCR, applications that are conformant to the ABR flow control should see minimum loss within the network; however, loss may occur at the ABR source if it is not tied to the application layer. When using GFR, the network attempts to carry the traffic above MCR on a best-effort basis.

Source: Modified from the ATM Forum Technical Committee, *Traffic Management Specification*, version 4.0, af-tm-0056.000, April 1996.

require less bandwidth allocation. Different tariff structures can be applied to different classes of service, thus providing high flexibility in designing cost effective network offerings. There are no requirements on what set of services or class of services are supported by a network.

Negotiating the Traffic Contract with the Network

This section discusses how the traffic contract is negotiated with the network. When setting up permanent virtual connections (PVC) or permanent virtual paths (PVP), the setting of the various elements of the traffic contract is done via the network management system. For switched virtual connections or paths, the signaling protocol handles the negotiation of the connection parameters [MCD94].

This section does not provide details of how the signaling protocol is designed, but views the negotiation mechanism from a high level. The reader should refer to [SIG4.0] for details on the ATM signaling protocol.

The PCR and SCR parameters are signaled in cells/second. The MBS is signaled in cells. The coding granularity has an impact on the amount of bandwidth that is allocated and the flexibility of contracting different rates.

If the CAC of a node in the path cannot allocate the bandwidth required to support the requested traffic descriptors, the node can reduce the value of the traffic descriptor. However, the value of the traffic descriptors cannot be reduced below that which may have been specified as the minimum acceptable value in the signaling message. If the value that can be handled by the network falls below these specified minimums, then the connection is rejected.

The P2P-CVD and Max-CTD are signaled with units expressed in microseconds. The CLR is expressed as a magnitude of n ($1 < n < 15$), where the CLR objective takes on the value of 10^{-n}.

As the signaling message proceeds from node to node, the Max-CTD and P2P-CDV are accumulated and carried in the signaling message, along with the requested objective value. When the signaling message reaches the last node, the accumulated QoS parameters represent the end-to-end objective that can be provided by the network. The connection setup is rejected if the accumulated value exceeds the requested objectives. The method for accumulating the Max-CTD and P2P-CDV through the network has a direct impact on the efficiency of the network as discussed below.

The CLR parameter is not explicitly accumulated. Each network element accepts or rejects the call based on a comparison between the loss rate supported by the network element and the requested CLR. The CLR is also usually used as the upper bound on the a parameter used to calculate the delay objectives. A network element may choose a smaller α (i.e., larger probability), which may have the effect of overestimating the cumulative Max-CTD and P2P-CDV.

Additive Accumulation of the P2P-CDV and Max-CTD

A simple accumulation that does not take into account the potential queuing points can lead to underestimation of the end-to-end delay, and the network may accept connections whose QoS cannot be met.

A worst-case accumulation approach for P2P-CDV is the following: A switch receives the accumulated P2P-CDV and adds its potential worst-case CDV contribution to the accumulated P2P-CDV.

However, the P2P-CDV is not additive; that is, it increases or decreases from one node to another (e.g., a node that performs traffic shaping resets the accumulated P2P-CDV to almost zero). Summing up the worst-case peak-to-peak measure provides a safe upper bound but may have the effect of rejecting many connections when the networks grow to a larger diameter. More sophisticated accumulation techniques that are proposed in the literature [KAT98] provide a better estimation of the end-to-end delay and can therefore minimize the number of connections rejected, but they tend to rely on assumptions about a cell arrival pattern or traffic-loading conditions that may jeopardize the QoS. Their complexity may also impact the call setup rate.

For example, Fig. 2.10 depicts the difference between an additive CDV accumulation and one based on Markov assumptions. If the CDV objective is less than 500 μsec, the network

Figure 2.10. Accumulation of CDV for CBR service as function of the number of hops.

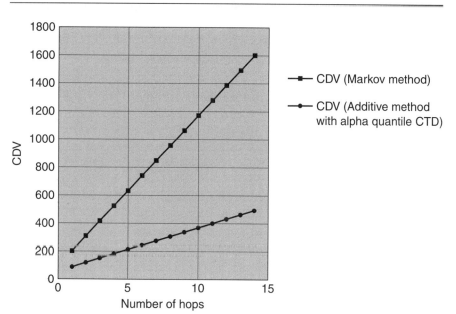

using an additive accumulation method rejects the call at the fourth hop. With a more sophisticated technique the call is accepted up to the fourteenth hop.

A simple accumulation for Max-CTD is the following: A switch receives the accumulated Max-CTD and adds its maximum CTD contribution to the accumulated Max-CTD. This additive method is also a worst-case assumption, since the probability that one cell suffers the maximum CTD at each switch in the path is very low.

Measuring the Delay Parameters

This section describes how to measure the network performance with respect to the delay parameters. More details on measurement procedures can be found in [I.356]. These measurements can be made in service, using special management cells (OAM cells), or out of service, using a target connection.

There are three performance measures associated with the CDV:

One-Point CDV describes the variability in the pattern of cell arrivals with reference to the PCR. It includes the variability present at the source and the cumulative effects of the variability introduced (or removed) by the network [I.356].

Two-Point CDV describes the variability in the pattern of cell arrivals with reference to the pattern generated by the source. It includes only the variability introduced (or removed) by the network [I.356].

Max-CDV measures the maximum CDV encountered in the cell flow.

One-Point CDV

One-point CDV describes the clumping in the pattern of cell arrival with reference to the PCR. Each cell arrival time is compared with its reference arrival time, which represents the time of the previous cell arrival plus the expected intercell arrival time (1/PCR). The one-point CDV for cell k (y_k) is defined as the difference between the cell's reference arrival time (c_k) and its actual arrival time (a_k) at the measurement point: $y_k = c_k - a_k$. The reference arrival time (c_{k+1}) is defined as follows:

$$\text{With } c_0 = a_0$$

$$c_{k+1} = \begin{cases} a_k + \frac{1}{\text{PCR}} & \text{if } c_k \le a_k \\[2ex] c_k + \frac{1}{\text{PCR}} & \text{otherwise} \end{cases} \tag{2.7}$$

One-point CDV measures the cell clumping. The gaps in the cell stream are accounted by a negative y_k. Figure 2.11 provides an example of the one-point CDV measurement. The figure isolates the cell flow resulting from the queuing of VC1 in the example provided in Fig. 2.5. In this example, VC1 sends cells at a PCR of one-fourth the line rate. The traffic stream is subsequently jittered at the multiplexer. Figure 2.11 should be read from right to left, where the first cell exits the system at time slot 2, assuming a fixed delay of one time slot (transmission delay).

Figure 2.11. One-point CDV measurement.

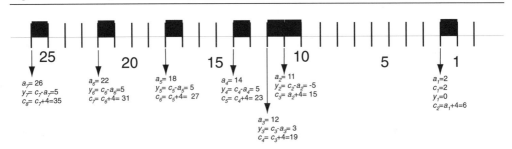

Negative values of the y_k represent gaps in the cell stream, and positive values represent clumping of cells. The one-point CDV measurement is relative to the PCR. For real-time VBR, a large negative value of y_k may represent a gap in the burst or a gap between the bursts.

Two-Point CDV

The two-point CDV (z_k) describes the clumping in the pattern of cell arrival with reference to the pattern of cells generated by the source. The measurement is taken between two reference points (MP1 and MP2) in the network (e.g., ingress and egress UNI).

For cell k, the two-point CDV is the difference between the *absolute CTD* (x_k) encountered by the cell and a *reference CTD* (d). The absolute cell transfer delay x_k is the difference between the cell arrival at MP2 and the cell arrival time at MP1. The reference CTD is defined as x_0, that is, the delay experienced by the first cell. This definition is still under study in the ITU-T.

A positive two-point CDV means that the cell encountered a CTD greater than x_0. A negative two-point CDV represents the case where the CTD of the cell is less than that of the reference cell.

Since the user cells are not time stamped, it is difficult to measure the two-point CDV. However, approximation based on one-point CDV and the max-CDV is described in Annex C of [I.356].

Figure 2.12 on page 30 demonstrates the calculation of the two-point CDV.

Maximum CDV for CBR

The maximum CDV can be measured using the one-point CDV defined above. It can be used in combination with the one-point CDV measurement to approximate the two-point CDV measurement (see Annex C [I.356]).

A positive value for y_k corresponds to a cell that experienced a smaller delay than the maximum delay experienced up to cell $(k - 1)$. A negative value for y_k corresponds to a cell with a delay larger than the maximum delay experienced by cells up to cell k. Figure 2.13 on page 30 provides a method for estimating the range of cell transfer delay for a succession of transferred cells. This method assumes that cells are input uniformly at the PCR.

Define Q_k as the maximum absolute CTD measurements. That is, Q_k represents the maximum clumping measured over a sample of consecutive cell arrivals.

When the first cell arrives,

$$\text{with } Q_0 = 0 \quad \text{and} \quad k = 0,$$

$$c_1 = c_0 + \frac{1}{\text{PCR}} \tag{2.8}$$

Figure 2.12. Illustration of the two-point CDV measurement.

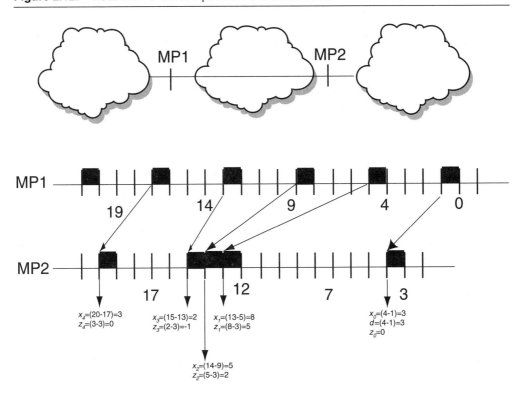

Figure 2.13. Illustration of the Max-CDV measurement.

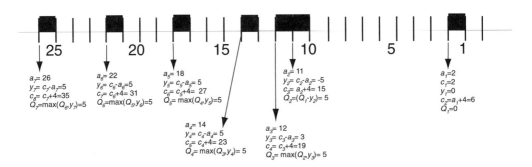

For each subsequent cell k (where $k = k + 1$), compute:

$$y_k = c_k - a_k$$

$$Q_k = \begin{cases} \max(Q_{k-1}, y_k) & \text{if } (y_k \geq 0) \\[2ex] Q_{k-1} - y_k & \text{otherwise} \end{cases}$$

$$c_{k+1} = \max(y_k, 0) + a_k + \frac{1}{\text{PCR}} \tag{2.9}$$

Note that the computation for y_k, and c_{k+1} is identical to the computation for the one-point CDV.

The value of Q_k can be used to engineer the tolerance of the policing function as described in Chap. 3.

Review

One key important feature of ATM is its ability to provide different levels of QoS to different types of connections. In order to allow inter-operability, a comprehensive set of service categories has been specified [TM4.0] and [I.371]. These categories of services are flexible and comprehensive enough to handle currently known applications and likely any foreseeable applications. The services are defined in terms of the traffic characteristics (traffic descriptors) and in terms of whether delay and or loss is considered in defining the level of QoS required. This information is conveyed to the network by means of a *traffic contract.*

References

[BON95a] Bonomi, F., and Fendick, K. *The Available Bit Rate Service.* ATM Forum 53-Bytes Publication, October 1995.

[BON95b] Bonomi, F., Fendick, K. "The Rate-Based Control Framework for the Available Bit Rate Service." *IEEE Network*, vol. 9, no. 2 (March/April 1995).

[I.356] ITU-Telecommunication Standardization Sector. *B-ISDN ATM Layer Cell Transfer Performance*, recommendation I.356, October 1996.

[I.371] ITU-Telecommunication Standardization Sector. *Traffic Control and Congestion Control in B-ISDN*, recommendation I.371, May 1996.

[I.610] ITU-Telecommunication Standardization Sector. *Integrated Service Digital Network (ISDN) Maintenance Principle—B-ISDN Operation and Maintenance.* November 1995.

[KAT98] Kataria, D. "Delay Based Path Selection Algorithms for PNNI Based Networks," submitted to *Computer Networks and ISDN Systems*, 1998.

[MCD94] McDysan, D.E., and Spohn, D.L. *ATM, Theory and Application*. McGraw-Hill Series on Computer Communications, 1994.

[SIG4.0] The ATM Forum Technical Committee. *User to Network Interface (UNI) Signalling Specification,* version 4.0, af-sig-0061.00. 1996.

[TAN92] Tanaka, T., Okubo, S., Hashimoto, H., and Yasuda, H. *A Study on Comparison Between VBR and CBR Video Service in ATM Environment*, paper 320-B.5.1. ICC, 1992.

[TM4.0] The ATM Forum Technical Committee. *Traffic Management Specification*, version 4.0, af-tm-0056.000, April 1996.

CHAPTER 3

Traffic Conformance

As discussed in Chap. 2, applications negotiate their QoS and bandwidth requirements via the traffic contract. The connection admission control (see Chap. 4) allocates sufficient bandwidth to the connection to meet these requirements.

However, the allocation of resources by the CAC is not sufficient to ensure that the QoS is met. That is, a connection could (intentionally or accidentally) exceed the contracted traffic descriptors and may suffer degraded QoS. Most importantly, that connection may impact the QoS of other well-behaving connections. Since the network is required to meet the QoS guarantees for at least the cells that are conforming, it is critical to have the capability of ensuring that the connection is *compliant* with the agreed upon traffic contract. This capability is achieved by the implementation of *traffic-shaping, traffic-policing,* and *soft-policing* mechanisms.

It is unlikely that the traffic of an application *naturally* behaves according to the traffic descriptors. To prevent QoS degradation, the connections (at the ATM interface) need to *shape* the traffic to ensure that it *complies* with the contracted traffic descriptors. Although the standards [TM4.0] and [I.371] do not *require* that traffic shaping be implemented, the applications do have to implement traffic shaping in order to conform to the negotiated traffic descriptors; otherwise the network can take drastic actions on the non-conformant traffic. A network that makes contractual commitments on the QoS cannot rely solely on the connection to comply with the traffic descriptors. The network is therefore allowed to monitor, or *police,* each connection to ensure that the cells *conform* to the contracted traffic descriptors and to take action on the *non-conforming* cells, preventing them from impacting the QoS. The monitoring is generally done at the entry point into the network (e.g., UNI) and between network boundaries.

For a given connection, a cell is qualified as conforming or non-conforming to a traffic descriptor through application of an algorithm called the *generic cell rate algorithm* (GCRA). The GCRA defines what it means to conform to a given set of traffic descriptors.

The network can implement the GCRA algorithm to *police* the traffic and take action on some of the non-conforming traffic. When the network finds a non-conforming cell, it can *tag* or *discard* the cell, or it can do nothing and let it enter the network as if it were conforming. *Tagging* refers to the action of degrading a high-priority cell (with CLP = 0) to a low-priority cell (with CLP = 1). Lowering the priority of a cell makes it ineligible for QoS guarantees, but it may still reach the destination if the network is not overloaded. *Discarding* simply refers to removing the cell from the stream. A cell with CLP = 1 that is found to be non-conforming cannot be degraded to a lower priority and may be discarded. Alternatively, the network can implement a shaping function, which ensures that the traffic entering the network conforms to the traffic descriptors but also allows some buffering of the user traffic that is non-conforming, until the traffic can be scheduled into the network as conforming. This capability is referred to as *soft policing.*

To prevent having its cells tagged or discarded, the traffic source performs a traffic-shaping function. The *traffic shaper* delays the emission of the cell until it would be qualified as conforming by the GCRA.

Therefore, if the source shapes its traffic according to the GCRA, then even if the network polices it, no cells should be affected. If the source cannot shape the traffic, the network can shape it instead of policing it.

Figure 3.1 demonstrates the multiple locations where traffic-shaping and traffic-policing functions may be located in a network.

Figure 3.1. Locations of the traffic shaping and traffic policing (assuming unidirectional traffic).

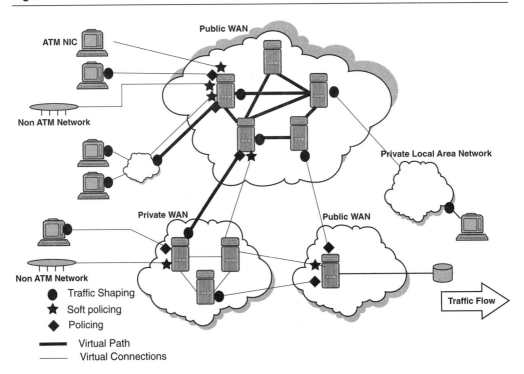

This chapter first presents the conformance definitions that apply to each service category. It then describes the GCRA and proceeds to a description of the policing and shaping functions.

The Conformance Definition

The conformance definition determines the types of cells (either CLP = 0 or CLP = 0+1) for which the QoS and the traffic descriptors are defined and what actions the network is allowed to take on non-conforming traffic. The conformance definition is included as part of the traffic contract. Since CLP = 1 cells have lower priority and are not generally eligible for QoS guarantee, no conformance definition applies to them unless they are included as part of the aggregate flow. The conformance definition does not mandate any actions from the network but defines the envelope (minimal set) of conforming cells that are eligible to receive the negotiated QoS. The network is required to provide the QoS to at least this minimal amount of conforming cells. Figure 3.2 depicts the conformance envelope and the relationship to QoS commitment.

When the QoS guarantee applies to the aggregate traffic (CLP = 0 + 1), the CLP = 0 and CLP = 1 cells are treated equally, without differentiating priority. The conformance definition is therefore *CLP transparent.*

Table 3.1 summarizes the conformance definitions that can be supported for each service category. There can be more than one conformance definition for a given service category to allow for flexibility in designing service offerings. The conformance definition also indicates

Figure 3.2. Conformance envelope.

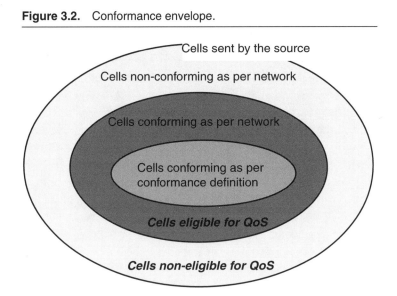

Table 3.1. Conformance definitions per service categories.

Name	Service category	PCR flow	SCR flow	MCR flow	Non-conforming action	CLR	Max-CTD P2P-CDV
CBR.1	CBR	0+1	N/A	N/A	Discard	0+1	0+1
VBR.1	rt-VBR, nrt-VBR	0+1	0+1	N/A	Discard	0+1	0+1 (rt)
VBR.2	rt-VBR, nrt-VBR	0+1	0	N/A	Discard	0	0 (rt)
VBR.3	rt-VBR, nrt-VBR	0+1	0	N/A	Tag	0	0 (rt)
ABR.1	ABR	0	N/A	0	Discard	0	N/A
GFR.1	GFR	0+1	N/A	0	Discard	0	N/A
GFR.2	GFR	0+1	N/A	0	Tag	0	N/A
UBR.1	UBR	0+1	N/A	N/A	Discard	N/A	N/A
UBR.2	UBR	0+1	N/A	N/A	Tag	N/A	N/A

which action the network can take for cells that are judged non-conforming. The possible actions are to discard or tag the cell, or let it enter the network as conforming (i.e., do nothing). If the cell enters the network as conforming, it is eligible for QoS (e.g., enough resources need to be allocated for all the conforming cells entering the network). Tagging only applies to the $CLP = 0$ flow. The PCR is always defined on the aggregate traffic ($CLP = 0 + 1$). Therefore a source can never send any cells (regardless of the CLP bit) at a rate higher than the PCR (see Fig. 2.3).

For the CBR service category, there is a single conformance definition that treats all the CLP cells equally; therefore the CBR conformance definition is CLP transparent.

For the VBR service category, the VBR.1 conformance definition is fully CLP transparent. This conformance definition is designed to support VBR VPs (see section on CLP transparency). The VBR.2 and VBR.3 conformance definitions allow the user to exceed the SCR up to PCR as long as the traffic is tagged. With VBR.3, the network tags the excess traffic, while VBR.2 assumes that the traffic is already tagged and discards the excess traffic.

For the ABR service category, there is a single conformance definition. However, since there are no $CLP = 1$ data cells specified in the flow control protocol (Chap. 6), the PCR and MCR are defined on the $CLP = 0$ flow only. The MCR is not used to define conformance of traffic but defines the minimum set of cells eligible for QoS regardless of the network's congestion status.

For the GFR service category, conformance applies only to the PCR of the aggregate traffic. The MCR is used to evaluate QoS eligibility but does not define conformance. The MCR is used to define the minimum set of frames that should receive a low frame loss rate.

For the UBR service category, all traffic below the PCR is conforming. However, that traffic is not guaranteed a QoS even though it is conforming. With the UBR.1 conformance, the network is not allowed to tag the traffic; in the UBR.2 conformance the network can tag any cell below the PCR. The tagging allows the network to carry the UBR traffic in the same queue as other traffic (e.g., VBR) and use the priority discard function (Chap. 7) to handle the congestion conditions.

CLP Transparency

The CLP bit is only meaningful at the VC level and that can create a problem in VP networks. Multiple VBR VCs containing cells with CLP = 0 and CLP = 1 can be aggregated into a VBR VP. At the aggregation point, the CLP bit cannot be reset to reflect the conformance of the cells within the VP-level traffic descriptors. The VP network cannot rely on this information to perform preferential discard of non-conforming cells.

For example, multiple VBR VCs carrying CLP = 1 and CLP = 0 cells are aggregated into a VBR VP, and traffic shaping is performed such that all the aggregated VP traffic conforms to the VP traffic descriptors. In this case there is no non-conforming traffic, and all cells as seen by the VP should have their CLP bit set to zero. Since the CLP bit cannot be modified, the traffic is carried into the VP network and CLP = 1 cells may be discarded.

This problem can lead to significant fairness issues. Consider a private network that carries 50 percent CLP = 1 cells (network A), and another private network whose traffic sources do not take advantage of the CLP = 1 bursting capability (network B). Both networks contract a VP VBR service of the same bandwidth with a public network. Assume that networks A and B are capable of shaping the aggregate traffic such that the VP fully conforms to the contracted traffic descriptor of the VP. In case of congestion in the public network, 50 percent of the traffic from network A is discarded before any of the traffic of network B, even though both networks contracted, paid, and conformed to the same service. Since the public network cannot reset the CLP bit (which has significance at the VC level only in this case) of the cells carried in the VP, it cannot ensure that cells of both connections are treated equally.

The CLP transparency option addresses this problem. It allows the VP-level network to carry the cells without considering the CLP bit. In the example above, both VPs would receive the same CLR, regardless of the mix of CLP = 0 and CLP = 1 cells at the VC level.

This solution does impact the bandwidth allocation. Since the CLP = 0 and CLP = 1 cells now have the same priority, bandwidth needs to be allocated to the CLP = 1 cells to ensure that they do not affect the performance of the CLP = 0 cells. The CAC (Chap. 4) should allocate bandwidth as if the SCR could be occupied only by CLP = 0 cells.

Although the CLP-transparent conformance definitions (where the QoS applies on all the cells regardless of the value of the CLP bit) are designed for use with VPs, they can also be used to offer services at the VC level. In this case, all cells of the VCs are treated as high-priority traffic.

Analyzing Cell Conformance

The generic cell rate algorithm (GCRA) is a theoretical algorithm used to define what it means to conform to the traffic descriptors. If the arrival rate is within the contracted rate, taking into account potential jitter, then the cell is qualified as conforming; otherwise it is non-conforming. The same algorithm can be used for shaping and policing.

Conformance for the CBR Service

In the case of the CBR service, the conformance definition applies to the peak cell rate of the aggregate traffic. An algorithm that verifies the conformance of a single source to the PCR can be very simple. If a cell arrives earlier than 1/PCR with respect to the previous cell, then the arrival rate exceeds the contracted rate and the cell is non-conforming.

However, if multiple connections are multiplexed together on a link, the initial traffic pattern can be disturbed or jittered, or cell delay variation can be introduced (see Fig. 2.5). Because of this phenomenon, this simple conformance test cannot be applied; otherwise, conforming traffic that encountered jitter might be treated as non-conforming.

To account for jitter, a *tolerance* factor is introduced to determine conformance. This tolerance is referred to as *cell delay variation tolerance* (CDVT) and is expressed in time units (usually microseconds).

The generic cell rate algorithm provides a means for applying this test on a per cell basis. The GCRA has two parameters, an increment (I = 1/PCR) and a limit (L = CDVT). The GCRA(I,L) can be expressed as a *leaky bucket algorithm* or as a *virtual-scheduling algorithm*. These two algorithms are standardized [I.371, TM4.0] and they both define the minimal amount of conforming cells. Both algorithms determine the same cell to be non-conforming for any combination of arrival patterns. In general, CDVT is greater than the measured Max-CDV (Chap. 2).

Leaky Bucket

The leaky bucket algorithm is based on the following analogy. A bucket (B) fills with I units every time a conforming cell arrives and continuously leaks one unit every unit of time. The bucket has finite capacity of L. If at cell arrival the bucket capacity is less than or equal to L, then the cell is conforming; otherwise it is non-conforming. The bucket overflows when cells arrive at a rate faster than the drain rate. The overflowing cells are non-conforming. The algorithm is triggered by the arrival of a cell, so fill and drain are performed according to the previous arrival time of a conforming cell (last conformance time, or LCT). That is, at the arrival of the cell at time t_a, the bucket drains by (t_a – LCT), which is equivalent to continuously leaking the bucket by one unit every unit of time. A negative bucket results from a cell arriving later than expected: In this case, the bucket is reset to zero to prevent accumulation of credits, which would allow for eventual generation of large bursts. If the cell is found to be conforming, the bucket is filled by I. At the arrival of the first cell at time t_a, B = 0 and LCT = t_a. The algorithm is applied to subsequent cell arrivals as depicted in Fig. 3.3.

Figure 3.3. Leaky bucket algorithm for CBR (PCR of aggregate flow).

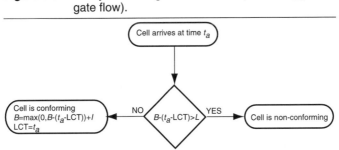

Virtual Scheduling

The virtual-scheduling algorithm keeps track of when the next conforming cell is expected to arrive, the theoretical arrival time (TAT). When a cell arrives at time t_a, if t_a is greater than TAT-L then the cell is conformant; if it is earlier then the cell is non-conforming. The TAT is always incremented by 1/PCR, unless the cell arrives later than TAT in which case it is set to t_a. At the arrival of the first cell at time t_a, TAT is initialized to t_a. Subsequent cell arrivals are subject to the algorithm presented in Fig. 3.4.

The following example demonstrates how the leaky bucket and virtual-scheduling algorithm behave. A conformant cell stream (PCR of one fourth of line rate) has been jittered by the ATM network (cloud), and the resulting stream is depicted in Fig. 3.5.

Figure 3.4. Virtual scheduling algorithm for CBR (PCR of aggregate flow).

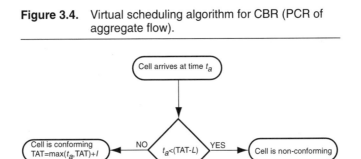

Figure 3.5. Cell stream originally equally spaced every 4 time units and jittered.

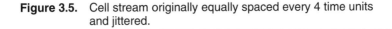

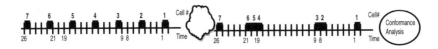

Table 3.2. Evolution of the leaky bucket and virtual scheduling on the cell stream of Fig. 3.5.
$l = 4$, $L = 2$.

Cell#	t_a	TAT	TAT-t_a	B	LCT	B-(t_a – LCT)	Conformance
1	1	1	0	0	1	0	Yes
2	8	5	−3	4	1	−3	Yes
3	9	12	3	4	8	3	No
4	19	12	−7	4	8	−7	Yes
5	20	23	3	4	19	3	No
6	21	23	2	4	19	2	Yes

Table 3.2 demonstrates the evolution of the algorithms based on the cell arrivals in Fig. 3.5, assuming a CDVT of two time units. The resulting cell stream is presented in Fig. 3.6, where gray cells are detected as non-conformant. In this case two cells are judged non-conforming.

Since the original cell stream was conforming, the CDVT should be set large enough to make all cells conform. Table 3.3 shows the behavior, assuming the CDVT is increased to three time units.

The resulting cell stream is depicted in Fig. 3.7, where the gray cells are non-conforming.

Figure 3.6. Cell stream after conformance monitoring with CDVT = 2. Gray cells are non-conforming.

Table 3.3. Evolution of the leaky bucket and virtual scheduling on the cell stream of Fig. 3.5.
$l = 4$, $L = 3$.

Cell#	t_a	TAT	TAT-t_a	B	LCT	B-(t_a-LCT)	Conformance
1	1	1	0	0	1	0	Yes
2	8	5	−3	4	1	−3	Yes
3	9	12	3	4	8	3	Yes
4	19	16	−3	7	9	−3	Yes
5	20	23	3	4	19	3	Yes
6	21	27	6	7	20	6	No

Figure 3.7. Cell stream after conformance monitoring with CDVT = 3. Gray cells are non-conforming.

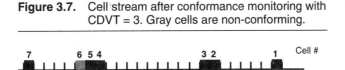

In order to detect all cells as conformant, the algorithm needs to set CDVT to six time units. Notice, though, that bandwidth allocation would need to be sufficient to handle potential simultaneous arrivals of three-cell bursts. Refer to Chap. 4 to understand the impact of CDVT on the bandwidth allocation and therefore on efficiency.

Conformance for the VBR Service

For the VBR service, the conformance is defined on both the SCR and the PCR. The PCR conformance is always defined on the aggregate of the cells. Depending on the type of conformance definition, the SCR may be defined on the aggregate (VBR.1) or on the CLP = 0 flow only (VBR.2 and VBR.3).

The SCR is evaluated by the same algorithm as for the PCR. In the case of SCR, a *burst tolerance* (BT) is defined to allow the connection to burst up to a maximum burst size (MBS) of cells at the PCR. The BT does not account for upstream jitter. Therefore the CDVT is added to BT when performing the conformance test. The tolerance is defined based on the average rate and the maximum burst size (MBS) in relation to the PCR. The BT is calculated as [TM4.0]:

$$BT = (MBS - 1) \times (1/SCR - 1/PCR) \tag{3.1}$$

The GCRA for the SCR is the same as for PCR, but in this case the increment is set to 1/SCR and the limit is set to BT + CDVT. As for PCR, the CDVT must also be included to account for the jitter. The SCR is always defined in conjunction with the PCR; therefore, in order to monitor conformance to SCR, one also needs to monitor the conformance to the PCR.

In the case of the VBR.1 conformance definition, a cell that conforms to the PCR must also conform to the SCR in order to be a conforming cell. For the VBR.2 and VBR.3 conformance definition, only cells with CLP = 0 that conform to the PCR need also conform to the SCR in order to be a conformant cell. Any CLP = 1 cells that conform to the PCR do not need to conform to the SCR in order to be conformant. The state of the algorithms are updated only if the cell conforms to both GCRAs. The resulting combined algorithm is referred to as dual leaky bucket and dual virtual scheduling.

Dual Leaky Bucket

The dual leaky bucket algorithm used to verify conformance for the VBR.1 definition is depicted in Fig. 3.8. This algorithm behaves like the single leaky bucket with limit and increment

Figure 3.8. Dual leaky bucket algorithm for VBR.1.

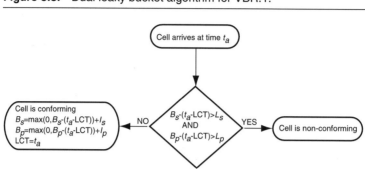

parameters for PCR and SCR—that is, L_p, I_p, L_s, I_s, respectively. B_p and B_s are the bucket sizes for the PCR and SCR. At the arrival of the first cell at time t_a, $B_s = B_p = 0$, LCT $= t_a$. Since the conformance definition is CLP transparent, only one LCT parameter is required.

The dual leaky bucket algorithm used to verify conformance for the VBR.2 or VBR.3 definition is depicted in Fig. 3.9. Again, this algorithm behaves like the single leaky bucket. In this case, two LCT parameters, LCT_p and LCT_s, are needed to keep track of the last conformance to PCR. At the arrival of the first cell at time t_a, $B_s = B_p = 0$, and $LCT_p = t_a$. At the arrival of the first CLP $= 0$ cell at time t_{a0}, $LCT_s = t_{a0}$.

Figure 3.9. Dual leaky bucket algorithm for VBR.2 and VBR.3.

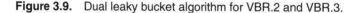

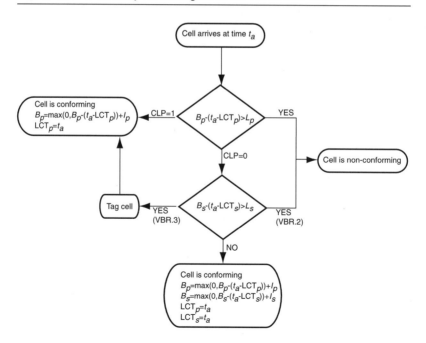

Dual Virtual-Scheduling Algorithm

Figures 3.10 and 3.11 present the dual virtual-scheduling algorithm applied to the VBR.1 and the VBR.2/VBR.3 conformance definitions, respectively. Two theoretical arrival time parameters, TAT_p and TAT_s, are needed to monitor the PCR and SCR, respectively.

Two examples are used to study the behavior of the dual conformance analysis. In both examples, the traffic contract consists of a PCR of half the line rate, a SCR one-fourth the line rate, an MBS of four cells and a CDVT of one time unit. With these parameters, the BT equals six time units, $I_s = 4$, $I_p = 2$, $L_s = 7$, $L_p = 2$.

Figure 3.10. Dual virtual-scheduling algorithm for VBR.1.

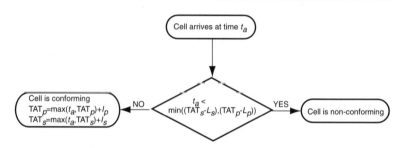

Figure 3.11. Dual virtual-scheduling algorithm for VBR.2 and VBR.3.

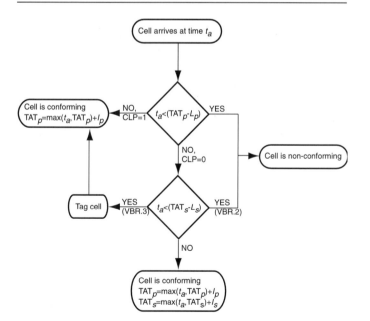

Table 3.4. Evolution of the leaky bucket and virtual scheduling for VBR.1 and VBR.2 with no shaping.

Cell#	t_a	TAT$_s$	TAT$_p$	B_s	B_p	LCT	TAT$_s$-t_a = B_s-(t_a-LCT)	TAT$_p$-t_a = B_p-(t_a-LCT)	Conformance
1	1	1	1	0	0	1	0	0	Yes
2	2	5	3	4	2	1	3	1	Yes
3	3	9	5	7	3	2	6	2	No
4	4	9	5	7	3	2	5	1	Yes
5	5	13	7	9	3	3	8	2	No
6	6	13	7	9	3	3	7	1	Yes
7	7	17	9	11	3	6	10	2	No
8	8	17	9	11	3	6	9	1	No
9	9	17	9	11	3	6	8	0	No
10	10	17	9	11	3	6	7	−1	Yes

In the first example, the source sends cells with CLP = 0 continuously at the line rate, without shaping. The result of applying VBR.1 conformance to the cell stream is depicted in Table 3.4 and Fig. 3.12. The same result would be obtained with the VBR.2 conformance definition.

Figure 3.12. Cell stream after conformance analysis. Gray cells are non-conforming.

Table 3.5. Evolution of the leaky bucket and virtual scheduling for VBR.3 with no shaping.

Cell#	t_a	TAT$_s$	TAT$_p$	B_s	B_p	LCT$_s$	LCT$_p$	TAT$_s$-t_a = B_s-(t_a-LCT$_s$)	TAT$_p$-t_a = B_p-(t_a-LCT$_p$)	Conformance
1	1	1	1	0	0	1	1	0	0	Yes
2	2	5	3	4	2	1	1	3	1	Yes
3	3	9	5	7	3	2	2	6	2	No
4	4	9	5	7	3	2	2	5	1	Yes
5	5	13	7	9	3	3	3	8	2	No
6	6	13	7	9	3	3	3	7	1	Yes
7	7	17	9	11	3	6	6	10	2	No
8	8	17	9	11	3	6	6	9	1	Yes/CLP = 1
9	9	17	11	11	3	6	8	8	2	No
10	10	17	11	11	3	6	8	7	1	Yes

Figure 3.13. Cell stream after conformance analysis.
Gray cells are non-conforming; dotted cell is
conforming and tagged.

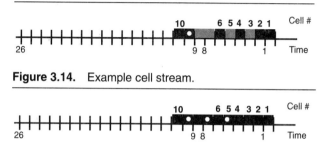

Figure 3.14. Example cell stream.

The resulting cell stream is depicted in Fig. 3.12, where the gray cells are non-conforming.

The result of applying the VBR.3 conformance is demonstrated in Table 3.5, the resulting cell stream is depicted in Fig. 3.13, where the gray cells are non-conforming.

In the second example, the source sends four cells with CLP = 0 and, alternatively, sends cells with CLP = 0 and CLP = 1 at the line rate, without shaping, as shown in Fig. 3.14, the results of applying the VBR.1 would be the same as the ones presented in Table 3.4 and Fig. 3.12. The results of applying the VBR.3 conformance definition are shown in Table 3.6 and Fig. 3.15.

Table 3.6. Evolution of the leaky bucket and virtual scheduling for VBR.3.

Cell#/ CLP	t_a	TAT_s	TAT_p	B_s	B_p	LCT_s	LCT_p	TAT_s-t_a = B_s-(t_a-LCT)	TAT_p-t_a = B_p-(t_a-LCT)	Conformance/ CLP
1/0	1	1	1	0	0	1	1	0	0	Yes/0
2/0	2	5	3	4	2	1	1	3	1	Yes/0
3/0	3	9	5	7	3	2	2	6	2	No/0
4/0	4	9	5	7	3	2	2	5	1	Yes/1
5/1	5		7		3		4		2	No/1
6/0	6	9	7	7	3	2	4	3	1	Yes/0
7/1	7		9		3		6	5	2	No/1
8/0	8	13	9	7	3	6	6	5	1	Yes/1
9/1	9		11		3		8		2	No/1
10/0	10	13	11	7	3	6	8	3	1	Yes/0

Figure 3.15. Cell stream after VBR.3 conformance
analysis. Gray cells are non-conforming, and
dotted cells are tagged.

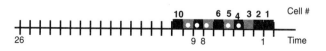

Table 3.7.   Evolution of the leaky bucket and virtual scheduling for VBR.2.

Cell#/ CLP	t_a	TAT$_s$	TAT$_p$	B_s	B_p	LCT$_s$	LCT$_P$	TAT$_s$-t_a = B_s-(t_a-LCT$_s$)	TAT$_p$-t_a = B_p-(t_a-LCT$_p$)	Conformance/ CLP
1/0	1	1	1	0	0	1	1	0	0	Yes/0
2/0	2	5	3	4	2	1	1	3	1	Yes/0
3/0	3	9	5	7	3	2	2	6	2	No/0
4/0	4	9	5	7	3	2	2	5	1	No/0
5/1	5		5		3		4		0	Yes/1
6/0	6	9	7	7	2	2	5	3	1	Yes/0
7/1	7		9		3		6		2	No/1
8/0	8	13	9	7	3	6	6	5	1	No/0
9/1	9		9		3		6		0	Yes/1
10/0	10	13	11	7	2	6	9	3	1	Yes/0

Figure 3.16.   Cell stream after VBR.2 conformance analysis. Gray cells are non-conforming; dotted cell is conforming and tagged.

The results of applying the VBR.2 conformance definition are shown in Table 3.7 and Fig. 3.16.

The above examples demonstrate the outcome of applying different conformance definitions to incoming traffic. The VBR.1 results in more discarded cells without differentiating the incoming CLP bit. The VBR.3 conformance definition results in fewer discarded cells but a higher number of cells with CLP set to one. For VBR.1, bandwidth needs to be allocated for the aggregate traffic; in the case of VBR.2 and VBR.3, bandwidth is only allocated for the CLP = 0 cells.

Conformance for the ABR Service

The conformance definition for the ABR service is network specific. For ABR traffic, the conformance is defined by the source/destination behavior specification (Chap. 6). The conformance definition needs to identify all cells as conformant if they are conformant to the GCRA (1/MCR, CDVT$_{MCR}$) (see Figs. 3.3 and 3.4).

An example conformance definition for ABR is the dynamic GCRA (D-GCRA) which applies to the explicit rate mode only. The D-GCRA differs from the GCRA in that the increment I varies over time, based on the content of the backward resource management cell, and considers various delays for response time (see [TM4.0], Appendix III). The algorithm is dynamic because it evaluates the conformance of a rate that varies with time. The algorithm needs to keep track of the feedback information to compute the source cell rate, but it also has to take into account the delays that can be encountered before the source modifies its rate. These requirements translate into a complex conformance analysis algorithm sensitive to many unknown parameters (e.g., delay)[TM4.0].

Conformance for the GFR Service

In the case of GFR, conformance is differentiated from service eligibility. Non-conforming frames are discarded, while tagging may be used to identify frames that are not eligible for the MCR guarantee. Conformance to the GFR service is governed by the following three tests:

- conformance to GCRA($1/PCR_{0+1}$, $CDVT_{PCR}$) for the aggregate (CLP = 0, CLP = 1) flow.
- all cells of the frame have the same CLP value.
- conformance to the maximum frame size (MFS). A cell conforms to this test if the number of cells from the last frame boundary up to and including this cell is less than MFS.

A frame conforms only if all cells in the frame conform. If a cell does not conform to these three tests, the following actions may be taken:

- If it is the first cell of a frame, the network should discard the whole frame.
- If the cell is not the first cell of the frame, the network should discard it and all the remaining cells of the frame, except for the last cell (frame boundary).

The MCR guarantee applies to complete unmarked frames declared conformant. That is, the GFR service is *CLP significant*. Eligibility of a conformant frame for the GFR service guarantee can be verified using a frame-based GCRA, the F-GCRA($1/MCR_0$, $BT+CDVT_{MCR}$), where BT = (MBS – 1)(1/MCR – 1/PCR) and MBS is greater than or equal to MFS.

The F-GCRA (I, L) is defined as per the flow chart of Fig. 3.17. Frames sent in excess of the MCR are not eligible for the service guarantees but may still be conformant. Frames not eligible for the service guarantee may be discarded or tagged. Frame discard would only apply to partial packets and complete frames that are ineligible for service guarantees.

Partially tagged frames are not allowed. There are two service definitions of the GFR service, based on allowing or not allowing network tagging of frames ineligible for the service guarantee. They include:

GFR.1 the network is not allowed to tag cells of an unmarked frame that is ineligible for the MCR service guarantee.

GFR.2 the network is allowed to tag cells of an unmarked frame that is ineligible for the MCR service guarantee. The network should attempt to tag only complete frames.

Figure 3.17. F-GCRA algorithm for GFR.1.

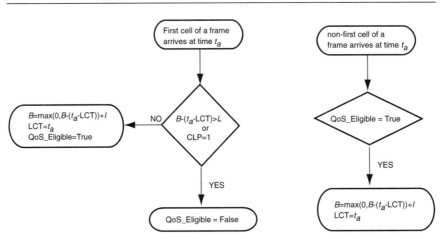

It should be noted that networks are not required to implement a frame-based GCRA to verify service eligibility of conforming frames. The network element can implement scheduling mechanisms that can guarantee the MCR of each VC while allocating the excess bandwidth according to a fair, network specific policy (see Chap. 5).

Conformance for the UBR Service

In the case of UBR, the conformance definition only applies to the PCR of the aggregate flow. It is therefore the same as for the CBR service.

Traffic Policing

The network needs to ensure that the incoming traffic is conforming, because it allocates bandwidth and guarantees QoS to the conforming cells. The network acts on the non-conforming cells by enabling a *policing* function for the VC. Policing is generally enabled at the UNI. This function is referred to as usage parameter control (UPC). Policing may be enabled between two networks, in which case it is referred to as network parameter control (NPC). Traffic need be policed only at its entry into a network. The policing function implements an algorithm that is equivalent to the corresponding GCRA algorithms, either single or dual leaky bucket or virtual scheduling [BuT91, DiT91, GAL89].

The policing function is nonintrusive [TM4.0, I.371], therefore it does not delay or modify the characteristics of the cell flow, other than by removing cells or lowering the priority by setting the CLP bit to one.

If originally conforming traffic is slightly jittered upstream, these drastic actions by the policing function can impact the service quality. For this reason policing functions generally are located only at the network ingress or just following a traffic shaper.

The implementation of the policing function is not standardized. An implementation that finds more cells to be non-conformant than the GCRA is not acceptable, because it would impact the guaranteed QoS (see Fig. 3.2). However, a lenient algorithm allowing non-conformant cells to enter the network as conformant cells is acceptable, but then the network has to guarantee their QoS and allocate a larger amount of resources.

Implementations may only be able to police a fixed set of predefined rates. When a connection is set up, its traffic descriptors are then mapped to the next higher rate supported. For example, if the policing function supports only rates in increments of 10Mbps and a connection requests a rate of 11Mbps, then the connection is policed at 20Mbps. The granularity of the policing function directly affects the efficiency of the network, because the traffic descriptor values used to allocate bandwidth in the CAC are the values at which the connection is policed. The CAC needs to consider that a greedy user could be filling all the extra bandwidth allowed by the policing function with data the network regards as conformant and eligible to receive QoS. Therefore, the 11Mbps connection mentioned above would be allocated 20Mbps, a waste of 9 Mbps in bandwidth. The smaller the granularity of the policing, the more efficient the bandwidth allocation. The ITU [I.371] has standardized the required granularity to allow handling a variety of link rates with equal precision. The policing function is required to handle a cell rate at most one percent larger than the contracted rate.

There are many other algorithms that can approximate the behavior of the leaky bucket and the virtual-scheduling algorithm. One example is a *fixed-window-monitoring* mechanism that uses fixed monitoring intervals to calculate the rate of arrival of cells. The fixed window uses a counter incremented by 53 bytes at the arrival of a cell and resets the counter at the end of the fixed interval. Whenever the counter exceeds a threshold, all cells arriving before the interval expires are non-conforming. Such algorithms may be easier to implement, but the granularity of the monitoring interval affects performance and the results are not necessarily equivalent to the algorithms discussed earlier. The application of a fixed-window function results in a more bursty stream of conforming cells, which requires a larger allocation of bandwidth. Refer to [RAT90] for detailed performance comparisons of the different implementations.

Policing CBR Connections

When traffic policing is applied to a CBR connection, the result is the same as applying the conformance algorithm to CBR described in the previous section, where some of the non-conforming (gray) cells are removed from the stream (see Figs. 3.4–3.7).

Policing VBR Connections

The policing function for VBR connection implements an algorithm that is equivalent to a dual leaky bucket or a dual virtual-scheduling algorithm, as described in the section on conformance monitoring for VBR. Again, in the case of policing, cells judged non-conforming after applying the algorithm are discarded. For the examples presented in the "Conformance for the VBR Service" section, the output of the policing function would be the same but the non-conforming (gray) cells would have been removed from the stream (see Figs. 3.12–3.16).

Policing ABR Connections

Implementing a D-GCRA to police ABR traffic is complex, because of the multiple delay variables and the granularity mismatch of the shaping and policing functions. The implementation of the policing function requires the processing of every backward resource management (BRM) cell, as well as complex timers to adjust the policing rate appropriately while guessing the reaction time of the source. Simpler, more approximate policing functions can also be implemented [I.371.1].

An alternative solution is the use of a virtual source. This solution is discussed in the soft-policing section of this chapter and in Chap. 6. To avoid complexity, the network can use virtual sources (VS) and virtual destinations (VD) (Chap. 6) to control the ABR traffic of each connection by reproducing the expected behavior of the source. If the source behaves properly, the use of the virtual source and destination is transparent (except for modification of some signaling parameters); otherwise the virtual source may take action on the excess traffic.

Policing GFR Connections

The GFR-policing function monitors the PCR of the aggregate traffic and can discard excess traffic, like the CBR-policing function. In addition, the GFR-policing function can verify that the maximum frame size (MFS) is not exceeded and can take actions (e.g., discard remainder of frame) if it is violated.

Policing UBR Connections

A UBR VC may be policed on the PCR. The UBR policing is similar to the CBR-policing function. In the case of UBR, the CDVT value should be larger to account for the likelihood of large queuing and jitter in the upstream nodes.

Policing of OAM Traffic

The OAM cells that are inserted in the cell flow of a given VC may impact the conformance of user cells. OAM traffic also needs to be policed to prevent a user from taking advantage of these cells to carry data while potentially avoiding the tarriffing structure. The policing of OAM traffic is also necessary to prevent a malfunctioning device from sending OAM cells that may affect the QoS of other connections.

Policing functions may not discriminate the OAM cells from user cells when deciding whether a cell is conformant. However, the conformance analysis of a fully conforming user cell stream with even a few OAM cells inserted in the flow may result in many user cells deemed non-conforming, because the insertion of cells can jitter the data flow. This problem can be compensated by providing some head room on the signaled parameter, usually a two percent increase of the traffic descriptors. This somewhat arbitrary solution does impact bandwidth allocation as well as network efficiency.

The ITU [I.371] allows for the use of a separate information element to signal the traffic descriptors of the OAM cell flow. This element allows implementation of a parallel policing function in order to police only the OAM traffic, not the user data cells. With this capability the traffic descriptors do not need to be inflated, but the CDVT does need to be increased to take into account the potential jitter effect of the OAM insertion.

Traffic Shaping

The source, the adaptation device, or the network can apply a traffic-shaping function to a VC or a VP. The traffic-shaping function modifies the traffic characteristics to conform to the contracted traffic descriptors. Although traffic shaping is an optional traffic management capability [I.371, TM4.0], it is a fundamental for efficient use of the network resources. As described in the previous section, the network can take drastic actions on the non-conforming traffic (tag or discard), which leads to retransmission of information by higher-layer protocols (Chap. 9) and therefore inefficient use of the network resources. It is highly unlikely, if not impossible, that traffic from an application magically conforms to a set of predefined traffic descriptors like SCR and PCR. In order to create a conforming cell flow, the device generating the cells needs to "shape" the traffic.

The objective of traffic shaping is to create a cell flow that conforms the traffic descriptors as per the conformance algorithm defined above. The shaped cell stream should have minimal CDV. Chapter 5 describes different algorithms to implement traffic shaping. This section provides a description of the results expected from a traffic shaper.

As demonstrated in Fig. 2.7, the effect of jitter in a multiplexer is very important. Even if a source does shape the traffic, some cells may be judged non-conforming because the cell stream suffered jitter in its path. In some cases, therefore, it is necessary to have the capability to reshape the traffic prior to having it enter a public network that polices the traffic [LAN97]. It may also be necessary for a public network to reshape the traffic prior to entering another public network with which it has contracted bandwidth.

Shaping is also extremely important for handling VPs. It is impossible to characterize a priori the traffic characteristics resulting from aggregating multiple VCs onto a VP. As VCs are added and removed from the VP, the characteristics are also modified. The resulting traffic characteristics could be highly bursty or very smooth. The VP is created with specific traffic descriptors, and the only way it can conform to these regardless of the mix of VCs aggregated at a given time is by traffic shaping.

To illustrate the complexity, assume PCR equal to 0.10 the line rate, SCR equal to 0.05 the line rate, and an MBS of 10 cells for each of six VCs aggregated onto a VBR VP. It is practically impossible to characterize the behavior of the aggregated stream. As a worst case, one can assume that the VBR VP's PCR would be equal to the line rate, that the MBS would be 60 cells, (e.g., the sum of the MBSs) and that the SCR is the sum of the individual SCRs (i.e., 0.30 the line rate). The SCR assumption is the most realistic. The PCR and MBS assumptions are worst case and lead to under-utilization of the VP, since the cells of each VC do not necessarily arrive at the same time. The lower bound on the PCR is 0.60 the line rate, and the lower bound on the MBS is 1. Furthermore, if ten additional VCs are set up, the original assumptions do not hold. Since the VP is provisioned ahead of time without prior knowledge of the mix of VCs aggregated on it, it is important to set up an efficient combination of traffic descriptors for the VP and to use traffic shaping to ensure conformance at any time. This problem also applies to the aggregation of CBR VCs onto a CBR VP. Aggregating ten CBR VCs with a PCR of 0.05 the line rate does not naturally result in a CBR VP with a PCR of half the line rate. The resulting traffic characteristics of the VP may be closer to a VBR VP with a PCR equal to the line rate, an SCR half the line rate, and an MBS of ten cells. As discussed in Chap, 4, this phenomenon has significant impact on the bandwidth allocation and on the efficiency of the network. Again, shaping the VP to half the line rate produces a conforming cell stream and resolves the problem of traffic characterization.

Traffic shaping may also be performed at the egress of the network, prior to delivering the cells to the end customer. A network provider can then guarantee minimum jitter in the cell stream entering the customer network, which would require less buffering in the end systems or in the downstream switches. This capability can be advertised as a value-added service.

The shaping function requires the traffic to be queued on a per VC/VP basis and allows cell transmission only when they would comply with the GCRA function with a zero CDVT. Because of the buffering and the rescheduling of the cells, the shaping function may increase the end-to-end delay. However, reapplying a shaping function within the network to traffic previously shaped should only increase delay slightly as the traffic is already behaving properly. Obviously, shaping the cells of a frame or PDU at a given PCR instead of sending them back to back at line rate increases the delay to reassemble the frame or PDU at the other end of the network. However, a lower PCR, which translates into higher statistical gains, should allow a lower service cost to compensate for the increased delay.

A traffic shaper can be implemented in various ways as long as it produces a conformant cell stream (Chap. 5). Therefore, the implementation has to follow the principles of a reverse leaky bucket or *cell-spacing* (or reverse virtual-scheduling) algorithms.

A traffic shaper should never take advantage of the CDVT parameter by intentionally sending cells back to back at the line rate. The goal of the shaper is to minimize the measured Max-CDV at its output. However, because many VCs can contend for the same link and be processed by the same shaper, there is a chance that, at a given instant, cells could be scheduled for transmission at the same time slot (cell collisions). The shaping function then transmits the cells as soon as possible, taking into account the delay requirement of the connections. The collisions create jitter in the shaped traffic pattern; therefore, even though the traffic is shaped, a nonzero CDVT is required in a downstream policing function to account for the collisions. Fig-

Figure 3.18. Impact of collisions in the traffic shaper.

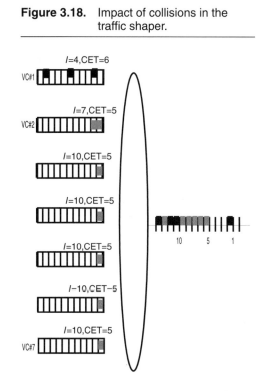

ure 3.18 demonstrates the impact of collisions on the resulting cell flow, assuming VC1 is real-time sensitive (e.g., CBR). In this case VC2 to VC7 are scheduled to transmit at time unit 5. The cell from VC6 is delayed by 4 units and the cell from VC7 is delayed by 7, because two cells from VC1 were transmitted at higher priority.

The shaping function never transmits cells too early, but in the case of collisions where the cell is transmitted late, the next conformant cell time is calculated based on the time the cell should have been transmitted rather than on the effective transmission time. The collisions can therefore create some level of clumping, but the shaping function allows the source to obtain the contracted bandwidth; otherwise, collisions would cause a long-term reduction in bandwidth.

Shaping CBR Traffic

Shaping CBR traffic can be implemented using various algorithms. The reverse leaky bucket and the spacing function are two common shaping techniques.

Reverse Leaky Bucket for PCR

The reverse leaky bucket, as its name implies, uses the concept of leaky bucket for scheduling a conforming departure time for a cell.

A cell is transmitted if the bucket (B) is empty. When the cell is transmitted, the bucket fills by $I = 1/PCR$ units and continuously leaks by one unit every unit of time until emptied. Therefore, when a cell is scheduled for emission, the bucket fills by I units. As discussed, the cell may not be transmitted at that time because of collisions, but the leaky bucket assumes transmission to prevent bandwidth loss.

Spacing for PCR

The "spacer" uses the virtual-scheduling concept to shape the traffic. A spacer keeps track of a conforming emission time (CET) for each connection. The spacer transmits the cells whose CET is lower or equal to the current clock time. When a cell is scheduled to be transmitted at time t_a, the CET for the next cell is set to $t_a + I$, where $I = 1/PCR$.

Table 3.8 provides an example of the behavior of the reverse leaky bucket and the spacing function. This example assumes a source that sends cells at line rate, and the shaping function makes the cell stream compliant to a PCR of half the line rate. In this example there is a single VC and no collisions.

Shaping VBR

For VBR traffic, the shaper can be implemented, as for the CBR, using a reverse dual leaky bucket or a dual spacer.

Reverse Dual Leaky Bucket

The reverse dual leaky bucket algorithm applied to the VBR.1 conformance definition works as follows: A cell, regardless of the value of the CLP bit, is scheduled for transmission if the PCR bucket (B_p) is empty and if the SCR bucket fill (B_s) is lower than BT. When the cell is scheduled to be transmitted, the B_p bucket fills by I_p units and the B_s bucket fills by I_s units. Both buckets continuously leak by one every unit of time; $I_s = 1/SCR$ and $I_p = 1/PCR$ until the bucket is empty.

Table 3.8. Evolution of the reverse leaky bucket and spacing algorithms for a source sending at the line rate; $I = 2$.

Cell#	time	CET	B	Cell scheduled
1	1	1	0	Yes
2	2	3	1	No
3	3	3	0	Yes
4	4	5	1	No
5	5	5	0	Yes
6	6	7	1	No
7	7	7	0	Yes
8	8	9	1	No

When shaping to the VBR.2 or VBR.3 conformance definitions, a similar algorithm is applied but the CLP bit of the cell is also taken into account. A CLP = 0 cell is scheduled for transmission if the PCR bucket (B_p) is empty and if the SCR bucket fill (B_s) is lower than BT.

If B_p is empty but B_s is greater than BT, then the cell can be tagged to CLP = 1 and scheduled immediately. Alternatively, the cell can be held in the buffer until B_s drains to a value lower than BT. These two approaches generate a conforming cell stream, with the former approach minimizing delay but increasing the amount of lower-priority cells sent into the network.

When a cell with CLP = 0 is scheduled, the B_p bucket fills by I_p units and the B_s bucket fills by I_s units. When a cell with CLP = 1 is scheduled, the B_p bucket fills by I_p units and the B_s bucket is not filled. Both buckets continuously leak by one every unit of time.

Dual Spacing

For VBR.1, the dual spacing algorithm keeps track of a CET_s and a CET_p for each connection. These parameters represent the cell emission time respective to the SCR and PCR. The CET for the connection is equal to $\max(CET_s - BT, CET_p)$. A cell whose CET is lower or equal to the current clock time is scheduled for transmission. When the cell is scheduled at time t_a, the CET_p is set to $t_a + I_p$, where $I_p = 1/PCR$ and CET_s is set to $t_a + I_s$, where $I_s = 1/SCR$.

When shaping to the VBR.2 or VBR.3 conformance definitions, the spacer takes into account the CLP value via a delay or tagging approach. Both approaches can be used for both conformance definitions. If the spacer implements a tagging function and a CLP = 0 cell is next to be scheduled on a given connection, then the cell is tagged and the CET for the connection is set equal to CET_p. If the spacer does not implement a tagging function and a CLP = 0 cell is next to be transmitted on a given connection, then the CET for the connection is equal to $\max(CET_s - BT, CET_p)$. If the next cell to be scheduled is a CLP = 1 cell, then $CET = CET_p$.

Cells with connections whose CET is lower or equal to the current clock time are scheduled for transmission. When a CLP = 0 cell is scheduled, the CET_p is increased by $I_p = 1/PCR$ and CET_s by $I_s = 1/SCR$. When a CLP = 1 cell is scheduled, the CET_p is increased by $I_p = 1/PCR$.

Table 3.9 presents the behavior of the reverse dual leaky bucket and the dual spacing function. The example assumes a source that sends CLP = 0 cells continuously at line rate and that is being shaped to a VBR.1 conformance definition. The PCR is half the line rate, the SCR is one fourth the line rate, and MBS is four. In this case, BT is six. This example assumes a single VC with no collision.

Since the incoming cells have a CLP = 0, Table 3.9 also demonstrates the effect of applying the VBR.2 and VBR.3 conformance definition with a shaper that delays instead of tagging.

Table 3.10 presents the same example, but the shaper applies the VBR.2 or VBR.3 conformance definition. The source continuously sends CLP = 0 cells at line rate. The example demonstrates the effect of a shaper that tags the traffic. In this case two more conforming cells are emitted during the 13 units of time.

Table 3.11 presents an example assuming that the source alternatively sends CLP = 0 and CLP = 1 cells at line rate and the same traffic descriptors as previously. The shaper applies the

Table 3.9. Evolution of the leaky bucket and virtual scheduling. $I_p = 2$, $I_s = 4$, BT = 6. VBR.1.

Cell#	time	CET_p	CET_s-BT	B_p	B_s	Output Cell #
1	1	1	−5	0	0	1
2	2	3	−1	1	3	None
3	3	3	−1	0	2	2
4	4	5	3	1	5	None
5	5	5	3	0	4	3
6	6	7	7	1	7	None
7	7	7	7	0	6	4
8	8	9	11	1	9	None
9	9	9	11	0	8	None
10	10	9	11	0	7	None
11	11	9	11	0	6	5
12	12	13	15	0	9	None
13	13	13	15	0	8	None

Table 3.10. Evolution of the leaky bucket and virtual scheduling. $I_p = 2$, $I_s = 4$, BT = 6 for VBR.2 and VBR.3.

Cell#	time	CET_p	CET_s-BT	B_p	B_s	Output Cell #/CLP
1	1	1	−5	0	0	1/0
2	2	3	−1	1	3	None
3	3	3	−1	0	2	2/0
4	4	5	3	1	5	None
5	5	5	3	0	4	3/0
6	6	7	7	1	7	None
7	7	7	7	0	6	4/0
8	8	9	11	1	9	None
9	9	9	11	0	8	5/1
10	10	11	11	1	7	None
11	11	11	11	0	6	6/0
12	12	13	15	1	9	None
13	13	13	15	0	8	7/1

Table 3.11. Evolution of the leaky bucket and virtual scheduling with a traffic shaper that delays the traffic. $I_p = 2$, $I_s = 4$, BT = 6 for VBR.2 and VBR.3.

Cell#/ CLP	time	CET_p	CET_s-BT	B_p	B_s	Output cell #/CLP
1/0	1	1	−5	0	0	1/0
2/1	2	3	−1	1	3	None
3/0	3	3	−1	0	2	2/1
4/1	4	5	−1	1	1	None
5/0	5	5	−1	0	0	3/0
6/1	6	7	3	1	3	None
7/0	7	7	3	0	2	4/1
8/1	8	9	3	1	1	None
9/0	9	9	3	0	0	5/0
10/1	10	11	7	1	3	None
11/0	11	11	7	0	2	6/1
12/1	12	13	7	1	1	None
13/0	13	13	7	0	0	7/0

VBR.2 or VBR.3 conformance definition. This example demonstrates the effect of a shaper that delays the traffic.

Shaping ABR

Shaping the allowed cell rate (ACR) of an ABR connection is similar to shaping the PCR of a CBR connection, except that the rate changes upon reception of a resource management (RM) cell. The shaping function is described by the source behavior, which is discussed in detail in Chap. 6.

Shaping GFR

The PCR of a GFR has to be shaped as for CBR. If the application wants to identify specific frames to be eligible for QoS, then the application can shape to the MCR according to the F-GCRA. That shaping is performed at the frame level and, if applicable, complete frames are tagged. The network can usually evaluate which frames are eligible for QoS, therefore the source does not necessarily have to implement the frame-based shaping.

Shaping UBR

Shaping UBR traffic is the same as shaping CBR traffic. The only difference is that, in case of collisions, the UBR traffic may suffer more jitter and the CDVT required to police a shaped UBR stream should be larger.

"Soft" Policing

The policing function described above is not forgiving and depends highly on the appropriate setting of the CDVT parameter and the statistical behavior of the queues in the upstream network. Engineering the CDVT parameter is complex and depends on many factors, such as the number of nodes between the traffic-shaping function and the traffic-policing function, the amount of buffering and the type of scheduling, along with the amount of higher-priority traffic present at a given instant.

To ensure that a conforming traffic stream "disturbed" prior to entering a network is not judged non-conforming, the CDVT can be set very large. The large CDVT prevents application of drastic actions like tagging or discarding on originally conforming traffic. On the other hand, a large setting of the CDVT impacts the efficiency of the network as its value is taken into account at connection admission (Chap. 4). One solution to this problem is to replace the policing function by a traffic-shaping function. The traffic-shaping function schedules the cells into the network only when they would be conforming and buffers the non-conforming or jittered cells [BOY92, BOY92-2, DAN94]. We refer to this function as a *soft-policing function*. The buffering can be limited and actions (tagging or discarding) are possible only when the buffer exceeds some predetermined limit. The limit can be a function of the CDVT and the number of active VCs at a given instant.

If the connection properly shapes its traffic, then the soft-policing function has no effect on the traffic stream. Furthermore, if the connection properly shapes its traffic but the traffic is going through multiple large buffers and is jittered, then the soft-policing function buffers the traffic and makes it a conforming stream into the network, while allocating only very minimal resources due to CDVT in the network. In this case, the CDVT allocation is much easier to characterize, because it only needs to cover the worst-case jitter encountered in the shaping function due to collisions. If the connection does not shape its traffic then, the soft-policing function buffers it up to a limit and then takes actions (e.g., discard). Priority discard or frame discard functions (Chap. 8) can also be applied to the soft-policing buffers.

Table 3.12 provides an example of the behavior of the reverse leaky bucket and the spacing function. This example assumes a source that sends cells at line rate, and the shaping func-

Table 3.12. Evolution of the soft-policing function for a PCR half the line rate and an unshaped source.

Cell#	time	CET	B	Buffer size	Cell # scheduled
1	1	1	0	0	1
2	2	3	1	1	No
3	3	3	0	1	2
4	4	5	1	2	No
5	5	5	0	2	3
6	6	7	1	2	No
7	7	7	0	2	4
8	8	9	1	2	No

tion makes the cell stream compliant with a PCR of half the line rate. In this example, there is a single VC and no collisions. It demonstrates the application of a soft-policing function to a CBR connection that is not shaping but is sending cells continuously at line rate. In this example, the buffer is limited to two cells per connection.

The soft-policing function discards cells 6 and 8 because the buffer reached its capacity when they arrived. If strict policing (no shaping) had been applied, with a CDVT of 2, then three cells would have been discarded (cells 3, 6, and 8). In the examples provided in the conformance analysis section, a buffer limit would have allowed transmission of all the cells instead of discarding the non-conformant cells. Since the buffers can be shared by all the VCs using the soft-policing function, the buffer limit can be larger, thereby allowing more conformant cells for a given VC to enter the network. Fair congestion control techniques (Chap. 7) can be applied to the shared buffer.

For ABR, the use of the virtual source instead of a dynamic-policing function is equivalent to applying soft policing. In this case, it allows handling the unpredictable delays that arise before the source adapts to the new rate contained in the RM cell without causing discard of multiple cells. Refer to Chap. 6 for more details on virtual sources.

Engineering the CDVT Value

As discussed in this chapter, proper engineering of the CDVT parameter is very important to ensure that a conforming cell stream jittered in a network is not judged to be non-conforming. However, the CDVT has an impact on network efficiency and cannot be counted on by itself to account for jitter. When a connection is set up using the ITU-T signaling capability, the CDVT value is modified at each node. It is modified based on the node configuration, architecture (e.g., scheduling), and whether shaping is performed. For example, a worst-case approach is to add together the Max-CDV of each node in the path. This additive method is a conservative worst case, as CDV is not simply additive but depends on the design of each node and in some cases on loading. Upon reaching a node that implements a traffic-shaping function, the CDVT can be reset to a lower value representative of the CDV resulting from collisions in the shaper.

The ATM forum signaling does not currently allow the signaling of the CDVT, but the ITU-T signaling allows the system to carry the CDVT information.

For real-time traffic, the CDVT can be theoretically bounded, since the end-to-end Max-CDV is guaranteed. However, for non–real-time traffic, which is prone to placement in very large buffers served at a variable service rate, the characterization of the CDVT is a very difficult task and somewhat arbitrary. However it directly impacts the efficiency of the network (Chap. 4). Traffic shaping prior to entering a policing function or soft policing are better solutions to resolve the CDVT characterization problem.

Performance of the GCRA

The GCRA may detect an excessive amount of non-conforming cells, due to the slotted nature of ATM. If a connection violates its contract, the number of cells judged non-conforming should be less or equal to the amount of traffic sent in excess. However, the leaky bucket and virtual-scheduling

Figure 3.19.   GCRA excess discard for CDVT = 0.

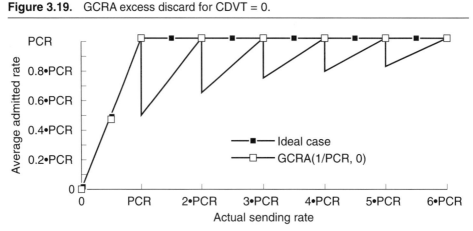

algorithms demonstrate some excessive discard behaviors [NAN15]. The problem can best be illustrated by taking the simple case of CDVT = 0, as illustrated in Fig. 3.19, which depicts the average rate of cells judged to conform (admitted) as a function of an actual sending rate. The problem is explained using the virtual-scheduling algorithm, however it also applies to the leaky bucket.

When a cell is regarded non-conforming, the TAT is not modified until the next arrival. When a late arrival occurs, the reference clock TAT *skips* to the arrival time of the late cell.

The intention of gap skip is to prevent the conforming traffic from exceeding the CDVT. However, solely enforcing CDVT can cause a significant reduction of the admitted cell rate of VCs, violating traffic contracts, sometimes as low as half of the declared PCR. Figure 3.19 demonstrates an example of a CBR VC sending constantly at a rate R higher than the contracted PCR. The rate of conforming cells after applying the GCRA(1/PCR, 0) is $R/\lceil R/\text{PCR} \rceil$, where $\lceil x \rceil$ denotes the minimum integer larger than x.

The above example shows that when a source sends slightly above its contracted rate (e.g., $1.01 \times \text{PCR}$), the resulting rate of conforming cells can be as low as half the contracted PCR. Furthermore, a smaller violation in the rate results in a lower average admitted rate. This behavior is obviously unfair due to the fact that the higher the rate violation, the higher the rate admitted by GCRA. The example is based on a zero CDVT, which is not realistic. However, such behavior is present until the CDVT is increased significantly.

In reality, once the GCRA judges one cell non-conformant, the following cell is likely to come late with respect to the TAT. At the arrival of that cell, the GCRA resynchronizes the TAT to the arrival time of the cell. Since the stream violates the contract, it likely finds the next cell non-conformant and resynchronizes. This cycle can repeat periodically. The result is excessive cell discard due to previous late arrival of cells. Furthermore, the ratio of cells discarded is highly dependent on the value of CDVT.

The problem of excessive discard can be resolved by setting the CDVT to a value larger than 1/PCR [I.371]. However, this inflated CDVT can reduce efficiency (see Chap. 4). Using a soft-policing function instead of strict policing also addresses the issue.

Review

In order to guarantee QoS, the ATM network has to allocate a proper amount of bandwidth for the connection. The allocation of bandwidth is done based on the negotiated traffic descriptors. However, the network can only meet the QoS objectives if the traffic behaves as per the traffic descriptors. The generic cell rate algorithm (GCRA), combined with conformance definitions, is used to specify unambiguously how the traffic should behave in order to conform to the traffic descriptors. Applications *shape* their traffic to ensure that it behaves as required, and the network can apply policing functions to monitor the traffic and take action on non-conformant traffic, while allowing some tolerance for jitter that may have affected the cell stream. Alternatively, the network can shape the traffic before allowing entry to the network. If the connection's traffic exceeds the contracted bandwidth by a large amount, the shaping function can discard the excess traffic.

References

[BOY92] Boyer, P., Servel, M.J., and Guillemin, F.P. "The Spacer-Controller, an Efficient UPC/NPC for ATM Networks." *XIV International Switching Symposium* (October 1992).

[BOY92-2] Boyer, P., Guillemin, F.P., Servel, M.J., and Coudreuse, J.P. "Spacing Cells Protects and Enhances Utilization of ATM Networks." *IEEE Networks* (Sept. 1992), 38–49.

[BUT91] Butto, M., Cavalero, E., and Tonietti, A. "Effectiveness of the Leaky Bucket Policing Mechanism in ATM Networks." *IEEE Journal on Selected Areas in Communications*, vol. 9, no. 3 (April 1991).

[DAN94] Danthine, O., Boyer, P. *Benefits of a Spacer-Controller in ATM WAN: Preliminary Traffic Measurements*. Exploit Traffic Workshop, Basel (September 1994).

[DIT91] Dittman, L., Jacobson, S., and Moth, K. "Flow Enforcement Algorithms for ATM Networks." *IEEE Journal on Selected Areas in Communications*, vol. 9, no. 3 (April 1991).

[GAL89] Gallasi, G., Rigolio, G., and Fratta, L. "ATM: Bandwidth Assignment and Enforcement Policies." *Proceedings of IEEE Globecom*, paper 49.6, Dallas, Texas (November 1989).

[I.371.1] ITU-Telecommunication Standardization Sector. *Traffic Control and Congestion Control in B-ISDN—ABR and ABT Conformance Definitions*, recommendation I.371.1, June 1997.

[I.371] ITU-Telecommunication Standardization Sector. *Traffic Control and Congestion Control in B-ISDN*, recommendation I.371, May 1996.

[LAN97] Landry, R., and Stavrakakis, I. "Study of Delay Jitter With and Without Peak Rate Enforcement." *IEEE/ACM Transactions on Networking*, vol. 5, no. 4 (August 1997).

[NAN15] *Throughput Behavior of the Generic Cell Rate Algorithm*. Newbridge Application Note, 31NAN0015, version 2, May 1997.

[RAT90] Rathgeb, E. "Modeling and Performance Comparison of Policing Mechanisms for ATM Networks." *IEEE Journal on Selected Areas in Communications*, vol. 9, no. 3 (April 1991).

[TM4.0] The ATM Forum Technical Committee. *Traffic Management Specification*, version 4.0, af-tm-0056.000, April 1996.

Connection Admission Control

An ATM connection traverses a set of switching nodes in the network. Even within a switching node, a connection may traverse a number of queuing points (see Chap. 5). To set up a connection on such a path, resources must be reserved at each queuing point to guarantee the contracted quality of service (Chap. 2). Generally, they comprise the buffer space and the bandwidth required to serve the connection at a queuing point. The sets of rules (or procedures) that determine admissibility of a connection in an ATM switch are commonly termed *connection admission control* (CAC).

As discussed in Chap. 2, an ATM connection can carry traffic of a particular service category (e.g., CBR, VBR, ABR, GFR or UBR). Furthermore, each of these service categories possess differing QoS objectives. Thus, the CAC rules are likely to be different for each service category.

To verify the admissibility of a connection, the CAC follows the general procedures outlined below to set up a connection at each queuing point:

1. Map the traffic descriptors associated with a connection onto a traffic model. Since each service category has specific traffic descriptors associated with it, different traffic models are necessary.
2. Use this traffic model with an appropriate queuing model to estimate whether there are enough system resources to admit the connection in order to meet the QoS objectives.
3. Allocate resources if they are suficient and admit the connection.

Depending on the traffic models used, the CAC procedures can be too conservative by overallocating the resources. This reduces the *statistical gains* (defined later in the chapter) that can be obtained. An efficient CAC produces maximum statistical gain without violating the QoS. The efficiency of the CAC thus depends on how closely the traffic and queuing models capture reality. Both the traffic and queuing models are well researched and widely discussed in the literature.

It should be noted that the CAC algorithms cannot be computationally intensive as these are executed in real time by the ATM switches. This execution directly affects the connection setup rate and the setup delay because the CAC algorithm is executed on every connection setup. Since connections are setup and torn down in real time, handling a high setup rate is crucial for efficient support of switched virtual circuits (SVCs).

There may be other techniques to allocate bandwidth based on heuristics, or long-term measurements. These types of connection admission control procedures cannot guarantee the QoS and do not allow for safe overbooking of the resources (see Sec. "Tuning the Connection Admission Control").

The CAC algorithms are not specified by the ATM Forum or the ITU-T, because each switch architecture, queuing, and scheduling implementations may be more suited for a specific type of CAC implementation. Other limitations, such as processing capacity or buffer size, may dictate the use of a specific CAC implementation. It is not necessary to have the same CAC function on every switch or even on every queuing point within a switch to achieve end-to-end QoS guarantees.

This chapter details some of the CAC procedures that can be adopted by ATM switches. Comprehension of these algorithms is not necessary to understand the remainder of this book. First, we look at the traffic models, queuing models, and CAC functions for the CBR traffic. The CAC methods for CBR traffic are divided into two areas: the methods that neglect CDV and the methods that account for the CDV. Then the CAC functions for VBR are discussed. There are two distinct CAC methods for VBR traffic: methods that consider each connection independently and methods that consider all the connections together. The former is also called the "effective bandwidth" method. The CAC rules for ABR, GFR, and UBR services are also discussed. The CAC extensions to multiclass traffic and the effect of CDV are also discussed. The CAC procedures based on measurement techniques are presented. Finally, different ways of tuning the CAC function are described.

Statistical Gain

Since a connection's maximum possible data rate is the peak cell rate (PCR), ignoring the jitter (or CDV), a CAC need not allocate more than PCR to a connection. However, since connections do not continuously send data, it is possible to allocate less resources when many connections are multiplexed at a queuing point. This means that statistical gain is possible and more connections can be admitted than if PCR is allocated to each connection. Thus, the term *statistical gain* can be defined as

$$\text{Statistical Gain} = \frac{\text{Number of connections admitted with statistical multiplexing}}{\text{Number of connections admitted with peak rate allocation}}$$

An efficient CAC should try to achieve as much statistical gain as possible without risking a congestion condition that would impair QoS. The gain (equivalently, the amount of statistical multiplexing that can be achieved), is generally a function of buffer size, traffic characteristics, and QoS objectives of the connections that are being multiplexed. For a given set of traffic and QoS parameters, larger statistical gain can be obtained with larger buffers up to a point of diminishing return. Thus, the occurrence of congestion at a queuing point [RMV96] can be analyzed into two parts:

1. Cell-scale congestion that occurs in a small buffer due to simultaneous arrivals of cells from different connections
2. Burst-scale congestion that occurs typically in a large buffer due to arrivals of bursts of cells from different connections

The CBR and real-time VBR (rt-VBR) service categories have nodal delay requirements. That is, the nodal delay experienced by cells of these services should not be more than a given value D (e.g., 250µs) with a given quantile Q (e.g., 10^{-10}); that is, $P(\text{nodal delay} > D) \le Q$. This delay requirement forces the buffer sizes to be small, and cell-scale congestion will be prevalent for these services. It is therefore difficult to achieve large statistical multiplexing gain for CBR and rt-VBR services. For nrt-VBR, the ATM switches provide larger buffers to absorb the bursts, and burst-scale congestion will occur frequently for these services. As a result, it is generally possible to achieve large statistical gain for nrt-VBR services.

CAC for CBR Traffic

A pure CBR traffic source emits a cell periodically at every 1/PCR units. Ignoring the CDV and the cell-scale congestion, a simple rule of CAC is to assign the PCR as the bandwidth required for each CBR connection and admit connections such that

$$\sum_i \text{PCR}_i \le \text{Link capacity} \tag{4.1}$$

This CAC algorithm is based on "peak rate allocation." As ATM cells traverse through various queuing points, the periodicity of a pure CBR source will be lost. The cells may clump together or disperse due to buffering and the effects of other intervening traffic (e.g., CDV). When cells are clumped together, the effective peak rate will be higher than the source actual peak rate. Due to the presence of CDV, this simple CAC rule may not be sufficient to ensure that the cell loss ratio (CLR) of the admitted connections is within the objective limits. Even without this jitter, the simultaneous arrival of cells due to the multiplexing of periodic cell streams can also cause cell loss. The buffer overflow can occur typically in a small buffer. In general, there are two approaches to account for CDV [RMV96]: negligible CDV methods and nonnegligible CDV methods.

Negligible CDV Methods

Negligible CDV methods do not directly account for the CDV and assume that the jitter in the traffic streams is negligible. One such method is to model the multiplexer queue as an $M/D/1$ queue. Given the buffer size B, the link capacity C, and the peak cell rate of the connection PCR_i, the method determines a load ρ such that the probability of queue length exceeding B is less than ε, where ε is a small number such as 10^{-10}. The CAC then admits the connections until

$$\sum_i PCR_i \leq \rho \times \text{Link capacity} \tag{4.2}$$

The second method is to use a $nD/D/1$ multiplexer model [DRS91, RV91, RMV96, FLV94] that assumes n identical periodic CBR cell streams being multiplexed. This method produces less conservative results than an $M/D/1$ model for high loads ($>80\%$). Asymptotic complementary queue length distributions in references [DRS91, RMV96, and FLV94] are not computationally intensive and serve as good approximations for these models. For example, in [FLV94], the $M/D/1$ approximation is given as:

$$P(\text{Buffer length} > x) \approx -\frac{1-\rho}{\ln(\rho)} \exp(-x(1 - \rho - \ln(\rho))) \tag{4.3}$$

The $nD/D/1$ approximation based on a Brownian Bridge approximation is given by [FLV94]:

$$P(\text{Buffer length} > x) \approx -\frac{1-\rho}{\ln(\rho)} \exp\left(-x\left(\frac{2x}{n} + 1 - \rho - \ln(\rho)\right)\right) \tag{4.4}$$

Here it is assumed that the service duration is one cell slot and the units of buffer length and x are in number of cells. Figure 4.1 compares these two methods for various buffer sizes. As indicated by Fig. 4.1, $M/D/1$ model is conservative and the $nD/D/1$ model can obtain better capacity. For large n, both models give nearly the same result, as the system is well approximated by the Poisson arrivals.

The $M/D/1$ and $nD/D/1$ models assume a homogeneous system of sources; that is, all sources have identical PCR. In reality, the sources will have different PCR requirements. Therefore, models like $\Sigma D_i/D/1$ [RMV96], $\Sigma n_k D_k/D/1$ [RV91] are useful for this purpose. Another way to deal with heterogeneous connections is to map them onto an equivalent homogeneous system. One such example is shown in [FLV94] by Fiche et al.

Figure 4.1.   Cell loss probability vs. buffer size.

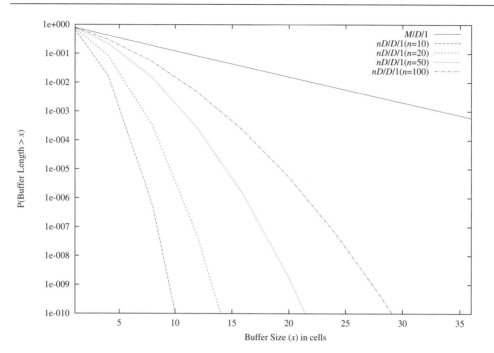

Nonnegligible CDV Methods

The negligible CDV method generally models the multiplexing of pure CBR, nonjittered sources. However, the CDV may not be negligible when CBR traffic streams are multiplexed with other traffic streams, such as rt-VBR. In this case, the traffic stream may become bursty, and the CAC needs to take into account the CDV to estimate the burst-scale congestion. Each ATM connection is generally policed at the network edges using the generic cell rate algorithms (GCRA) (Chap. 3). For CBR connections arriving on a link with a link rate (LR), the peak rate policing is enforced with GCRA(1/PCR, CDVT). The worst-case output traffic pattern of such a policing function will be a periodic on-off process with a maximum burst size $BS = 1 + \lfloor CDVT/(T\text{-}\delta) \rfloor$ where $T = 1/PCR$ and $\delta = 1/LR$.

Therefore, to account for the CDV, in addition to Eq. (4.1) another constraint is placed on the buffer such that $\Sigma BS_i \leq B$, where B is the buffer size of the queue and BS_i is the maximum burst size of connection i. This worst-case estimate assumes that no cell loss occurs with the simultaneous arrivals of bursts from all the connections (also called *lossless multiplexing*). However, this constraint can be overly pessimistic. Another way is to consider the on-off process of the leaky bucket model and map it to an equivalent VBR traffic with parameters $SCR' = PCR$, $PCR' = LR$ and $MBS' = 1 + \lfloor CDVT/(T\text{-}\delta) \rfloor$. Then, the same CAC as for the VBR traffic can be applied with SCR′, PCR′, and MBS′. Here, PCR is the peak cell rate of CBR connection; LR is the link rate of the CBR connection. The CAC methods for the VBR traffic are described in the next section.

CAC for VBR Traffic

As noted in Chap. 2, the variable bit rate (VBR) traffic is generally characterized by an average rate (SCR), peak cell rate (PCR), cell delay variation tolerance (CDVT) and maximum burst size (MBS). The QoS specifications for rt-VBR traffic are cell loss ratio (CLR) and delay, while nrt-VBR traffic has only the cell loss.

The ratio SCR/PCR defines the *burstiness* of a VBR connection and has a strong impact on the statistical gain. If the burstiness (or SCR/PCR)$<<$ 1, a CAC based on peak-rate allocation will be very inefficient and conservative. It is shown [WK90] that the link utilization can go as low as 5 percent when SCR/PCR is small. Even if the buffer for VBR traffic is very small, peak-rate allocation is unnecessary. It is possible to admit connections such that

$$\sum_i \alpha_i \leq \text{Link capacity} \tag{4.5}$$

where, $SCR_i \leq \alpha_i \leq PCR_i$ for connection i. While peak-rate allocation does not provide any statistical gain, Eq. (4.5) does provide the statistical gain. The statistical gain at a queuing point can then be defined as the ratio $\Sigma PCR_i / \Sigma \alpha_i$. The α_i is called the *effective bandwidth, equivalent bandwidth,* or *virtual bandwidth* of a connection.

In the case of a small-buffer or no-buffer scenario, a *rate envelope multiplexing* (REM) [RMV96] technique can be used. That is, the connections are admitted such that the total aggregate arrival rate (rate envelope) of the connections is less than the link capacity with a high probability. On the other hand, if there is a very large buffer ($\rightarrow\infty$) available for the VBR traffic, it would absorb the bursts so that allocating more than SCR for each VBR connection is unnecessary. In practice, the buffer is finite and the bandwidth allocation falls in between that of SCR and PCR. This method is called *rate sharing* (RS) technique.

Rate Envelope Multiplexing (REM)

The *rate envelope multiplexing* (REM) [RMV96] method assumes that there is little or no buffering available to the VBR traffic. Thus, it is also called the *zero buffer* or *bufferless* approximation. This method is well suited for real-time traffic due to the assumption of small buffers, and it models the cell-scale congestion well. By the REM method, connections are admitted so that the aggregate arrival rate AR (i.e., rate envelope) of the connections is less than the link capacity C of the queuing point with large probability. The cell loss ratio (CLR) can be estimated as

$$CLR = \frac{E\{(AR - C)^+\}}{E\{AR\}} \tag{4.6}$$

Here, the CLR is defined as the ratio of amount of cells lost to the amount of cells submitted. It depends solely on the connection parameters and not on the queuing behavior of the system. The operator $(\cdot)^+$ takes into account only the positive differences (i.e., when $AR > C$) and is zero when $AR < C$. For call admission purposes, the aggregate rate AR can be measured in real time or estimated from the traffic models. Once AR is known, the CLR is estimated using Eq. (4.6) before admitting a new connection. The connection can be accepted if the resulting CLR is lower than the objective. For example, when N identical on-off sources with peak rate PCR and mean rate SCR are multiplexed on a link of capacity C, the CLR is given by [RMV96]

$$\text{CLR} = \sum_{i \times \text{PCR} > C} (i \times \text{PCR} - C) \binom{N}{i} \left(\frac{\text{SCR}}{\text{PCR}}\right)^i \left(1 - \frac{\text{SCR}}{\text{PCR}}\right)^{N-i} \times \left(\frac{1}{N \times \text{SCR}}\right) \quad (4.7)$$

Alternately, one can use the equivalent bandwidth approach. This is described in Sec. "Effective Bandwidths," later in the chapter.

Rate Sharing (RS)

The REM method relies on the fact that the total aggregate input rate does not exceed the link capacity or that the probability of exceeding is very small. If this assumption is not true, buffering is needed to absorb any rate mismatch. This is especially true for bursty traffic, the average rate of which is small compared to its peak rate. For example, given VBR traffic with SCR $<<$ PCR, there could be a small number of connections simultaneously sending at PCR but the sum of PCR can be much larger than the link capacity. To guarantee a certain QoS to the connections, such as CLR, a buffer is needed to store the traffic temporarily and the link capacity is shared among the contending connections. Thus, the queuing models should also be incorporated into the connection admission rules. There are two approaches to do this:

1. Consider all the traffic streams that are multiplexed together and estimate the cell loss probability to obtain maximum possible statistical gain.
2. Consider each connection independently and estimate bandwidth requirements of the connection so as to guarantee a given QoS. This method is also referred to as the effective bandwidth approach.

The effective bandwidth approach is explained in detail in the next section. The first approach considers the connections that have already been admitted plus the one being considered for admission together, and checks whether the new connection would violate the QoS guarantees of any of the connections. That is, the method considers the presence of other existing connections in determining the QoS objectives. The new connection will be accepted if the QoS objectives are met.

In [BC92], a large class of VBR sources and their superposition is taken into account. A point process belonging to the class of discrete-time batch Markovian arrival processes (D-

BMAP) is proposed. Buffer occupancy and cell loss probabilities of a statistical multiplexer are derived based on this process, using a matrix-analytical approach.

Buffet and Duffield [BD94] developed exponential upper bounds for the queue distribution of a FCFS (first-come-first-serve) queue, which is fed by superposition of homogeneous Markovian on-off sources. Using the theory of Martingales, a bound of the form $P[\text{queue length} \geq B] \leq cy^{-B}$ for any $B \geq 1$ where $c < 1$ and $y > 1$ is given explicitly as a function of parameters of the model. The model assumes that L independent markovian sources are multiplexed, each with mean silence length of $1/a$ units, and the mean burst length of $1/d$ units. Let the service rate of the multiplexer be σL. Define $k = (1-a-d)$; then the explicit bound for the cell loss probability is given by

$$P[Q \geq B] \leq \frac{a(1 - a - \sigma k)}{d(a + \sigma k)} \left[\frac{(1 - \sigma)(a + \sigma k)}{\sigma(1 - a - \sigma k)} \right]^{B} \left[\frac{1}{(a + d)} \left(\frac{d}{1 - \sigma} \right)^{1 - \sigma} \left(\frac{a}{\sigma} \right)^{\sigma} \right]^{L} \quad (4.8)$$

An *MMDP/D/1/K* queuing system is used in [YT95] to estimate the cell loss probability of an ATM multiplexer loaded with homogeneous on-off sources. As per the Markov Modulated Deterministic Process (MMDP), a source can be in one of two states: *on* or *off*. When the source is on, it generates a stream of cells that are equally spaced at PCR. When it is off, the source generates no cells. Both on and off periods are distributed as independent exponential random variables. Exact and approximate methods are used to estimate the cell loss probability.

Diffusion process approximation of a statistical multiplexer is considered by Ren and Kobayashi [RK94]. The sources are modeled as Markov Modulated Rate Process (MMRP), and a diffusion process approximation for the superposition of such rate processes is developed in [RK94]. This model is not restricted to the exponential distribution for the duration of each state.

There are many more traffic as well as queuing models proposed in the literature for the CAC purposes than can be listed here. However, it should be observed that all these methods estimate the tail probabilities—that is, $P(\text{Queue Length} > \text{Buffer})$—as a function of N, the number of connections. Although these methods may achieve better statistical gain than the methods based on *effective bandwidths* (see next section), the stated dependence on the number of connections (N) makes them generally difficult to implement in real switches. These methods tend to be computationally intensive and such processing power may be limited in the switches. The CAC function should be able to dynamically add or remove connections in real time. Consequently, methods that translate the source traffic parameters into one number, called the equivalent or effective bandwidth, have become very popular. Many ATM network-engineering tools use the effective bandwidths approach to estimate the required bandwidth of connections.

Effective Bandwidths

The effective bandwidth approach views each connection in isolation, as if it were alone at the queuing point. This model maps each connection's traffic parameters into a real number α_i, called the *effective bandwidth* or *equivalent bandwidth* of the connection, such that the QoS constraints are satisfied. Thus, the effective bandwidth is derived as a source property, and with this mapping the CAC rule becomes very simple:

$$\sum_i \alpha_i \leq \text{Link capacity}$$

That is, a connection is admitted if there is available spare capacity, or else it is rejected. For a connection with an average rate SCR_i and peak rate PCR_i, the effective bandwidth is a number between the SCR_i and PCR_i. That is, $SCR_i \leq \alpha_i \leq PCR_i$. The value of effective bandwidth depends on the statistical properties of the connection being admitted as well as on the queuing properties of the congestion point under consideration. In general, for a given connection it is intuitive that the effective bandwidth will be close to the PCR for very small buffers and close to the SCR for very large buffers.

Two properties constitute the main advantages of the effective bandwidth method:

1. *Additive Property*: Effective bandwidths are additive; that is, the total effective bandwidth needed for N connections equals to the sum of effective bandwidths of each connection.
2. *Independence Property*: Effective bandwidth for a given connection is only a function of that connection's parameters.

The additive property of the effective bandwidth method makes it widely accepted and used in ATM technology. Since connections are set up and torn down dynamically, with the effective bandwidth method, the CAC function can add (or subtract) the effective bandwidth of the connection being set up (or torn down) from the total effective bandwidth. This is not easily possible with any method that lacks the independence and additive properties. However, it should be noted that, as well due to the independence property, the effective bandwidth method could be far more conservative than a method that considers the true statistical multiplexing (i.e., a method that considers the presence of other connections). The main reason for this is that the actual bandwidth needed to serve N connections could be far less than the sum of the bandwidths of N connections. In the sections that follow, effective bandwidths for rate envelope multiplexing and rate sharing are presented.

Effective Bandwidths for Rate Envelope Multiplexing

The CLR for rate envelope multiplexing is estimated by Eq. (4.6). Kelly [Kel91] developed the effective bandwidths for a heterogeneous system of sources producing an aggregate load:

$$AR = \sum_{j=1}^{J}\sum_{i=1}^{n_j} AR_{ji} \qquad (4.9)$$

Here, AR_{ji} is the load produced by source i in class j, and n_j is the number of sources in class j. Using large deviation approximations, Kelly [Kel91] showed that

$$\log P(AR \geq C) \approx \inf_s \left[\sum_{j=1}^{J} (n_j M_j(s) - sC) \right] \tag{4.10}$$

where

$$M_j(s) = \log E\left[e^{sAR_{ji}}\right] \tag{4.11}$$

is the logarithmic moment-generating function of the random variable AR_{ji} and C is the link capacity. Let s attain an infimum at s^*. Then, the constraint on the tail behavior $\log P\{AR \leq C\} \leq -CLR$ implies that the call acceptance region is

$$A(n^*) = \left\{ n : \sum_{j=1}^{J} \alpha_j^* n_j + \frac{CLR}{s^*} \leq C \right\} \tag{4.12}$$

Here $\alpha_j^* = M_j(s^*)/s^*$ is the *effective bandwidth* of source j, and $\log P\{AR \leq C\} \leq -CLR$. For on-off sources with peak rate PCR_j and average rate SCR_j, the moment-generating function $M_j(s)$ is given by,

$$M_j(s) = \log\left(1 + \frac{SCR_j}{PCR_j}(e^{sPCR_j} - 1)\right) \tag{4.13}$$

Effective Bandwidths for Rate Sharing

The rate-sharing technique uses a buffer to absorb momentary bursts of data when the aggregate arrival rate can momentarily exceed the service capacity. The buffer can be dimensioned to allow small loss probabilities. The effective bandwidth method should consider the cell loss ratio and the buffer size. The techniques of effective bandwidths for rate sharing can be divided into lossless and loss-tolerant models. As the name implies, lossless models do not allow cell loss to occur and thus CLR is not explicitly taken into account.

Kelly [Kel91] developed effective bandwidth for a $M/G/1$ model for lossless performance. Here it is assumed that bursts from a source of class j arrive in a Poisson stream of rate r_j. The bursts are assumed to have a length distribution G_j. Let μ_j and σ_j^2 be the mean and variance of G_j and L the buffer size. Then the effective bandwidth of a source of type j is found to be

$$\alpha_j = r_j \left[\mu_j + \frac{1}{2L}(\mu_j^2 + \sigma_j^2) \right] \tag{4.14}$$

Elwalid [EMW95] developed the effective bandwidth assuming a worst-case traffic pattern of a source according to the leaky bucket algorithm. The departure process of such a policing function is assumed to be on-off and periodic. Let B_T be the token buffer size of such leaky bucket. Let SCR_j, PCR_j be the average and peak cell rates of connection j. The maximum burst size (MBS) allowed by the conformance definition will be $MBS_j = B_T \lfloor PCR_j/(PCR_j - SCR_j) \rfloor$. The effective bandwidth of such a connection for lossless performance is given by

$$\alpha_j = \begin{cases} \dfrac{PCR_j}{1 + \dfrac{B(PCR_j - SCR_j)}{B_T C}}, & \text{if } SCR_j \leq \dfrac{B_T}{B/C} \\[4ex] SCR_j, & \text{if } \dfrac{B_T}{B/C} \leq SCR_j \leq PCR_j \end{cases} \tag{4.15}$$

The loss probability is considered in realistic models through the *asymptotic slope* of the queue length distribution. There is a plethora of research on this topic. In general, for a given buffer size B, the queue length tail probabilities are asymptotically exponential:

$$P(\text{queue length} \geq B) \approx e^{-f(\alpha_i)B} \tag{4.16}$$

The function $f()$ is determined from the statistical properties of the traffic stream. The term α_i is the effective service rate or effective bandwidth needed to serve the connection in order to guarantee a given CLR; that is, $P(\text{queue length} > B) \leq CLR$. From these two equations, the effective bandwidth of a connection can be determined as

$$\alpha_i = f^{-1}(-(\log CLR)/B) \tag{4.17}$$

Let $(\log CLR)/B = \zeta \in [-\infty, 0]$. For on-off sources with exponentially distributed on and off periods, Gibbens and Hunt [GH91] derived the effective bandwidths of a source. Let a source mean on period be $1/\mu_i$ and its mean off period be $1/\lambda_i$. When the source is on, it is assumed to produce information at a constant rate γ_i. The effective bandwidth α_i of the source is given by Gibbens and Hunt [GH91] as

$$\alpha_i = \frac{(\zeta\gamma_i + \mu_i + \lambda_i) - \sqrt{(\zeta\gamma_i + \mu_i - \lambda_i)^2 + 4\lambda_i\mu_i}}{2\zeta} \tag{4.18}$$

Equation (4.18) implies that for large B, $\zeta \to 0$ and α_i equals the mean rate of the source $\lambda_i\gamma_i/(\lambda_i + \mu_i)$. For a small buffer B, $\zeta \to -\infty$ and the effective bandwidth of the source will be $\alpha_i = \gamma_i$, the peak information rate. For a connection that generates traffic using the on-off model with traffic descriptors of SCR, PCR, CLR and ABS (average burst size), the above parameters can be mapped as $\mu_i = PCR/ABS$, $\lambda_i = \mu_i \times SCR/(PCR - SCR)$, $\gamma_i = PCR$. Note that for VBR connections, MBS and not ABS is indicated in the traffic descriptor. Therefore, in order to use this function as a CAC for VBR traffic, another mapping is needed to translate the ABS into an MBS. One method for such mapping is to use truncated distributions with ABS as the mean and the distribution truncated at MBS. Another method is to choose the ABS value such that the probability of the burst size exceeding MBS is very low.

Using Eq. (4.18), Fig. 4.2 shows the effective bandwidth as a function of buffer size for various traffic parameters. A connection with PCR = 100 Mb/s, CLR = 10^{-7} and ABS = 50 cells is chosen for this graph. The effective bandwidth as a function of buffer size is plotted for various values of SCR. Figure 4.2 clearly shows that the effective bandwidth is close to PCR for small buffers and tends to approach SCR as the buffer size increases. Figure 4.3 shows the amount of statistical gain that can be achieved for the same connections.

The result of Gibbens and Hunt [GH91] is extended in [EM93]. Elwalid and Mitra [EM93] obtain two sets of results: one for a statistical multiplexing with general Markov-modulated fluid sources and the other for queues in which traffic sources are Markov-modulated Poisson or phase-renewal processes. Based on large deviation calculations, for large B, an approximate measure of effective bandwidth is given by Courcoubetis et al. [CFW94] for stationary sources as

$$\alpha_i = m_i + \frac{\delta \xi_i}{2B} \tag{4.19}$$

Figure 4.2. Effective bandwidth as a function of buffer size.

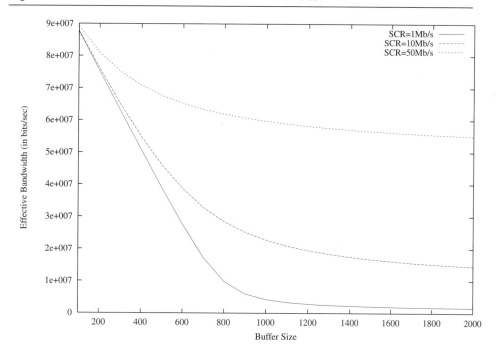

Figure 4.3. Statistical gain as a function of buffer size

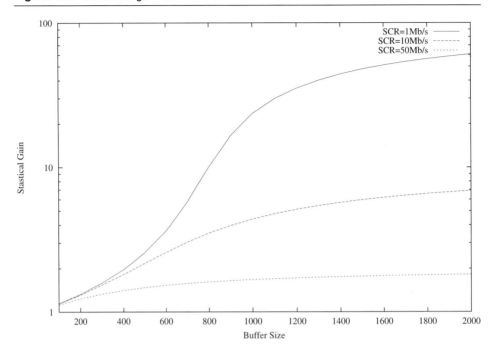

where, m_i is the mean rate of the source, $\delta = -log$ (CLR) and ξ_i is called the index of dispersion. For an on-off Markov fluid model with a mean on period $1/\mu_i$, a mean off period $1/\lambda_i$, and peak information rate γ_i, the effective bandwidth will be

$$\alpha_i = \frac{\lambda_i \gamma_i}{\lambda_i + \mu_i} + \frac{\delta \lambda_i \mu_i \gamma_i^2}{B(\lambda_i + \mu_i)^3} \tag{4.20}$$

To see how these approximations of effective bandwidth compare, consider:

1. The Gibbens and Hunt method given by Eq. (4.18)
2. The Courcoubetis et al. method given by Eq. (4.20)
3. The Buffet and Duffield method given by Eq. (4.8)

Note that Eq. (4.8) does not yield any explicit effective bandwidth. Instead, Eq. (4.8) is used to calculate the effective service rate required for serving a single connection so that the loss probability is less than a given value. Figure 4.4 shows such a comparison for connections with PCR = 100Mb/s, CLR = 10^{-7}, line rate = 150 Mb/s, average burst size (ABS) = 50 cells. However, the comparison is limited because the degree of conservatism for each method varies

Figure 4.4. Comparison of effective bandwidth function

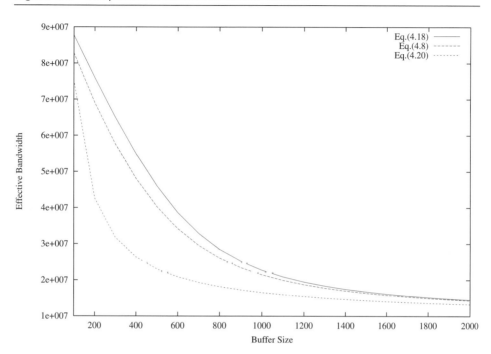

with changes in traffic parameters. Figure 4.4 does not show, for example, that for large ABS, Eq. (4.20) can be more conservative than others for small buffer sizes.

Effective bandwidth methods are generally conservative because they do not consider the effect of multiplexing many sources together (e.g., smoothing of aggregate traffic). However, Guérin et al. [GAN91] used an aggregate stationary bit rate approximation to account for this multiplexing. First, a fluid-flow approximation is used by Guérin et al. [GAN91] in deriving the effective bandwidth for a single two-state Markov source. Let the peak rate of the source be PCR_i, utilization ρ, and mean burst period b. With queue size B and $\gamma = \ln(1/CLR)$, the effective bandwidth of the source is approximated by

$$\alpha_i = \frac{\gamma b(1-\rho)PCR_i - B + \sqrt{[\gamma b(1-\rho)PCR_i - B]^2 + 4B\gamma b\rho(1-\rho)PCR_i}}{2\gamma b(1-\rho)} \quad (4.21)$$

It is possible that Eq. (4.21) can be very conservative for large bursts. As a result, an aggregate stationary bit rate approximation is used. The distribution of the stationary bit rate is assumed to be Gaussian. Thus, when N connections are multiplexed, the total capacity needed is approximated as

$$C_s = m + \alpha'\sigma \quad (4.22)$$

where m is the mean aggregate bit rate ($\sum_{i=1}^{N} SCR_i$), σ is the standard deviation of the aggregate bit rate and $\alpha' = \sqrt{-2\ln(CLR)} - \ln(2\pi)$. The flow and stationary approximations are then combined into a single approximation. That is, the total equivalent capacity needed to multiplex N connections is taken as the minimum of stationary and fluid approximations:

$$\min \left\{ m + \alpha'\sigma, \sum_{i=1}^{N} \alpha_i \right\}$$

The key element in effective bandwidth approximation is shown in Eq. (4.16), where queue length tail probabilities are assumed to be asymptotically exponential. This method is too conservative and a better approximation can be achieved by introducing more variables to this equation, as described in [CLW96]. The waiting time probabilities are generalized as here in the form

$$P(W > x) \approx \beta e^{-\eta x} \text{ as } x \to \infty$$

where β is the asymptotic constant and η is the asymptotic decay rate. Introducing more terms further refines this equation. The actual effective bandwidth lies between this approximation and that of Eq. (4.16).

Much of the work presented so far is based on Markovian models for the traffic sources. However, network traffic measurements have shown that network traffic can be self-similar. That is, the traffic has shown both short- and long-range dependence in its correlation. Markovian models cannot generally capture this behavior. Measurements have also shown that with increased buffer capacity the resulting cell loss is not reduced exponentially but decreases slowly. To reflect this behavior, an asymptotic upper bound to an overflow probability that decreases hyperbolically with buffer size is developed by Tsybakov [TG97]. Norros [Nor94, Nor95] developed an effective bandwidth model for the self-similar traffic:

$$\alpha_i = m + \left(H^H (1-H)^{(1-H)} \sqrt{-2\ln(CLR)} \right)^{1/H} a^{1/(2H)} B^{-(1-H)/H} m^{1/(2H)} \qquad (4.23)$$

where m is the mean bit rate of the traffic stream, a is the coefficient of variation, B is the buffer size, H is the Hurst parameter of the stream ($0.5 \le H \le 1$), CLR is the target cell loss ratio. Note that this equation does not follow the asymptotic exponential queue length distribution.

CAC for ABR, UBR, and GFR Traffic

The connection admission control procedures for ABR, GFR, and UBR are quite simple. Both ABR and GFR traffic have minimum cell rate (MCR) guarantees. Thus the CAC function has to assign this bandwidth for each connection. Based on current definition of GFR and depending on the available buffer size and buffer management techniques, the CAC needs to take into account the MFS and MBS parameters. However, since UBR traffic does not have such bandwidth guarantees, the CAC can theoretically admit connections without limit, but it may be designed to limit the number of UBR connections so that each connection gets some level of throughput in the long term.

Admission Control for Multiclass Traffic

Until now, the CAC functions discussed are designed for a single service category. In the real world, traffic flow consists of multiple service classes (see Chap. 2), where the services may be partitioned and queued separately (see Chap. 5). Even within a given service category, multiple subclasses can be differentiated depending on their QoS requirements (see Chap. 2).

To guarantee QoS for such multiclass traffic, a certain amount of bandwidth (or capacity) is reserved for each of the service classes. With an effective-bandwidth approach, this assignment becomes very simple. Let N_j be the number of sources for class j, and let α_j be the effective bandwidth of a source belonging to class j. Let there be K such classes. The CAC for multiclass traffic should then check that the total estimated capacity is less than the service rate; that is,

$$\sum_{j=1}^{K} N_j \alpha_j \leq \text{link capacity} \tag{4.24}$$

Priority queuing is a simple architecture to provide a multiple QoS (see Chap. 5) structure. An example is shown in Fig. 4.5 below. Equation (4.24) is sufficient to guarantee QoS of such structure as long as there are no or few CLP = 1 cells from CLP-significant VBR services.

Berger and Whitt [BW98] considered modifications of effective bandwidths for priorities. Generally, high-priority traffic has stricter performance criteria than the low-priority traf-

Figure 4.5.   An example priority-queuing structure

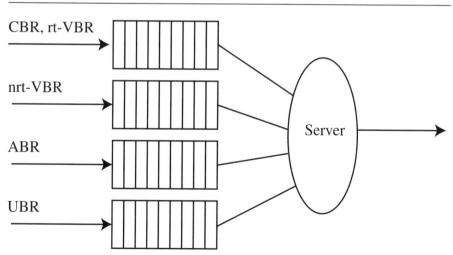

fic class. It is therefore possible to admit more connections of low-priority traffic. Instead of the linear constraint used in Eq. (4.24), the method in [BW98] uses a set of constraints. If these are N priority levels, N such constraints are needed. At each level k, the constraint considers the effective bandwidths of connections of the levels above, as seen at level k. Let α_{ij}^k denote the effective bandwidth of a priority-i, class-j connection as seen by priority-k, and n_{ij} the number of connections of priority-i, class-j connections. Then the bandwidth constraints are defined as

$$\sum_{i=1}^{k}\sum_{j=1}^{J_i}\alpha_{ij}^k n_{ij} \leq \text{link capacity} \tag{4.25}$$

Here, i denotes the priority level and j denotes the service class, and $1 \leq j \leq J_i$. By doing this, it is shown that the number of connections admitted is greater than the number admitted by the linear constraint of Eq. (4.24).

The existence of effective bandwidths for multiclass Markov fluids and other types of sources that are used to model ATM traffic is shown in [KWC93]. Hsu and Walrand [HW96] proposed an admission control scheme for multi-class ATM traffic in which it is assumed that real-time traffic is not buffered. In this case, the real-time traffic uses peak rate allocation and provides multiple service classes. However, the total bandwidth assigned to the real-time traffic for each class is limited to $min(\sum PCR, C_k)$, where C_k is the capacity estimated to meet the QoS objectives of the aggregate traffic of class k.

An effective bandwidth vector for two-priority ATM traffic is presented by Kulkarni et al. in [KGC94]. This model provides a CAC for two service classes sharing a single buffer. The effective bandwidth function is extended to such two-priority traffic in [KGC94].

Effect of Cell Delay Variation on CAC

Due to the buffering at various contention points in an ATM network (see Chap. 5), each cell of a connection suffers a different amount of delay jitter. To account for this cell delay variation, connections are policed with a CDVT parameter at an UPC point. For example, a connection with a peak cell rate PCR and cell delay variation tolerance CDVT is policed by a UPC function GCRA(PCR,CDVT). This means that the output of a policing function for a CBR source emitting cells at PCR would be bursty and jittered within the limits of the specified CDV tolerance. This added burstiness should be considered in the CAC, as this may require more resources.

The nonnegligible CDV methods described earlier in the section "CAC for CBR Traffic" did not explicitly consider the CDV tolerance. As described in that section, one way is to consider the on-off process of the leaky bucket model and map it to an equivalent VBR traffic descriptor. Then the same CAC as for the VBR traffic can be applied.

A novel way was devised by Skilros [Skl94] to adapt the CDVT parameter for the CAC. Specifically, the output of the policing function is characterized by a generalized geometric

Figure 4.6.   *GGeo* CAC function. Source: Reprinted from Skliros, A. "A Connection Admission
                    Control Algorithm for ATM Traffic Distorted by Cell Delay Variation," *Proceedings of
                    ITC14* (1994), 1385–1394, copyright 1994, with permission from Elsevier Science.

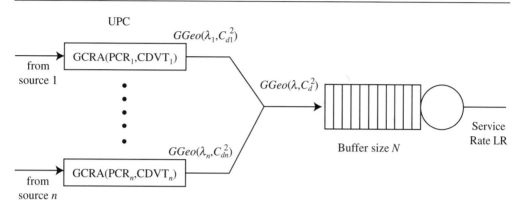

(*GGeo*) distribution with two moments, the mean λ and the squared coefficient of variation C_d^2.
For CBR traffic, if the connection passes through a multiplexer with a link rate LR, then the
worst-case burst size will be MBS $= 1 + \lfloor$CDVT$/(T - \delta)\rfloor$, where $T = 1$/PCR and $\delta = 1$/LR.
The mean (λ) and coefficient of variation (C_d^2) of the output process of the policing function are
then approximated by $\lambda = 1$/PCR and $C_d^2 = ($MBS $- 1)(1 - ($PCR/LR$))^2$. As shown in Fig. 4.6,
the individual *GGeo*(λ_i, C_{di}^2) process can then be merged into one single *GGeo*(λ, C_d^2). A maximum entropy solution is formed for the resulting *GGeo*/*GGeo*/1/*N* queue, which is used as a
CAC function.

CAC Based on Measurements

The CAC procedures described thus far are based on analytical modeling of the behavior of both
the traffic sources and queuing structures. In reality there are varieties of traffic sources, behaving quite differently, and it is impossible to model all of them accurately. Analytical methods
used to estimate the resource needs for one given class of traffic sources could severely overes-
timate or underestimate the resource requirements for some other class. It is also possible that
sources may not fully utilize their traffic descriptors. Hence, CAC procedures based on real-time
measurements of resources can predict the resource usage more accurately. These procedures
measure certain resources in real time and attempt to estimate whether the QoS objectives could
be maintained if a new connection is admitted.

Courcoubetos et al. [CKW95] proposed one such method. This procedure monitors the
traffic at a queuing point and makes decisions of admitting more connections based on the fraction of cells lost in the queue. Given a buffer size *B*, a number of connections *N*, a service rate

C, and *F(N,B,C)* as the fraction of cells lost due to buffer overflows, the fraction of cells lost $F(N(1 + \varepsilon),B,C)$ is estimated. Here $N(1 + \varepsilon)$ represents the additional connections admitted. The function *F* is represented in terms of the buffer overflow probability φ in a busy cycle. For large *B*, the function $\varphi(N(1 + \varepsilon),B,C)$ is approximated as $\varphi(N,B,C/(1 + \varepsilon))$. Since *F* is expressed in terms of φ, it is assumed that $F(N(1 + \varepsilon),B,C)$ can also be approximated as $F(N,B,C/(1 + \varepsilon))$. The problem now simplifies to estimating the function $F(N,B,C/(1 + \varepsilon))$. Since the measured probabilities are very small (of the order of 10^{-7} or less), the function *F* is estimated by using three smaller virtual buffers.

A scheme that relies on aggregate statistics and cell loss measurements for ongoing traffic is proposed by Zukerman and Tse [ZT97]. It assumes that new connections are considered as transmitting at their PCR for a certain warm-up period. This implies that, if the warm-up period is very long, peak rate allocation will be used. The system is adaptive; when the measured cell loss rate is higher than the required rate, the warm-up period is increased. The cell loss ratio is estimated using Reich's approach, which does not assume any specific model for the traffic. The method in [DJM97] uses both the traffic descriptors and the traffic measurements to estimate the aggregate equivalent bandwidth required by the connections. The optimization framework uses a linear Kalman filter for the estimation. It takes into account the connection-level dynamics and provides information for evaluation of bandwidth to be reserved to meet the QoS objectives. A new connection is accepted if the reserved bandwidth is less than the link capacity. The dynamic CAC in [SS91] uses the measured number of cells arrived during a fixed interval and the traffic descriptors to estimate the CLR.

Besaou et al. [BLCT97] proposed a fuzzy-logic algorithm to predict the CLR. The fuzzy approximation estimates the cell loss ratio using (1) the CLR when the system size is small (e.g., small buffer, low service rate, etc.) and (2) the asymptotic behavior of the CLR when the system size is large. The CAC mechanism (Fig. 4.7) employs two components. The first one consists of a set of virtual buffers with reduced service capacity to observe high cell loss with a small variance within a short measurement interval. The second component is a fuzzy approximation and a decision process. The fuzzy algorithm determines the required bandwidth for ongoing calls, while the decision process makes a decision to accept or reject a new call based on the outputs of the algorithm.

Tuning the Connection Admission Control

Applications derive the required traffic descriptors based on some delay or response-time requirements while trading off the cost of different connection bandwidths. It is quite unlikely that the connection will need the full amount of negotiated bandwidth on a continuous basis. For data applications, connections make use of the bandwidth for transferring large amounts of data. Smaller amounts of data can also be exchanged periodically, but the usage is generally much lower than the SCR. In the case of permanent connections (PVCs), the actual utilization compared to the negotiated SCR can be orders of magnitude smaller when measured over the life-

Figure 4.7. A CAC mechanism based on fuzzy logic. Source: Bensaou, B., Lam, S.T.C., Chu, H., and Tsang, D.H.K. "Estimation of the Cell Loss Ratio in ATM Networks with a Fuzzy System and Application to Measurement-Based Call Admission Control," *IEEE/ACM Transactions on Networking*, vol. 5, no. 4 (August 1997), 572–584. © 1997 IEEE.

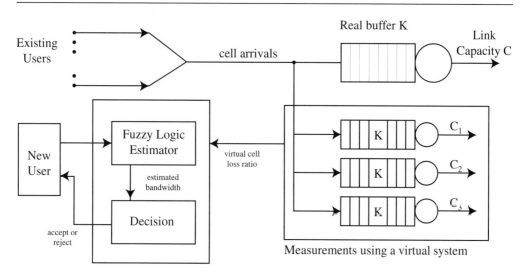

time of the connection. For switched connections (SVCs) this difference is usually smaller, since the connection is torn down when the transfer of information is completed.

The underutilization of the allocated bandwidth coupled with the fact that the CAC allocates bandwidth conservatively can lead to loss of efficiency with respect to the network's ability to carry CBR and VBR traffic. With appropriate measurement of the resource utilization, it is possible to quantify the amount of underutilization and to tune the CAC function appropriately. The CAC *booking* and *scaling factors* are generally available to allow the actual usage of the bandwidth to be taken into account when artificially reducing the amount of bandwidth statically allocated for each connection, thus allowing more connections to be admitted. It should be noted that the statistical gain achieved through booking or scaling factors is completely different from the gains achieved through statistical multiplexing. In the former case, the gain is possible due to connections not utilizing their bandwidth; in the latter, the gain is possible due to multiplexing many sources together.

There are two ways of tuning the CAC function: by applying some *overbooking factor* to the calculations of effective bandwidth, or by *scaling* (using *scaling factors*) the traffic descriptors before applying the calculations to derive the effective bandwidth. Since the relationship between the traffic descriptors and the allocated bandwidth is not linear, the use of the booking and scaling factors results in different overbooking levels. In both cases, if not carefully engineered, overbooking can result in not acheiving the QoS objectives for all the connections sharing the overbooked resource.

The scaling factor is engineered by measuring the usage of the bandwidth over a long period of time on a per-connection basis, for example. If it is determined that connections of a given range of traffic descriptors, or traffic coming from a given type of applications, do not use more than 50 percent of their SCR, then the SCR can be scaled down by at most 50 percent, leaving room for error and unpredictable trends. The scaled-down value is used for CAC purposes only and is not used for policing, since the connection should be allowed to generate bursts according to the negotiated traffic descriptors. If further measurements indicate that usage is growing or reducing, the scaling factors can be modified accordingly.

Booking factors are engineered by measuring the growth trends of the queues. Congestion measures are often available to provide insights as to whether the queue can be overbooked without affecting QoS. Congestion measures indicate whether the queue size has exceeded specific thresholds for a given period of time. Based on that information, it is possible to decide how aggressively the resource can be overbooked.

It is difficult to provide a definite recipe to tune CAC perfectly to achieve very high utilization using only traffic with statically allocated bandwidth. The dynamics of an SVC-based network renders the task more complex, because measured statistics are likely to vary with the mix of connections at a given time. It is important to note that underutilized allocated resource can still at any time be effectively used by bandwidth-on-demand services (ABR, GFR, UBR). Therefore the overall network can remain efficiently utilized.

Review

The connection admission control (CAC) is a very important function in ATM switches. The CAC function determines the admissibility of a new connection into the network by checking the availability of various system resources. The ATM network efficiency thus depends on how well the CAC function models the traffic and queuing behavior of the underlying congestion point. This chapter presented some of the modeling approaches. As this area is widely researched and published in the literature, it is difficult to enumerate or discuss all of the models here. The reader may want to review other interesting approaches, such as:

1. Gibbens et al. [GKK95] discuss admission procedures based on Bayesian rules, where acceptance decisions are based on whether the load is less than a precalculated load.
2. Duffield et al. [DLORT95] proposed an empirical entropy function to estimate QoS parameters, by-passing the modeling procedures.
3. A regression approach is used in [ROAG98], where simulation data is used to develop regression models for cell loss and delay; these estimates are used in computing the effective bandwidths.

References

[BC92] Blondia, C., and Casals, O. "Statistical Multiplexing of VBR Sources: A Matrix-Analytical Approach," *Performance Evaluation*, vol. 16 (1992), 5–20.

[BD94] Buffet, E., and Duffield, N.G. "Exponential Upper Bounds via Martingales for Multiplexers with Markovian Arrivals," *Journal of Applied Probability*, vol. 31 (1994), 1049–1061.

[BLCT97] Bensaou, B., Lam, S.T.C., Chu, H., and Tsang, D.H.K. "Estimation of the Cell Loss Ratio in ATM Networks with a Fuzzy System and Application to Measurement-Based Call Admission Control," *IEEE/ACM Transactions on Networking*, vol. 5, no. 4 (August 1997), 572–584.

[BW98] Berger, A.W., and Whitt. W. "Extending the Effective Bandwidth Concept to Networks with Priority Classes," *IEEE Communications Magazine* (August 1998), 78–83.

[CFW94] Courcoubetis, C., Fouskas, G., and Weber, R. "On the Performance of an Effective Bandwidth Formula," *Proceedings of the International Teletraffic Congress*, ITC14 (1994), 201–212.

[CKW95] Courcoubetis, C., Kesidis, G., Ridder, A., and Walrand, J. "Admission Control and Routing in ATM Networks using Inferences from Measured Buffer Occupancy," *IEEE Transactions on Communications*, vol. 43, no. 2/3/4 (February/March/April 1995), 1178–1784.

[CLW96] Choudhury, G.L., Lucantoni, D.M., and Whitt, W. "Squeezing the Most Out of ATM," *IEEE Transactions on Communications*, vol. 44, no. 2 (February 1996), 203–267.

[DJM97] Dziong, Z., Juda, M., and Mason, L.G. "A Framework for Bandwidth Management in ATM Networks-Aggregate Equivalent Bandwidth Estimation Approach," *IEEE/ACM Transactions on Networking*, vol. 5, no.1 (February 1997), 134–147.

[DLORT95] Duffield, N.G., Lewis, J.T., O'Connell, N., Russell, R., and Toomey, F. "Entropy of ATM Traffic Streams: A Tool for Estimating QoS Parameters," *IEEE Journal on Selected Areas in Communications*, vol. 13, no. 6 (August 1995), 981–990.

[DRS91] Dron, Lisa G., Ramamurthy, G., and Sengupta, B. "Delay Analysis of Continuous Bit Rate Traffic Over an ATM Network," *IEEE Journal on Selected Areas in Communications*, vol. 9, no. 3 (April 1991), 402–407.

[EM93] Elwalid, A., and Mitra, D. "Effective Bandwidth of General Markovian Traffic Sources and Admission Control of High Speed Networks," *IEEE/ACM Transactions on Networking*, vol. 1, no. 3 (June 1993), 329–343.

[EMW95] Elwalid, A., Mitra, D., and Wentworth, R.H. "A New Approach for Allocating Buffers and Bandwidth to Heterogeneous, Regulated Traffic in an ATM Node," *IEEE Journal on Selected Areas in Communications*, vol. 13, no. 6 (August 1995), 1115–1127.

[FLV94] Fiche, G., Lorcher, W., Veyland, R., and Oger, F. "Study of Multiplexing for ATM Traffic Sources," *International Teletraffic Congress ITC14* (June 1994), 441–452.

[GAN91] Guérin, R., Ahmadi, H., and Naghshineh, M. "Equivalent Capacity and Its Application to Bandwidth Allocation in High-Speed Networks," *IEEE Journal on Selected Areas in Communications*, vol. 9, no. 7 (September 1991), 968–981.

[GH91] Gibbens, R.J., and Hunt, P.J. "Effective Bandwidths for the Multi-Type UAS Channel," *Queueing Systems*, vol. 9 (1991), 17–28.

[GKK95] Gibbens, R.J., Kelly, F.P., and Key, P.B. "A Decision-Theoretic Approach to Call Admission Control in ATM Networks," *IEEE Journal on Selected Areas in Communications*, vol. 13, no. 6 (August 1995), 1101–1113.

[Hui88] Hui, J.Y. "Resource Allocation for Broadband Networks," *IEEE Journal on Selected Areas in Communications*, vol. 6, no. 9 (December 1988), 1598–1608.

[HW96] Hsu, I., and Walrand, J. "Admission Control for Multi-Class ATM Traffic with Overflow Constraints," *Computer Networks and ISDN Systems Journal*, vol. 28, no. 13 (1996), 1739–1752.

[JSD97] Jamin, S., Shenker, S.J., and Danzig, P.B. "Comparison of Measurement-Based Admission Control Algorithms for Controlled-Load Service," *Proceedings of IEEE Infocom '97*, Kobe, Japan (1997), 973–980.

[Kel91] Kelly, F.P. "Effective Bandwidths at Multi-Class Queues," *Queuing Systems*, vol. 9 (1991), 5–16.

[KGC94] Kulkarni, V., Gun, L., and Chimento, P. "Effective Bandwidth Vector for Two-Priority ATM Traffic," *Proceedings of IEEE Infocom '94*, Toronto (1994), 1056–1064.

[KWC93] Kesidis, G., Walrand, J., and Chang, C. "Effective Bandwidths for Multiclass Markov Fluids and Other ATM Sources," *IEEE/ACM Transactions on Networking*, vol.1, no. 4 (August 1993), 424–428.

[Nor94] Norros, I. "A Storage Model with Self-Similar Input," *Queueing Systems*, vol. 16 (1994), 387–396.

[Nor95] Norros, I. "On the Use of Fractional Brownian Motion in the Theory of Connectionless Networks," *IEEE Journal on Selected Areas in Communications*, vol. 13, no. 6 (August 1995), 953–962.

[NRSV91] Norros, I., Roberts, J.W., Simonian, A., and Virtamo, J.T. "The Superposition of Variable Bit Rate Sources in an ATM Multiplexer," *IEEE Journal on Selected Areas in Communications*, vol. 9, no. 3 (April 1991), 378–387.

[RK98] Ren, Q., and Kobayashi, H. "Diffusion Approximation Modeling for Markov Modulated Busty Traffic and Its Applications to Bandwidth Allocation in ATM Networks," *IEEE Journal on Selected Areas in Communications*, vol.16, no. 5 (June 1998), 679–691.

[RMV96] Roberts, J., Mocci, U., and Virtamo, J. *Broadband Network Teletraffic*. Berlin, Heidelberg: Springer, 1996.

[ROAG98] Ramaswamy, S., Ono-Tesfaye, T., Armstrong, W.W., and Gburzynski, P. "Effective Bandwidths for Real-Time Traffic." To appear in *Journal of High-Speed Networks*, 1998.

[RV91] Roberts, J.W., and Virtamo, J.T. "The Superposition of Periodic Cell Arrival Streams in an ATM Multiplexer," *IEEE Transactions on Communications*, vol. 39, no. 2 (February 1991), 298–303.

[Skl94] Skliros, A. "A Connection Admission Control Algorithm for ATM Traffic Distorted by Cell Delay Variation," *Proceedings of ITC14* (1994),1385–1394.

[SS91] Saito, H., and Shiomoto, K. "Dynamic Call Admission Control in ATM Networks," *IEEE Journal on Selected Areas in Communications*, vol. 9, no. 7 (September 1991), 982–989.

[TG97] Tsybakov, B., and Georganas, N.D. "Overflow Probability in an ATM Queue with Self-Similar Input Traffic," *Proceedings of IEEE ICC '97*, Montreal (June 1997), 822–826.

[WK90] Woodruff, G., and Kositpaiboon, R. "Multimedia Traffic Management Principles for Guaranteed ATM Network Performance," *IEEE Journal on Selected Areas in Communications*, vol. 8, no. 3 (April 1990), 437–446.

[YT95] Tang, T., and Tsang, D.H.K. "A Novel Approach to Estimating the Cell Loss Probability in an ATM Multiplexer Loaded with Homogeneous On-Off Sources," *IEEE Transcations on Communications*, vol. 43, no. 1 (January 1995), 117–126.

[ZT97] Zukerman, M., and Tse, P.W. "An Adpative Connection Admission Control Scheme for ATM Networks," *Proceedings of IEEE ICC '97*, Montreal (June 1997), 1153–1157.

CHAPTER 5

Queuing and Scheduling

A multiservice ATM network provides support for a wide variety of services with differing QoS requirements to be carried on the same switching nodes and links. Multiple services share the network resources (e.g., link bandwidth, buffer space, etc.) and may try to access a resource simultaneously. Resource contention arises because of this sharing, and a queuing structure is required to temporarily store cells. The point at which this resource contention occurs is generally referred to as a *queuing* or *contention point*. Depending on the architecture, a switching node can be implemented with one or more queuing structures. A scheduling mechanism is implemented at each queuing structure to appropriately select the order in which cells should be served to meet the QoS objectives. The term *scheduling* refers to the mechanism that determines what queue is given an opportunity to transmit a cell. A queuing structure and the corresponding scheduling algorithm attempt to achieve the following objectives:

Flexibility: to support a variety of services, and to easily evolve in support of new services (see Chap. 2)

Scalability: to be simple enough to allow scaling up to large number of connections while allowing cost-effective implementation

Efficiency: to maximize the network link utilization (i.e., maximize the throughput)

Guaranteed QoS: to provide low jitter and end-to-end delay bounds for real-time traffic; to allow implementation of simple CAC functions (see Chap. 4)

Isolation: to reduce interference among service classes and connections

Fairness: to allow fast and fair redistribution of bandwidth that becomes dynamically available. The fairness can be defined by a flexible policy

This chapter focuses on the design of queuing structures and scheduling algorithms at a contention point. Other related buffer management techniques are discussed in Chap. 7. After a brief introduction to ATM switch architectures, the queuing structures are discussed, followed by the scheduling mechanisms.

Overview of ATM Switch Architectures

This section provides an overview of a generic ATM switch architecture. It does not provide an exhaustive description of all possible architectures and related physical layout issues, but aims at describing the generic location of the queuing structures.

As shown in Fig. 5.1, an ATM switch switches traffic between L links. The switch can simultaneously support a variety of link speeds ranging from 1.5Mb/s (i.e. DS-1) up to 2.4Gb/s (i.e., OC-48). The switching function is performed by a *switching fabric* (or *switching core*). The switching fabric switches between N *fabric links*, which are generally of the same speed. The number (N) and speed of the fabric links define the capacity of the switching fabric. In order to maximize the utilization of the fabric links, multiple input links can be concentrated onto a fabric link through different combinations of multiplexers. Corresponding demultiplexers are used to separate the outgoing traffic to the appropriate link.

The switch fabric routes cells from a fabric input link (FIL) to the appropriate fabric output link (FOL). In the case of multicast operation, the switch fabric routes a cell from a FIL to two or more FOLs.

A physical link is bidirectional and therefore interfaces to both an input and output port. For example, in Fig. 5.1, Input Link 1 and Output Link 1 are on the same physical port.

Figure 5.1. Generic switch architecture.

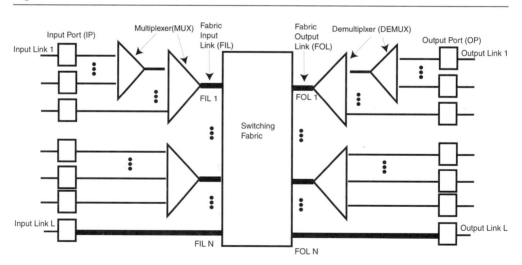

A queuing structure may be required at different points on the switch in order to temporarily store the cells awaiting access to an internal link or to the output link. In order to meet the QoS objectives, it is necessary for each queuing structure to implement appropriate queue definitions, scheduling (as discussed later in this chapter), and buffer management techniques (see Chap. 7). Queuing structures are generally required at the following points:

Input port: Generally, the link rate is lower than the rate at which the input port inserts cells into the switch, so a queuing structure is not required. However, traffic shaping may be implemented on the input port for soft policing (see Chap. 3), in which case a queuing structure would be required. The size of the input port buffers would depend on how many connections are being shaped at the same time.

Multiplexers: A multiplexer requires a queuing structure if the sum of its input rates exceeds its output rate. Otherwise, only a single small queue is required to absorb simultaneous arrivals from the different inputs. The amount of buffering required at a multiplexer is a function of the speed mismatch ratio, that is, the ratio of the sum of the input rates over the multiplexer's output rate.

Switching fabric: There are many ways to implement a switching fabric, each of which have different queuing structure requirements. Switching fabric are discussed later in this section.

Demultiplexers: A demultiplexer (DEMUX) requires queuing structures for each output that has a rate lower than the DEMUX input. The amount of buffering required at a DEMUX is a function of the speed mismatch ratio.

Output port: An output port requires a queuing structure if its input rate is greater than the link rate, or if shaping is implemented. The amount of buffering required at a DEMUX is a function of the speed mismatch ratio and, in some cases, the round-trip delay of the connection (see Chap. 9).

In some architectures, the switching fabric may employ *backpressure* or *flow control* methods to push the congestion to the edge of the switch or move it outside the switching fabric. In this case, the queuing structure of the input multiplexers or input ports also absorbs the contention at the switch fabric.

The design of a switch fabric is a complex topic. Switch fabrics can be classified into three general categories [Tob90]:

Shared memory: A shared-memory switch fabric consists of a single dual-ported memory, which is shared by all FILs and FOLs. The memory is partitioned (or grouped) per FOL. Cells arriving on a FIL are multiplexed onto a single stream, which feeds the common memory. Cells are retrieved from the output queues and transmitted on the corresponding FOL.

Shared medium: A shared-medium switch fabric uses a common high-speed medium (such as a parallel bus). Cells arriving on various FILs are multiplexed onto this medium. Each FOL uses an address filter and a queue to retrieve cells destined for it.

Space division: A space-division switch fabric uses many concurrent spatial paths from each FIL to a given FOL. Each path operates at the same data rate.

In all three types, the technology used in implementing the switch fabric places limitations on the size and speed of the fabric links. To build larger switches, many switching fabrics are interconnected in a multistage configuration. Since this chapter does not focus on the switching architectures, readers are referred to [Tob90] and [AD89] for more information on this topic.

ATM switch fabrics can be classified, in a broad sense, as "blocking" or "nonblocking." Internal blocking occurs when a switching fabric cannot route a cell from a FIL to a FOL while simultaneously routing a cell from a different FIL to a different FOL (assuming no broadcast or multicast operation). A queuing structure is necessary to handle the cells waiting for access to the switching fabric in the case of internal blocking.

However, there could be multiple cells simultaneously destined to a given FOL from different FILs. In this book, this phenomenon is referred to as *FOL contention*. A queuing structure becomes necessary to handle this resource conflict. Figure 5.2 depicts potential locations for queuing structures in a nonblocking switching fabric [HK88].

Figure 5.2. Queuing options for nonblocking switches. Source: Hluchyj, M.G., and Karol, M.J. "Queuing in High-Performance Packet Switching" *IEEE Journal on Selected Areas in Communications*, vol. 6, no. 9 (December 1988), 1587–1597. © 1988 IEEE.

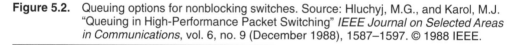

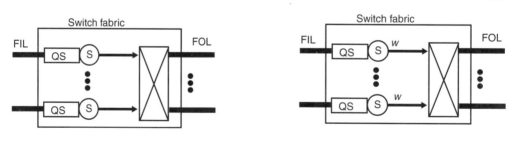

a) Input queuing   b) Window selection

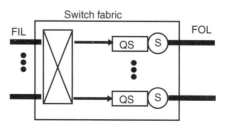

c) Output queuing

The following sections provide a description of these queuing options and their respective performance when applied to a nonblocking fabric.

Switch Fabric without Buffers

For a switch fabric without any buffers, when FOL contention occurs, only one cell is successfully transferred to the destination port in a given cell time, and remaining contending cells are dropped. It is assumed that the speed of the switch fabric is equal to the FIL rate; that is, the switch transfers at most one cell per slot from each of the N inputs. When $N{\rightarrow}\infty$, the probability of success p(success) that a cell wins the FOL contention is given by p(success) $= (1 - e^{-\rho})/\rho$, where ρ is the input traffic load, assuming a Bernoulli arrival process. That is, a cell arrives in a given slot with a probability ρ. The value $(1 - e^{-\rho})$ is the throughput of the switch fabric and attains a maximum value of 0.632 when $\rho = 1$. This value is attained at the expense of cell loss; that is, 36.8 percent of incoming cells are dropped. Such high loss cannot be tolerated by many services, so buffers are necessary to limit the cell loss.

Switch Fabric with FIFO Input Buffers

When buffers are used at the input of the switch fabric (Fig. 5.2(a)), cells that did not win the FOL contention are stored in a buffer with any new cells that have arrived. The switch fabric transfers at most one cell from each FIL in a given time slot; buffers at output of the fabric are not necessary in this case. When a first-in-first-out (FIFO) [KLE75] service discipline is assumed for the buffers, the maximum switch throughput for $N{\rightarrow}\infty$ is shown to be 0.586 [HK88] when the FILs are saturated (i.e., each input queue always has a cell to transmit). A FIFO discipline services the cells in the order of their arrival. The performance of this type of switch fabric is summarized in Table 5.1. The maximum throughput of a nonblocking switch with a FIFO input buffer is lower than that of the switch fabric, which does not have any buffers because of the effect of head-of-line (HOL) blocking. However, unlike a switch without any buffers, cells are not dropped immediately and buffering improves the cell loss performance. When a cell at the head of the line in a buffer is blocked due to FOL contention, remaining cells in the same input buffer are also blocked due to FIFO service discipline. Even though there could be some cells destined to other FOLs, they cannot be routed by the switch. When $N{\rightarrow}\infty$, Hui [JH87], assuming a Bernoulli arrival process, obtained an expression for the upper bound on the cell loss probability at the input buffers:

$$P_{\text{loss}} < \frac{p(2 - p)}{2(1 - p)}\left[\frac{p^2}{2(1 - p)^2}\right]^B \tag{5.1}$$

Here p is the probability that a cell arrives in a given slot, and B is the input buffer size. The policy for selecting which FIL can transmit a cell to a given FOL also has an impact on the performance of the switch fabric. A random selection policy is the most common: One FIL is randomly chosen to transmit a cell among all the FILs contending for a given FOL. This behavior may not

Table 5.1. Switch Fabric throughput for FIFO and window discipline. Source: Hluchyj, M.G., and Karol, M.J. "Queuing in High-Performance Packet Switching" *IEEE Journal on Selected Areas in Communications*, vol. 6, no. 9 (December 1988), 1587–1597. © 1988 IEEE.

Size		Window size (w)							
N	FIFO	1	2	3	4	5	6	7	8
2	75.0%	75%	84%	89%	92%	93%	94%	95%	96%
4	65.5%	66%	76%	81%	85%	87%	89%	94%	92%
8	61.8%	62%	72%	78%	82%	85%	87%	88%	89%
16		60%	71%	77%	81%	84%	86%	87%	88%
32		59%	70%	76%	80%	83%	85%	87%	88%
64		59%	70%	76%	80%	83%	85%	86%	88%
∞	58.6%								

always be desirable, however. A priority selection was proposed for the knock-out switch by Eng [Eng88] in which newly arriving cells are given lower priority than previously blocked cells. When FOL contention occurs, a cell from the high-priority class (if any) is selected first and transferred to the destination. Cells that are not transferred due to contention are stored in the input buffers. If a cell is not transferred the second time, it is dropped from the input buffer. This scheme has lower buffering requirements than the random selection policy.

A number of techniques are possible to improve the throughput of an input-buffered switching fabric. One approach is to increase the switching capacity (also referred to as a *speed-up* of the switch fabric). Another approach is to use a non-FIFO service discipline: when a cell is blocked due to HOL, any cells behind not destined for the same FOL can be routed instead. This enhancement reduces HOL blocking and improves performance.

Switch Fabric with Non-FIFO Input Buffers

Servicing the cells in the input buffers using FIFO discipline leads to HOL blocking, which limits the throughput of a switch fabric to 58.6 percent, assuming no speed-up. An alternative to improve the throughput of the switch is to implement a non-FIFO service of the input discipline, called the "window selection discipline" or "look-ahead contention resolution."

In this servicing scheme (Figure 5.2(b)) when FOL contention occurs, the first "w" cells in each of the input buffers sequentially contend for the FOL again. The cells at the head of the buffer contend first for access to FOL. The contention process repeats up to w times at the beginning of each time slot, sequentially allowing "w" cells in an input buffer's window to contend for any remaining idle FOLs until the input is selected to transmit a cell. The variable w is called the "window size." Several names have been used for this service discipline-priority scheme, window policy, bypass queuing, input smoothing, to name a few. Table 5.1 shows the maximum throughput of a switch fabric with various window sizes. The throughput that is indicated in the

FIFO column is derived using an input saturation analysis that assumes inputs always have a cell to send. The throughput indicated for various window sizes is obtained from simulations. The window discipline is most effective when N is small and w is large. For example, when $N = 2$ and $w = 8$, a maximum throughput of 96 percent is possible. Parallel buffers at inputs can implement the window-selection discipline at the expense of additional hardware.

Switch Fabric with Input and Output Buffers (Switch Fabric Speed-Up)

Another technique to avoid HOL blocking is to speed up the switch fabric and use buffering at the output. It is assumed that up to L ($1 \leq L \leq N$) contending cells are accepted to a FOL per cell slot. The variable L is referred to as the *speed-up* or *switching capacity* of the switch. Such a switch can also transfer up to a maximum of L cells from FILs to each FOL. In this type of switch, the cells at the heads of input buffers contend for FOL, and only one cell out of the contending cells is sent to a given FOL. This process is repeated L times per slot on a FIFO basis. For each repetition, the contention process is tried again with cells that lost the previous contention round(s) trying with any new cells that moved to the head position. Therefore, buffers are needed at both FILs and FOLs.

The cell loss probability is given by replacing p with p/L in Eq. (5.1). Oie [YO89] summarizes some of the past research done in this area. When $L = N$, cell queuing does not occur at the input but occurs at the FOLs. The switch fabric achieves a maximum throughput in this case. Even if N cells arrive at different FILs that are destined to the same FOL, these N cells can be switched at once. However, it is difficult to implement such switches as N becomes very large. For large N, the switch throughput is 99.9% for $L = 5$ [YO89].

Switch Fabric with Output Buffers

With output queuing (Fig. 5.2(c)) all queuing is done at the outputs of the switch fabric, with a separate queuing structure provided for each FOL. In this case, the switch fabric operates N times as fast as the FIL, so that if k ($k = 1, 2, \ldots, N$) cells arrive in a time slot on different FILs all addressed to the same FOL, all k cells can be routed through the switch fabric to the proper output queue in one time slot. However, only one cell can be removed from the output buffer during a FOL time slot, and remaining cells wait in the output buffer. Note that there is no HOL blocking introduced by the output queuing, but there can be cell loss due to congestion in the FOL buffer caused by simultaneous arrival of multiple cells from different FILs. Output queuing achieves the best waiting-time performance. The memory available in the switch fabric can be shared in many ways among the FOLs (Chap. 7).

Queuing Structures for QoS Guarantees

The previous section dealt with how and where queuing structures are necessary in switches. Queuing structures are also required in the receiving end system, if there is a speed mismatch.

The sending end-system may also require a queuing structure if shaping is performed. This section addresses how individual connections are queued up for service at a contention point or how a contention point is configured. To guarantee QoS for each connection, distinctions need to be maintained among the service categories with respect to the way they are serviced. In general, queuing structures can be organized as

1. Per-group queuing
2. Per-VC/VP queuing

With per-group queuing, many connections share the same queue in a FIFO arrangement; with per-VC/VP queuing, the cells of each VC or VP is queued independently. These two methods are described below. Note that at a contention point, a combination of both per-group and per-VC queuing is also possible.

Per-Group Queuing

In this queuing structure, the connections are categorized into *groups*. The cells from each group are queued up separately. The definition of a group can vary from one implementation to another. Typical groups consist of connections belonging to the same

• Service category
• Service class
• Conformance definition

Group as Per-Service Category

Connections can be grouped according to their service category, so cells from each service category are separately queued (see Fig. 5.3). Through this method, one can achieve per-service

Figure 5.3.   Per-group queuing: a group is defined as per-service category.

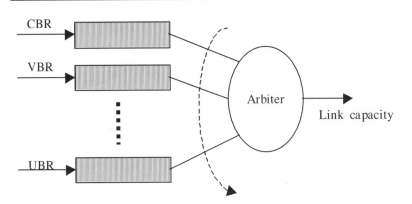

isolation, partition of the link capacity, and hence separate QoS guarantees to each service. Ideally, the number of queues in such a structure should be equal to the number of service categories.

However, as can be seen later in this chapter, an increase in the number of queues significantly increases the complexity of the scheduling function. The initial designs of ATM switches consisted of only a few queues at a contention point. Thus, many switches in the market may mix some of the service categories together in the same queue. In general, when traffic from various service categories is mixed in the same queue, it is difficult to provide QoS guarantees for each service category independently because traffic from each category can interfere with the other. The keys to efficient service guarantees using such a queuing structure is the appropriate dimensioning of buffers and setting of discard thresholds, such as CLP1, EPD, PPD, EFCI, and the like (Chap. 7), as well as selecting the correct scheduling disciplines. By setting of some of these thresholds, one can achieve partial service isolation between services sharing a queue.

Group as Per-Service Class

ATM networks can provide one or more classes of service (Chap. 3) within each service category. For example, an ATM network can provide two classes of CBR service, one with CTD $- 250\mu Sec$ and one with CTD $- 2.5mSec$. Or, it can provide a premium class with CLR of 10^{-10} and a normal class with CLR of 10^{-7}, with same CTD.

An example of per-group queuing, where a group is defined as a service class, is shown in Fig. 5.4.

Figure 5.4. Per-group queuing: a group is defined as per-service class.

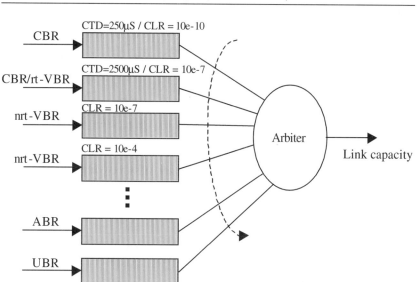

There are many ways to accomplish different CLR classes for a given service category. One method is to set cell discard thresholds on a given queue, whereby cells of low QoS connections are dropped when the queue depth reaches the discard threshold. Another method is to use a separate queue for each class. Proper connection admission control and bandwidth allocation procedures are required when a single queue is used with multiple discard thresholds. See Chap. 7 on congestion control for other methods of selective cell discard policies, such as buffer push-out, to provide multiple QoS service classes within a service category.

Since cell delay is directly proportional to the queue size for a given service rate, multiple-delay classes can be obtained by using separate queues for each class in a given service category. It is also possible to obtain multiple-delay classes by using admission thresholds on the buffers. In either case, proper buffer dimensioning, bandwidth allocation, and priority servicing of the delay classes are necessary to achieve required delay guarantees.

Group as Per-Conformance Definition

Another way of grouping the connections is by their conformance definition (see Chap. 3). For example, VBR services (both real-time and non-real-time) are classified into VBR.1, VBR.2, and VBR.3 based on the definition of the traffic descriptors and the meaning of the CLP bit. Figure 5.5 demonstrates a queuing structure that uses the conformance definition as a group. The main advantage with this structure is easy handling of CLP transparency issue, which is discussed in the section labeled "Other Issues" at the end of the chapter.

Figure 5.5. Per-group queuing: a group is defined as per conformance definition.

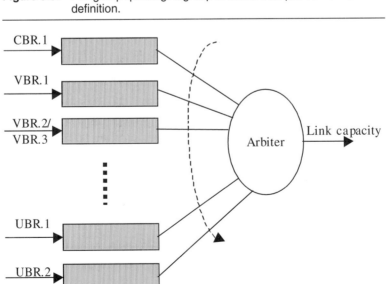

The main problem with per-group queuing is the difficulty of achieving per-connection isolation and QoS guarantees. This system offers isolation per group. It cannot prevent a traffic source from interfering with others within a given group. Policing or soft policing needs to be implemented to ensure that the connections behave as per their traffic contract. For example, each ABR connection needs a different minimum cell rate (MCR) guarantee. If all the ABR connections are multiplexed together into a single queue and if there are misbehaving ABR connections, it is only possible to guarantee aggregate MCR (ΣMCR_i) for the connections. Aggregate MCR guarantee does not necessarily mean the guarantee of MCR_i for each VC_i. One possible way to achieve per-VC isolation with such queuing structures is to use "per-VC accounting," which keeps a record of the cell statistics and performs intelligent discards when congestion occurs (see Chap. 7).

Various cell-scheduling mechanisms that can be implemented for the per-group queuing structures are priority scheduling, round robin (RR), weighted round robin (WRR), weighted fair queuing, aggregate traffic shaping (TS), or combinations thereof. These schemes are discussed in detail later in the "Scheduling Mechanisms" section.

Per-VC/VP Queuing

With per-VC/VP queuing, the cells arriving on each VC or VP are queued separately. Per-VC (or VP) isolation for access to bandwidth can be achieved using a per-VC (or VP) queuing structure, which is depicted in Fig. 5.6. Isolation of buffer usage depends on the buffer management scheme used (see Chap. 7). However, per-VC queuing is more complex and expensive to implement and does not scale well to a large number of connections. This architecture builds

Figure 5.6. Per-VC queuing structure.

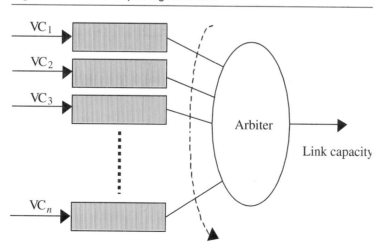

firewalls (achieves isolation) between the VCs/VPs so that a misbehaving connection cannot affect the QoS of other connections.

Some of the scheduling mechanisms that apply to the per-VC/VP queuing structure are priority scheduling, round robin, weighted round robin, weighted fair queuing, per-VC/VP traffic shaping, or combinations thereof.

Both per-group and per-VC structures need buffer management to manipulate how the physical memory is shared among the queues. The available buffer can be either completely partitioned or shared among the queues. This particular topic is addressed in Chap. 7. For the purpose of this chapter, it is assumed that the queues are properly engineered or dimensioned.

Scheduling Mechanisms

As described in the preceding section, a contention point can have a number of queues. An arbitration function is needed to extract cells from these queues and transmit (or serve) them appropriately to meet the QoS objectives of each connection. An *arbiter* or *arbitration function* or *scheduler* is responsible for this scheduling and allocation of bandwidth to the queues. An arbiter implements a *scheduling algorithm* or *scheduling mechanism*. A robust scheduling mechanism protects the traffic flows from malicious (or misbehaving) sources (or users) without relying solely on the policing function. It should also be efficient under any network load variations. The queues at a contention point can be divided into logical sets, each of which is served by an arbiter. Depending on how the queues and arbiters are organized, scheduling schemes can be divided into *flat-* (or *single-*) *level scheduling* and *hierarchical scheduling*.

In a flat-level (or single-level) arbitration, a contention point uses a single arbiter serving all the queues. The arbiter uses a single scheduling function among all the queues, as shown in Fig. 5.7.

However, in order to divide the bandwidth more flexibly and accurately, the arbitration can be performed in multiple levels, or *hierarchically*, as exemplified in Fig. 5.8.

Figure 5.7. Flat scheduling.

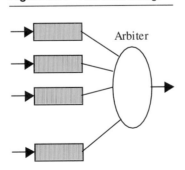

Figure 5.8. Hierarchical scheduling.

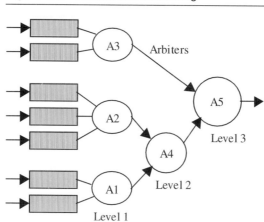

Hierarchical scheduling uses multiple-arbitration functions. One arbiter arbitrates between a set of queues, and a few other arbitration functions are used in hierarchical fashion to arbitrate between the arbiters. Each of the arbiters in the hierarchy can implement a different scheduling algorithm to achieve specific bandwidth partitioning and control.

Hierarchical scheduling (see also [BZ97]) is useful to divide the bandwidth on a link between different sets of queues (e.g., queues belonging to a given customer, to a given service, etc.). With hierarchical scheduling, the bandwidth left over by a connection is redistributed first between the connections within the same set. A flat arbitration scheme cannot achieve this type of bandwidth redistribution. For the remainder of this section, it is assumed that an arbiter handles queues; however, it should be understood that it could also handle the output of another arbiter. Using a hierarchical scheduler also simplifies the weight recalculation in the case of weighted scheduling (see sections below on fair-share scheduling), since only weights within a set need to be recalculated at connection setup or tear down.

The scheduling algorithms that an arbiter implements can be classified into four types:

1. Priority-based scheduling
2. Work-conserving fair-share scheduling
3. Non-work-conserving fair-share scheduling
4. Traffic shaping.

Priority-Based Scheduling

A priority-based scheduler assigns a priority to each queue and serves them in order of priority. A lower-priority queue is served only when there is no cell waiting for service in any higher-priority queue; that is, cells with higher priority are served first, even though cells of low priority waiting in their respective queues may have arrived earlier. The transmission opportunity of the low-priority queue depends on the traffic load of the high-priority queue, which may vary dynamically. Therefore, it is difficult to support multiple services with guaranteed QoS for each queue separately. Since CBR and rt-VBR services have stringent delay requirements, they are generally assigned higher priority. The nrt-VBR services have a low cell loss requirement but do not require any delay guarantees, so these services can be assigned a priority order lower than CBR and rt-VBR. The ABR and GFR services expect a long-term MCR objectives with a reasonably low cell loss. Therefore ABR and GFR connections are assigned the next priority level. Since UBR service does not have any cell loss or delay objectives, it can be served as the lowest priority.

The priority scheduling can be applied to both per-group queuing as well as per-VC queuing. In the case of per-VC queuing, all the VC queues belonging to a particular service category can be viewed as one priority level. If CBR service is assigned highest priority and UBR the lowest, then the CBR service gets the best possible delay and cell loss, while the UBR gets the worst. If the higher-priority queue gets a traffic burst, it can temporarily starve the low-priority queues. Thus, in a priority-scheduling scheme it is difficult to meet QoS objectives for lower-priority traffic (e.g., ABR). When multiple service classes share the same queue, it is possible to order a queue on a non-FIFO basis as long as the cells within a service class maintain a logical FIFO structure. That is, the cells from within a service class should be ordered as a FIFO. Though complex to implement, this kind of arrangement provides priorities within service classes when they share the same physical queue.

Priority-based scheduling provides very simple and efficient arbitration among a small number of queues. It can, for example, provide a class of real-time traffic, a class of non-real-time traffic with guaranteed loss rate, and a best-effort class. Increasing the number of classes beyond these three, however, may not provide sufficiently fine-grained QoS commitments unless some level of fair access to the bandwidth is provided as described in the next section.

Fair-Share Scheduling

An alternative approach to priority scheduling is fair-share scheduling, in which each queue is guaranteed to get its share of link bandwidth according to a defined weight. The scheduler divides the bandwidth among the queues based on the weighted fair share. Fair-share scheduling is a concept that introduces firewalls (or isolation) among various queues at a contention point in a way that minimizes interaction between the traffic in the different queues. Fair-share scheduling basically deals with how the bandwidth is distributed among the queues by attempting to distribute it in a fair manner. It is very useful for ABR, GFR, and UBR services where the bandwidth is assigned on the basis of availability. One can assign some weight for UBR traffic so that UBR connections get a share of link capacity. This flexibility would not be possible in priority-based scheduling scheme.

Note that the fair bandwidth allocation is possible only among the queues and not between connections sharing a queue, if the traffic is divided as such. For example, if connections from each service category are grouped in a queue, then a fair-allocation is possible among service categories but not among connections within a service category.

The fair-share scheduling algorithms guarantee a certain minimum rate allocated among the queues. These "rate-based" mechanisms can be classified into two categories [ZK91]: *rate-allocation* service discipline and *rate-controlled* service discipline (see Fig. 5.9).

In the rate-allocation service discipline, a queue may be served at a higher rate than the minimum service rate as long as the guarantees made to other services do not suffer. In the rate-controlled service discipline, the mechanism does not serve any queue at a rate higher than its assigned service rate under any circumstance. Figure 5.9 depicts the difference between the two. Each queue needs a *minimum bandwidth guarantee* of r_i in this example. The scheduler should try to achieve this minimum bandwidth guarantee for all queues.

These rate-based schemes are also classified as *work-conserving* or *non-work-conserving*. A work-conserving scheduler is never idle when there are cells to send in any queues. Since rate-controlled schedulers do not serve a queue with more than its allocated rate, these are classified as non-work-conserving while the rate-allocation schedulers are work-conserving. It can be expected that control of delay, jitter, and buffer requirements for each of the queues depends on the type of scheduler, that is, whether it is work conserving or not. Some of the rate-based schemes proposed in the literature are discussed below. Note that some of the schemes are developed within the context of data networks where the data unit is of variable length. However, they are presented here in the context of ATM, with fixed-sized cells.

An ideal fair-share scheduler is one that employs processor sharing (PS) among the connections. The processor divides the link capacity equally among the contending connections with a very fine granularity. When connections are given different weights and the link capacity is divided not as equal share but in proportion to the weight assigned, then the processor sharing

Figure 5.9. Rate-controlled versus rate-allocation.

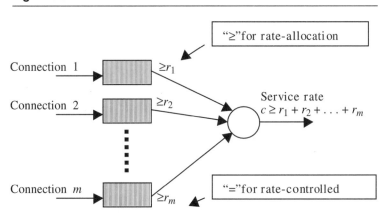

is referred to as generalized processor sharing (GPS). It is very difficult to implement the PS or GPS, because it assumes that the traffic is infinitely divisible and that all connections with non-empty queues can be served simultaneously. In reality, a cell can only be served in its entirety (i.e., cannot be split). Therefore, fair queuing or the weighted fair queuing can be thought of as a practical implementation of the PS or GPS. There are many schemes proposed in the literature that try to achieve this fair-share scheduling by various approximation algorithms. The fair-share schedulers can be implemented in two ways:

Method 1: Assign a *service deadline* F_i^j (or *time-stamp*, or *virtual finishing times*, or *finish number*) for each cell of connection j at instant i, and serve them in the increased order of the deadline. If there is a tie between cells, the cells are re-ordered randomly. Assuming a unit link capacity, the service deadline F_i^j assigned to the cells of each connection j at instant i has the following form:

$$F_i^j = \max \{F_{i-1}^j, v_i^j\} + (1/r^j)$$

$$F_0^j = 0 \tag{5.2}$$

Here r^j is the minimum guaranteed bandwidth for connection j, and v_i^j is the virtual time for connection j at instant i. The main difference between various algorithms is the way the virtual time is computed.

Method 2: Serve the queues in a round-robin fashion using frames or cycles. In each cycle all the queues are given a transmission opportunity to transmit a cell. Queues with larger weights can be given several transmission opportunities in each cycle. If all the queues have the same weight then it is a round-robin (RR) system, otherwise it is weighted round-robin (WRR). The RR and WRR schemes are described later in this chapter. The behavior is similar to that of a TDM system, except that if a queue is given a transmission opportunity when the queue does not have any cell to transmit, the scheme does not waste the bandwidth. Instead, the scheduler examines the rest of the queues for any possible cell transmission. With N backlogged connections, a round-robin discipline assigns a bandwidth of (link capacity)/N to each connection, while for each connection with weights w_i, a WRR scheme assigns a bandwidth of $w_i \times$ (link capacity)/$(\Sigma_{1 \leq i \leq N} w_i)$.

The two methods offer different levels of

• Minimum bandwidth guarantees for each connection
• Bandwidth granularity

In the following sections, the algorithms that use virtual finish times employ Method 1.

Work-Conserving Fair-Share-Scheduling Algorithms

Fair Queuing [DKS89]

The fair-queuing algorithm proposed by Demers et al. [DKS89] emulates bit-by-bit round-robin service discipline. It assumes per-VC/VP queuing. Each cell is assigned a service deadline, which is the finishing time if the cells are served using a bit-by-bit round-robin (BR) scheme. If each queue is served one bit at a time in a round-robin fashion, the service deadline is the time when a cell would have left under the BR servicing scheme. When cells are served in increasing order of finish times, it is shown that the system emulates the BR scheme. A virtual finish time is assigned to each cell:

$$F_i^j = \max \{F_{i-1}^j, R_i^j\} + 1 \tag{5.3}$$

Here R_i^j is the number of rounds made in the round-robin service discipline. The fair queuing assigns equal share of bandwidth to all connections.

Packet-Based Generalized Processor Sharing [PG93]

The packet-based generalized processor sharing (PGPS) concept is a generalized version of fair queuing that assigns virtual finish times and weights to each connection. The weight allows each connection to get a weighted share of link bandwidth rather than just an equal share. The cells are stamped with a virtual finish time F_i^j:

$$F_i^j = \max \{F_{i-1}^j, v_i^j\} + (1/r^j) \tag{5.4}$$

The virtual time v_i^j during a busy period $[t_1, t_2]$ is defined as:

$$\frac{\partial v(\tau)}{\partial t} = \frac{1}{\sum_{i \in B_k} \phi_i} \quad \forall t_1 \le \tau \le t_2; \, v(t_1) = 0$$

where B_k is the set of backlogged connections and ϕ_i is the weight of connection i. Parekh [PG93] has shown that, regardless of traffic arrival pattern, PGPS approximates to GPS within one cell transmission time. Delay bounds for connections traversing through a set of GPS or PGPS servers is derived in [PG94]. These bounds are tighter than those derived via summation of worst-case delays at each node.

Self-Clocked Fair Queuing [Gol94]

Both PGPS and WFQ algorithms developed the virtual finish times based on a hypothetical fluid-flow fair-queuing system. Computing the virtual finish times is very complex and may not be practical to implement. Therefore, self-clocked fair queuing (SCFQ) is proposed by Golestani [Gol94]. As per this scheme, the cells are stamped with a virtual finish time:

$$F_i^j = \max \{F_{i-1}^j, \hat{v}_i^j\} + (1/r^j) \tag{5.5}$$

where $\hat{v}_i^j$ is regarded as the system's virtual time and is defined as the service tag of the cell receiving at that time. That is, $\hat{v}_i^j$ is the virtual finish time of the last cell to leave (hence the name *self-clocked*) the queuing system during a busy period. Once the busy period is over and there are no more cells to serve in the queue, $\hat{v}_i^j$ is reset to zero.

The virtual spacing [Rob94] scheme is similar to SCFQ, independently developed and applied to the context of ATM with constant length cells. In this scheme, cells are stamped with a virtual finish time as:

$$F_i^j = \max \{F_{i-1}^j, \hat{v}_i^j\} + (1/r^j) \tag{5.6}$$

where $\hat{v}_i^j$ cannot be greater than the time stamp of any cell already waiting when its value is updated. This result implies that backlogged cells are spaced at an interval of $(1/r_i)$.

Virtual Clock [Zha90]

The virtual-clock scheduling algorithm is an emulation of TDM (time division multiplexing) service discipline. TDM is a slot-based system that does not allow any statistical multiplexing and guarantees a fixed bandwidth for the connections by assigning fixed slots. If a queue does not have any data to send in the assigned slot, the slot is not re-used and the bandwidth wasted. Thus TDM is a non-work-conserving service discipline. However, with virtual clock, statistical multiplexing is feasible and slots are utilized if there are any nonempty queues (i.e., work conserving). While a real-time clock is used in a TDM system to define the service slots, a virtual clock is used to stamp the cells in this virtual clock scheduling. Each cell is assigned a service deadline (or virtual time), which is the time a cell would leave if it were using a TDM system. Then, cells are sent in the order of virtual times. The virtual time v_i^j assigned to a traffic flow j is the real time itself, that is, the time t at which the cell of the queue arrived. In other words, the cells are marked with a time-stamp as

$$F_i^j = \max \{F_{i-1}^j, t\} + (1/r^j) \tag{5.7}$$

The delay bounds for a single server as well as a network of servers using VC discipline is derived in [FP95].

Deficit Round Robin [SV96]

Deficit round robin is an extension of the round-robin scheduler. This scheme maintains a "deficit counter" (DC_i) for each connection. The deficit counter is reset to zero whenever the queue falls empty. The deficit counter is initialized to the weight of connection (Q_i) when the queue becomes backlogged. The weight in this scheme is the number of cells a queue is allowed to send in a given round. Since a connection may not have enough cells to transmit in a round, a deficit can be built up for each connection. The current deficit is set equal to the previous deficit, if any, less the number of cells sent, so $DC_i = DC_i + (Q_i\text{-}cells\_sent_i)$. The connection can take advantage of the available deficit in its next round, which means that the amount of bandwidth the flow can use is the sum of DC_i added to the weight of the connection Q_i.

Pulse Scheduling [MLF92]

Pulse scheduling generalizes the virtual clock method of Zhang [Zha90] to bursty sources. Recall that virtual clock uses only the average rate (r^j) of the traffic source in the computation of finish times. Pulse scheduling extends this concept by taking into account the burst properties of the connection. Let a connection i transmit at a peak rate λ_i for a duration $t1_i$ and shut off (nothing transmitted) for duration $t2_i$. The pulse scheduling assigns finish times using the peak rate for $\lambda_i \times t1_i$ cells. The next cell is assigned a virtual time of $t2_i$ and the process is repeated. In this way, the virtual time follows the burst properties of the connection and the pulse scheduling thus provides preferential treatment to the connections based on their advertised peak rate. This scheme is identical to the virtual clock when $t2_i = 0$.

Delay Earliest Due Date [FV90]

The methods described to this point are concerned only with providing a fair amount of bandwidth to each queue. But delay guarantees are very essential for real time services. A method for guaranteeing delays in wide area networks is proposed by Ferrari et al. [FV90], called Delay Earliest Due Date (Delay-EDD). The scheme provides two services, one with deterministic delay bounds and the other with statistical delay bounds. Deadlines are assigned to cells based on the service. The deadlines for cells belonging to deterministic-delay-bound service are "aligned" in such a way that, if the deadlines of the cells overlap, the deadlines are appropriately reduced so that the delay guarantees are met. When it is time to serve the queues, the service compares the deadline stamps of the head-of-line cells waiting at both deterministic-delay and statistical-delay service queues. The comparison is with respect to the end time (i.e., deadline of statistical queue cell) and beginning time (i.e., deadline – service time) of the deterministic queue packet. If the latter is lower than the former, the deterministic delay queue is served immediately. The deadlines assigned to each cell are of the form

$$F_i^k = \max \{a_i^k + d_i^k, F_i^k + x_{min}^k\} \tag{5.8}$$

where a_i^k is the arrival time of the cell, d_i^k is the delay bound assigned by the server to the connection, and x_{min}^k is the minimum interarrival time for the connection.

Worst-Case Fair-Weighted Fair Queuing [BZ96]

All the fair-queuing systems described so far try to emulate the GPS system as closely as possible so that fair queuing is practical to implement. The main difference between the GPS and cell-based systems is that in a fluid system multiple cells are served simultaneously, while in cell-based systems only one cell can be served at a time. This effect causes the service provided by both systems to vary for a given connection. Bennet and Zhang [BZ96] show that this is exactly the case by considering the worst-case fairness properties. To minimize the difference between a cell system and the fluid system, [BZ96] proposed a policy called worst-case fair-weighted fair queuing (WF^2Q). In a WFQ system, the next cell chosen to serve is the one that would have completed service in the corresponding GPS system at time t. In a WF^2Q system, the server considers the set of queues that would have started and possibly finished receiving service in the corresponding GPS system. It is shown that, by doing so, WF^2Q provides service almost identical to GPS, not differing by more than one cell. To reduce the complexity of implementation, [BZ97] extends this scheme to a WF^2Q+ scheme using a lower-complexity virtual-time function.

Bennet and Zhang [BZ97] proposed a hierarchical-packet fair queuing (H-PFQ) as an approximation to hierarchical-generalized-processor-sharing (H-GPS), which is shown in Fig. 5.10.

Figure 5.10. Hierarchical GPS. Source: Bennet, J.C.R., and Zhang, H. "Hierarchical Packet Fair Queuing Algorithms" *IEEE/ACM Transactions on Networking*, vol. 5, no. 5 (October 1997), 675–689. © 1997 IEEE.

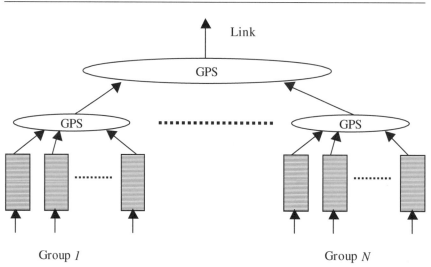

Here, individual physical groups are arranged into aggregate logical groups, each with its own GPS server. There is another GPS server at the top level, which serves the individual logical groups. With an hierarchical GPS server, each logical group gets its own fair share, which is further redistributed to the individual physical queues within that logical group. At the physical-group level, any of the fair-queuing techniques already discussed can be used. Bennet and Zhang [BZ97] presented an implementation framework for the logical-group level. The major difference is that at the logical-group level the queue need not be a FIFO.

Weighted Round-Robin (WRR) Scheduling

Unlike the schemes described above that are based on virtual finish times, the weighted round-robin (WRR) schemes can be built with frames. The simple case of WRR is the round robin. If there are N connections, each separately queued, the RR server in each cycle visits each of the queues and serves a cell if any is waiting. Thus, the RR server shares the link bandwidth equally among the queues. The cycle length of the RR server is N cell slots. Instead of equal share, a weighted share per queue is also possible by assigning weights to each queue and giving slots proportional to weight in each server cycle. This allows cycle length much larger than N, depending on the bandwidth granularity supported by the WRR server. For a cycle of F slots, the minimum bandwidth assigned for a connection is $1/F$ of the link capacity. By assigning slots proportional to weight w_i in a cycle, each queue gets a fair share of $w_i \times$ link capacity$/(\Sigma_{1 \leq i \leq N} w_i)$. To achieve finer bandwidth granularity, the cycle F can be made large, which has implications on the delay. A better way to achieve finer granularity is to implement a hierarchy of WRR schedulers as described earlier in the chapter.

Rotating Priority Queues⁺ (RPQ⁺) Scheduling [WL97]

The RPQ⁺ scheduler uses a set of prioritized FIFO queues. The order of the priorities is rearranged periodically to increase the priority of waiting cells. By doing so, it is proven [WL97] that RPQ⁺ can provide worst-case delay guarantees superior to static priority queuing and approximating the optimal Delay-EDD scheduler. The efficiency of RPQ⁺ increases with the priority re-labeling and approaches that of Delay-EDD in the limit. The RPQ⁺ employs $2P$ ordered FIFO queues. These queues are labeled from highest to lowest priority with indexes as: $0^+, 1, 1^+, 2, 2^+, \ldots, (P-1), (P-1)^+, P$. The RPQ⁺ always selects a cell from the highest-priority nonempty FIFO for transmission. Connections are divided into traffic sets as $C_1, C_2, \ldots, C_P$. Connections in the set C_i assumed to have identical delay bounds $d_i = i\Delta$, where Δ is the priority rotation (or relabeling) interval. The queue rotation is a two-step process, one a concatenation step and the second a promotion step. In the concatenation step, the current FIFO i and FIFO i^+ are merged to form a FIFO i for all $1 \leq i \leq P$. Cells from FIFO i^+ are concatenated to the end of FIFO i. In the promotion step, FIFO i is relabeled as FIFO $(i-1)^+$ for all $1 \leq i \leq P$. A new empty FIFO i is also created to hold arriving cells during the next rotation interval. All cells reside in FIFO i^+ queue after the promotion step.

Leap-Forward Virtual Clock [SVC97]

Leap-forward virtual clock (LFVC) is a modification to the virtual clock (VC) algorithm to provide throughput fairness using two mechanisms: a quarantine mechanism and a leap-forward mechanism. The original virtual clock generally has throughput fairness problems when some sources send bursty data while others remain idle. Also, when the rates of connections vary widely, it can give short-term unfairness. The LFVC tries to avoid this problem by providing two queues: a high-priority queue H and a low-priority holding-queue L. Traffic from well-behaved sources is always placed in queue H. When a connection becomes oversubscribed, the cells of that connection are placed in queue L. The server always serves cells from queue H. It is possible that cells in queue H may have larger virtual finish times than those in queue L, which is a departure from the original algorithm to serve in increasing order of finish times. For a given connection, the cell at the head of the low-priority queue is transferred to the high-priority queue before its delay condition is violated. Since the LFVC is work conserving, to serve a low-priority queue L when there are no cells waiting in the high-priority queue, the server clock is advanced as far as possible (called leap forward) without violating the delay objectives for any queues. The resulting scheme provides throughput fairness and end-to-end delay bounds.

Frame-based Fair Queuing [SVa96-1]

A frame-based fair-queuing algorithm that provides the same end-to-end delays as a PGPS server is proposed in [SVa96-1]. This algorithm uses a potential function $P_i(t)$ for connection i at time t, defined as: $P_i(t) - P_i(\tau) = (W_i(\tau,t)/\rho_i)$, where $W_i(\tau,t)$ is the amount of service received by the connection i during the interval (τ,t) and ρ_i is the rate allocated to the connection. The potential of a connection is a nondecreasing function of time during the system's busy period, and when the connection is backlogged it increases by the normalized service it received. A fair algorithm is the one that attempts to increase the potentials of all backlogged connections at the same rate.

The fluid version of the frame-based fair queuing (FFQ) is defined as the server that services the set of backlog connections with the minimum potential, and the connections in the set are served at a rate proportional to their requested rates. The time is split into frames of F bits. If LR is the link rate, then the frame period T is F/LR. Let $\varphi_i = \rho_i T$, which denotes the maximum amount of traffic connection i can send during the frame. If L_c is the size of a cell, then it is also assumed that $L_c \leq \varphi_i$. Let $f(t)$ be the frame in progress at time t. When the system is empty, $f(t)$ is reset to zero and the potentials of all backlogged connections are also reset to zero. When the potentials of all backlogged connections equals T, then $f(t)$ is increased by T. The system potential function is set as follows: Let the frame update occur at time τ. Then, $f(t)$ and $P(t)$ are set as: $f(\tau) = f(\tau^-)+T$ and $P(\tau) = \max(P(\tau^-),f(\tau))$. At other times, system potential is computed as $P(t) = P(\tau)+(t-\tau)$. The scheduler uses this potential function in order to compute the time stamp of the cell. This FFQ algorithm belongs to the general class of rate-proportional servers (RPS), which provide low latency and bounded fairness.

Two algorithms are executed on the arrival and departure of a cell. On arrival, a cell is stamped with its finishing potential, computed based on the cell length, the reserved rate, and starting potential. The starting potential itself is estimated as the maximum of the finishing potential of its previous cell and the system potential. When the cell finishes transmission, another algorithm is executed that updates the state of the system.

Variation Fluctuation Smoothing [MLG97]

To optimize CDV performance for circuit emulation services in ATM networks, a scheduling algorithm called variation fluctuation smoothing (VFS) is proposed in [MLG97]. The VFS algorithm estimates the clock of each connection by using on-line traffic measurements. Then it computes the lateness of the head-of-line cell for each connection and assigns highest priority to the latest cell. The algorithm stores two variables: lateness L_{i-1} and arrival time Y_{i-1} of the last cell. When the next cell i arrives, its lateness is computed as $L_i = \alpha L_{i-1} + (Y_i - Y_{i-1} - T)$, where T is the nominal assembly time of the connection corresponding to a given rate. When this cell is at the head-of-line position, its current lateness is calculated by adding the waiting time to L_i. This final lateness of the head-of-line cells for all streams is compared and the cell with greatest lateness is sent. With a jittered CBR traffic, it is shown in [MLG97] that this VFS scheme outperforms both FIFO and EDD in providing reduced jitter for connections.

Non-Work-Conserving Fair-Share Scheduling Algorithms

Many real-time services require bounded-delay guarantees for cells transmitted across a network. If the traffic stream is shaped or policed as per the conformance definition (see Chap. 3), it is possible to obtain delay performance bounds for some of the WFQ schemes discussed in the preceding section. So these schemes can be used at the edge of networks where policing functions are in place. But with work-conserving disciplines, traffic distortions take place within the network. Due to this problem, traffic characterization at downstream nodes in the network becomes very difficult, making it increasingly difficult to meet QoS objectives efficently. To address this issue, the traffic can be controlled at intermediate switches in the network by scheduling traffic with non-work-conserving disciplines. Cells are not serviced until a predetermined time and are held in their queues. This behavior may increase the average delay each cell experiences, but the end-to-end delay remains bounded. This section discusses some of the methods proposed for such service.

Stop-and-Go [Gol90]

This scheme is based on a framing strategy and assumes that traffic streams that need delay bounds are (r,T) smooth. A cell stream is defined to be (r,T) smooth if, during each frame of length T, the arrived cells have no more than $r \times T$ bits. Since cells are of fixed length, this scheme is equivalent to receiving $(r \times T)/(\text{cell size})$ cells during the interval T. In the stop-and-go service discipline, if a connection k is (r_k,T) smooth when it enters the network, the property continues to hold at any switching node. The service strategy is based on framing; that is, both incoming and outgoing links are assumed to carry fixed-size frames. These frames need not be synchronous across input and output, so output frames can be time lagged with respect to the input frames. The transmission of cells arriving on an input frames is postponed until the beginning of the next frame on the output link. When a connection traverses H links, the total delay experienced is a fixed value between HT and $2HT$, where T is the frame size. Since delay is proportional to T, the frame size for small-delay connections T should be small. However, the bandwidth granularity is inversely proportional to T; that is, since all cells are fixed size, the minimum bandwidth allocated to a connection is cell size/T bits/s. Thus, T should be large for smaller bandwidth granularity. These are two opposing requirements. Therefore, Golestani [Gol90] also proposed a multilevel framing strategy, a generalized version of stop-and-go.

Hierarchical Round Robin [KKK90]

The hierarchical round robin (HRR) also uses framing strategy like stop-and-go. The frames are divided into various levels and each level can be a different frame length. At each level, slots are assigned to connections directly on that level or reserved for usage by lower levels. Thus, a certain fraction of link bandwidth is assigned to lower-level frames. This behavior is depicted in Fig. 5.11, where the slot C is applied to any connection and the slot L is applied to next level.

Finer bandwidth granularity can be achieved by allocating slots at various levels for the same connection. Let b_i represent the number of slots allotted to the next level, and let f_i represent the slots in a frame at level i. If a connection is assigned k_i slots at level i, then the bandwidth a connection gets in an L-level HRR scheme is:

$$\text{Connection bandwidth} = \left(\sum_{i=1}^{L} k_i \frac{b_1 b_2 ... b_i}{f_1 f_2 ... f_i} \right) \times \text{Link capacity} \qquad (5.9)$$

Note that if there is only one level, the HRR turns into a WRR. It should also be noted that the last level is a simple WRR. The original HRR scheme is non-work-conserving: If there are no cells waiting for a connection when serving a given slot, instead of sending cells assigned to other slots, the server is left idle. This way the total duration of the cycle (i.e., cycling through all frames) is always constant. As a result HRR maintains the traffic smoothness inside the network. Keeping the frame size constant, the HRR can be made work conserving by assigning unused slots temporarily to the bandwidth on demand traffic. Queuing delays when HRR servers are used and with rate-controlled schedulers in general is developed in [BK93].

Figure 5.11. Levels in hierarchical round robin. Source: Kalamanek, C.R., Kanakia, H., and Keshav, S. "Rate Controlled Servers for Very High-Speed Networks," *Proceedings of IEEE Globecom '90*, San Diego (December 1990), 300.3.1–300.3.9. © 1990 IEEE.

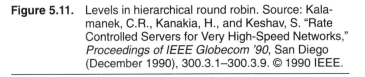
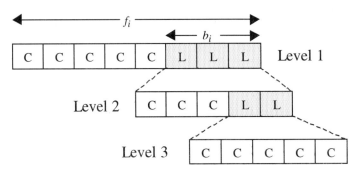

Dynamic Time Slice [Sri92]

In the dynamic time slice (DTS) method, each queue is assigned a time slice and the queue is served until the expiration of the time-slice duration or empty queue, whichever occurs first. If there are n queues and each is assigned a time slice T_i, then each queue gets a link bandwidth of $(T_i/\Sigma_i T_i)$ link capacity, $0 \le i \le n$ and $\Sigma_i T_i \le D_C$, where D_C is the DTS cycle time. Since the cycle time is fixed, delay guarantees can be met for the queues that require it.

Jitter Earliest Due Date [VZF91]

The jitter earliest due date (EDD) is an extension of delay-EDD to provide delay-jitter bounds. This method provides both minimum and maximum delay bounds. To guarantee a delay-jitter bound, each node in the network has to preserve the cell arrival traffic pattern on a given connection. In this scheme, each cell is stamped with a value (called *correction term*), which is the time difference between the instant the cell is served and the instant it was supposed to be served (its deadline). A traffic shaper is used at the next switch, which holds the cell for this duration before the cell is declared eligible. Note that this scheme requires participation of the next switch to control the delay. The holding time is defined as (correction term + delay bound-jitter bound). Then the cell's eligibility time = (holding time + arrival time) computed and the cell's deadline is determined as max{(eligibility time + jitter bound), (deadline of last cell + x_{min})}, where x_{min} is the minimum cell interarrival time. The scheme can be viewed as consisting of traffic shapers for each connection followed by a bounded-delay server that is shared by all connections.

Traffic Shaping

As discussed in Chap. 3, a source, an adaptation device, or the network can apply a traffic-shaping function. The objective of traffic shaping is to create a cell flow conformant to the traffic descriptors. In this chapter, the traffic-shaping function of a switch within a network is discussed. Traffic shaping can be applied to both per-group and per-VC queuing structures. The former application shapes the aggregate traffic, while application shapes the latter traffic per connection. However, in general, shaping is applied on a per-VC/VP basis using the traffic contract information. Since it is slightly different from the rate-controlled fair-share scheduling techniques, however, traffic shaping is considered as a separate scheduling discipline.

In rate-controlled scheduling described above, the cells are held (or delayed) to control delay jitter (e.g., stop-and-go, jitter-EDD, DTS) or rate jitter as in HRR. The rate control in HRR is based on the average connection rate and does not take into account the burst properties of the ATM connections. The traffic-shaping schemes control the rate of connections as per the traffic conformance definitions (such as GCRA or the leaky-bucket algorithm). This technique is becoming very popular and many modern switches implement it to shape the traffic flow (see Chap. 3). In some cases, it may not be necessary to reshape real-time traffic, which by definition will not accumulate much jitter as it proceeds downstream. Thus a combination of work-conserving and rate-controlled service disciplines makes a good compromise to support a multiservice platform. This section looks at a few such architectures.

An integrated traffic-shaping and link-scheduling architecture is described by Rexford et al. in [RBGW97]. The architecture assumes that connections are policed (Chap. 3) with parameters (σ,ρ), where σ is the token bucket size and ρ the token generation rate. The "conforming" cells are then fairly scheduled using rate-based algorithms. Instead of dropping, the traffic shaper delays the incoming cells until they conform to the traffic descriptors. Cell conformance times are estimated using a virtual-scheduling algorithm [TM4.0]. Let t be the cell arrival time, c the conformance time, X the estimated arrival time, and (σ, ρ) the leaky bucket parameters. The cell conformance computation is performed as in Fig. 5.12 [RBGW97].

The cells are stamped with this conformance time. The shaper can also enforce both PCR and SCR by incorporating a dual leaky-bucket algorithm conforming to $(\sigma, \rho, \rho_{peak})$ for each connection. The shaper then uses the conformance time c to schedule cells on the link. A calendar queue can be used to sort the cells in order of increasing conformance times. A calendar queue can be thought of as an array of linked lists. Each position of the array corresponds to a given conformance time, and the linked list at a given position corresponds to the cells that are to leave at that time. Normally there are many connections being multiplexed onto a given a link, so there is a chance that quite a few cells can have the same conformance time. This event is called cell "collisions" and was discussed in Chap. 3. Since it is only possible to transmit a single cell at a time on a given link, a transmission FIFO is used to hold the cells that have reached their conformance time.

Instead of including all the backlogged cells of a connection, only the head-of-line cell is scheduled onto the calendar queue to reduce the complexity of the shaper and prevent a large number of collisions. This simplification is possible because the head-of-line cell has a conformance time at most $1/\rho$ into the future; otherwise there would be a previous cell in the shaper for this connection. Therefore, a per-connection FIFO can be used to hold the backlogged cells of a connection, while the head-of-line cell is scheduled onto the calendar queue and waits to go at its scheduled time. This system is shown in Fig. 5.13. It is assumed that each traffic flow is separately queued. The conformance times for the waiting cells is shown as the label $c = x$. The cal-

Figure 5.12. Cell conformance computing. Source: Rexford, J., Bonomi, F., Greenberg, A., and Wong, A. "Scalable Architectures for Integrated Traffic Shaping and Link Scheduling in High-Speed ATM Switches," *IEEE Journal on Selected Areas in Communications*, vol. 15, no. 5 (June 1997), 938–950. © 1997 IEEE.

$X = X + 1/\rho$	// Estimated cell arrival time
$if (X \leq t)$	// Full token bucket : reset X
$\quad c = X = t;$	
$else\ if (X \leq t + \sigma/\rho)$	// Partially full token bucket
$\quad c = t;$	
$else$	// Empty token bucket : delay cell
$\quad c = (X - \sigma/\rho)$	

Figure 5.13. Calendar queue sorter. Source: Rexford, J., Bonomi, F., Greenberg, A., and Wong, A. "Scalable Architectures for Integrated Traffic Shaping and Link Schoduling in High-Speed ATM Switches" *IEEE Journal on Selected Areas in Communications*, vol. 15, no. 5 (June 1997), 938–950. © 1997 IEEE.

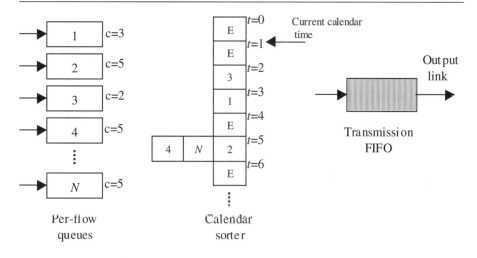

endar sorter lists either the connection identification or the actual cells at the heads of the queues at their respective conformance times. In Fig. 5.13, a slot E indicates that no cell is scheduled to go at that time and that it is empty. The calendar sorter reads the cells at the current calendar time and appends them to the transmission FIFO from which the cells are eventually transmitted.

But this scheme can complicate the implementation of exact sorting, because the new cell entering the calendar might have already reached its conformance time and may need to be inserted between other cells waiting for their service. Approximate-sorting algorithms become necessary to reduce these overheads. For example, head-of-line cells that have reached their conformance times can be sent directly to the transmission FIFO instead of being scheduled on the calendar. One of the problems with calendar queue implementation is that a low-bandwidth connection may be scheduled very far into the future, requiring a very large-array calendar sorter. This problem can be avoided by incorporating multiple-level (granularity) calendar sorters. For example, in Figure 5.13, the calendar granularity is shown to have one-cell transmission time (or one-cell slot). As the granularity (g) increases, the calendar sorter maps the conformance times between time t and $(t + g)$ onto the same slot on the sorter, requiring a smaller array of linked lists. As an example, if $g = 4$, then conformance times 0 to 3 time slots are mapped onto the same slot in the calendar sorter. As a result, the time "resolution" of the calendar is poor for large granularity, which causes an increase in the jitter of the transmitted cells. Generally, high-speed connections cannot tolerate large jitter and should therefore be mapped onto low-granularity sorters. In a network with a wide variety of traffic connections, it is possible to arrange the calendar sorter ingroups. Then a group-level arbitration becomes necessary.

Since the calendar sorter schedules head-of-line cells as per the traffic-shaping rules, it can also be used for implementing work-conserving scheduling, such as WFQ. That is, instead of using a leaky bucket shaper, virtual finish times can be used to schedule cells onto the calendar. The flexibility achieved by integrating the traffic shaping and WFQ is highly beneficial, allowing the selection of which connections are shaped or not on a per-queuing-point basis using the same implementation. One such example is shown in Fig. 5.14, where some traffic flows use the WFQ calendar and others use leaky-bucket shaping calendars.

Each of the traffic shapers and the WFQ shown in Fig. 5.14 are complete calendar sorters; each slot is a bin that holds multiple-connection identifiers scheduled to go at that instant. Note that it is also possible to avoid the use of a transmission FIFO by using two pointers for every traffic shaper. One points to the real calendar time and the other to the virtual calendar time. New connections are scheduled onto the calendar using the real calendar time pointer, while cells are actually read from the virtual calendar time pointer. The virtual calendar time pointer always lags behind the real calendar time pointer and tries to catch up whenever cell collisions occur.

A rate-controlled static-priority (RCSP) queuing is proposed by Zhang [ZF93]. This scheme uses traffic shapers for each connection, followed by a static-priority queuing structure (see Fig. 5.15). By constructing either a partial or full traffic pattern, both rate and delay-jitter control shapers can be used, respectively. Calendar sorting is used for traffic shaping. The scheduler consists of one more stage of queuing, which comprises a set of priority queues. This scheme is similar to the approach shown in Fig. 5.14, where the calendar arbitration is done by a set of priority queues.

A general methodology for designing integrated shaping and scheduling based on FFQ is presented by Stiliadis and Varma [SVa97]. The FFQ server belongs to the class of rate proportional servers (RPS) that aim to equalize the potential for all backlogged connections at each instant. See the definition of potential function in the FFQ description. A shaped-rate propor-

Figure 5.14. Integrated traffic shaping and WFQ.

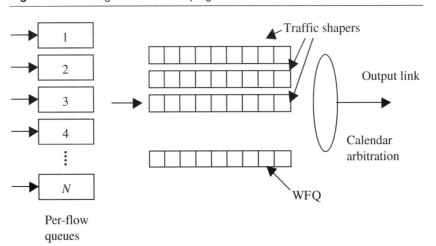

Figure 5.15.　Rate-controlled static-priority (RCSP) queuing. Source: Zhang, H., and Ferrari, D. "Rate Controlled Static-Priority Queuing," *Proceedings of IEEE Infocom '93*, San Francisco (April 1993).

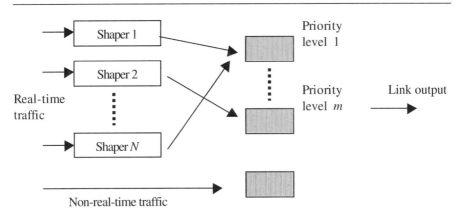

tional server (SRPS) uses both a shaper and scheduler. The shaper is used to admit eligible cells into the scheduler under the admission criterion that the current value of system potential in the RPS is equal to or greater than the finishing potential of the previous cell admitted from that connection. The logical structure is shown in Fig. 5.16. The scheduler has a separate queue to hold eligible cells for each connection. Stiliadis and Varma [SVa97] also proposed another scheduling algorithm called shaped-starting-potential-based fair queuing (SPFQ). It is also shown that RPS algorithms such as virtual clock, which are not fair, can yield worst-case fairness identical to WFQ.

Figure 5.16.　Structure of integrated shaper and scheduler in the SRPS class. Source: Stiliadis, D., and Varma, A. "A General Methodology for Designing Efficient Traffic Scheduling and Shaping Algorithms," *Proceedings of IEEE Infocom '97*, Kobe, Japan (1997), 326–335.

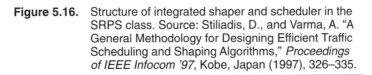

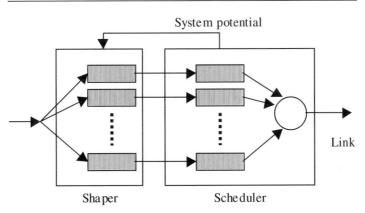

When rate-controlled (or non-work-conserving) servers (RCS) are used in conjunction with shapers, end-to-end delay bounds can be provided for connections traversing multiple hops. This scheme is shown in [GGPS96], where the traffic is reshaped at every hop before entering the next switch. The main disadvantage of RCS servers is that the end-to-end delay bounds are generally obtained as a sum of worst-case delays at each node. If this problem is alleviated by a proper reshaping function at every node, performance similar to a GPS system is obtained. The system can be made work conserving by maintaining two queues, a high priority and low priority, like in leap-forward virtual clock. The high-priority queue is used to hold cells eligible for scheduling (i.e., reshaped) and the low-priority queue is used to hold cells that are not yet eligible. A nonpreemptive arbitration is used to schedule cells, and cells from the low-priority queue are served only when the high-priority queue is empty. Delay guarantees are not affected when operating in the work-conserving mode.

Comparison of Scheduling Schemes

Several scheduling algorithms are reviewed and discussed in this chapter. Some metrics proposed in the literature can be used to compare these algorithms: fairness index, complexity, delay guarantees, latency, and minimum bandwidth property.

Golestani [Gol94] defined the notion of *fairness* as the difference between the normalized service received by different connections. The normalized service w_k of a connection k is defined as the ratio of aggregate traffic $W_k(t_1,t_2)$ served during an interval (t_1,t_2) of the connection to the service rate r_k allocated to that connection. Then the fairness index (*FI*) for two connections i and j is given by

$$FI = \left| w_i(t_1, t_2) - w_j(t_1, t_2) \right| = \left| \frac{W_i(t_1, t_2)}{r_i} - \frac{W_j(t_1, t_2)}{r_j} \right| \tag{5.10}$$

Bennet and Zhang [BZ96] defined *worst-case fairness* of a connection as follows: A connection i is called worst-case fair if, for any time t, the delay of a cell $d_i(t)$ arriving at t is bounded above by $C_i + Q_i(t)/r_i$, where r_i is the guaranteed throughput of the connection i, $Q_i(t)$ is the queue size of the connection at time t, and C_i is a constant independent of queues of other connection sharing the multiplexer. That is, worst-case fair index C_i is such that

$$d_i(t) \le C_i + \frac{Q_i(t)}{r_i} \tag{5.11}$$

The *minimum bandwidth property* of the schedulers is defined in [HuK96]. This metric looks at departure times from a processor-sharing node versus the departure times from a FIFO queue if the server is given a devoted bandwidth. Consider a scheduler for N queues. For connection j, let d_i^j be the departure time of the ith cell from the processor-sharing node using this scheduler. Then the scheduler is said to have a *minimum bandwidth property* with parameter μ, if $d_i^j = \lceil F_i^j \rceil + \mu$ for all cell arrival processes, where $\lceil F_i^j \rceil$ is the departure time of the ith cell from the queue having dedicated bandwidth. The parameter μ for some of the servers described in this chapter is as follows: $\mu = -1$ for PGPS, $\mu = N-2$ for SCFQ, $\mu = -1$ for virtual clock, where N is the number of connections.

Other comparison parameters are the per-connection buffer space requirements, the order of computational complexity of the algorithms, the end-to-end delay bounds, and the end-to-end delay-jitter bounds. Note that some of the delay bounds for work-conserving disciplines are obtained under the assumption that traffic is constrained. The models used are either a leaky bucket model or other constrained-traffic models, such as ($X_{\min}$, X_{ave}, I, $S_{\max}$). Here $X_{\min}$ is the minimum cell interarrival time, X_{ave} is the average cell interarrival time, I is the averaging interval over which X_{ave} is computed, and $S_{\max}$ is the cell size.

The classification introduced in this chapter as work-conserving and non-work-conserving scheduling is defined in a broad sense. Further classification is also possible based on the type of server mechanism used (i.e., whether a server uses a single scheduler or uses a rate controller and a scheduler), the type of queuing used (static priority versus sorted priority), and whether framing is used. Zhang [Zha95] introduced a taxonomy of service disciplines that provided the basis for Stiliadis and Varma [SVa96] to define a general class of latency rate (LR) servers capable of describing the worst-case behavior of numerous scheduling algorithms. A scheduling algorithm belongs to the class of LR servers if the average rate of service the scheduler offers to an active connection i at least equals its reserved rate over every interval starting at time θ_i from the beginning of the period of activity. The parameter θ_i is called the *latency* of the scheduler and is the worst-case delay seen by a first cell of the period of activity (i.e., a cell arriving to an empty queue). All the work-conserving schedulers belong to this model. If the traffic is constrained by a leaky bucket with parameters (σ_i,ρ_i), then the delay bound for connection i is given by $D_i \le \theta_i + (\sigma_i/\rho_i)$. The delay is also bounded when the traffic is passed through a series of n such servers, and the delay bound is given by $D_i^n \le \sum_{j=1}^{n} \theta_i^j + (\sigma_i/\rho_i)$.

Stiliadis and Varma [SVa96-1] further classified the LR servers to rate proportional servers (RPS) based on a system potential function with zero latency. Examples of such a server are based on frame-based fair-queuing strategy.

Table 5.2 shows some comparisons (see also [SVC97, SVa96-1, Zha95]) for various LR servers. The following notations are used: N is the number of connections; L_c is the cell size; F is the frame size; ϕ_i is the amount of traffic allocated in a frame to connection i for frame-based servers; ρ_i is the rate requested by the connection; r is the total service rate of the server; and ε is a small constant.

Table 5.3 compares (also see[ZK91]) some of the service disciplines, which provide delay guarantees. Some of these algorithms are non-work conserving, which are also referred to as Rate-Controlled Service disciplines.

Table 5.2.   Some comparisons of LR servers.

Server	Bandwidth fair?	Worst-case fairness	Latency	Complexity
GPS	Yes	Excellent	0	Not practical
PGPS	Yes	Poor	$(L_c/\rho_i) + (L_c/r)$	$O(N)$
Virtual clock	No	Poor	$(L_c/\rho_i) + (L_c/r)$	$O(logN)$
Frame-based fair Queuing	Yes	Poor	$(L_c/\rho_i) + (L_c/r)$	$O(logN)$
SCFQ	Yes	Poor	$(L_c/\rho_i) + (N\text{-}1)(L_c/r)$	$O(logN)$
WF^{2}Q	Yes	Good	$(L_c/\rho_i) + (L_c/r)$	$O(logN)$
Deficit round robin	Yes	Poor	$(3F-2\varphi_i)/r$	$O(1)$
Weighted round robin	Yes	Poor	$(F-\varphi_i+L_c)/r$	$O(1)$
Leap forward VC	Yes	Good	$(L_c/\rho_i)+(L_c/r) + \varepsilon$	$O(\log logN)$

Table 5.3.   Server comparison that provides delay guarantees.

Server	Bandwidth fair?	Delay guarantee?	Jitter guarantee?	Work conserving?
Stop-and-go	Yes	Yes	Yes	No
HRR	Yes	Yes	No	No
Delay -EDD	Yes	Yes	No	Yes
Jitter -EDD	Yes	Yes	Yes	No
DTS	Yes	Yes	No	No
RCSP	Yes	Yes	Yes	No

Other Issues

The implementation of the queuing and scheduling mechanisms should also consider the following issues:

1. CLP transparency
2. CLP flooding
3. Programming the weights

CLP Transparency

The CLP transparency support (Chap. 3) applies to the traffic conformance definition of CBR.1, VBR.1 (both real-time and non-real-time) classes. These service classes' conformance definition is based on CLP0 + 1 stream; that is, the QoS objectives apply equally to the CLP = 0 and CLP = 1 cells. The other VBR conformance definitions (VBR.2 and VBR.3) only provide QoS to CLP = 0 cells. When using per-group queuing, where CBR.1 and rt-VBR.1 are mixed with rt-VBR.2 and rt-VBR.3, or nrt-VBR.1 is mixed with nrt-VBR.2 and nrt-VBR.3, the CLP = 1 cells of CBR.1 and VBR.1 must be treated as CLP = 0 cells. One approach is to save the CLP status and reset it (i.e., mark it as CLP = 0) when the cell enters the switch. The saved status is copied back when the cell exits the switch. Generally, most of the switches maintain internal cell format, which is longer than 53 bytes, and one bit can be used for CLP transparency purposes. The CLP transparency issue can also be handled by using separate queues for the CLP-transparent connections and treating all cells in these queues with the same priority.

CLP Flooding

This CLP flooding problem applies to per-group or per-VC/VP queuing with priority scheduling. The VBR.2 and VBR.3 conformance definitions (Chap. 3) allow the user to exceed the SCR up to PCR, as long as the traffic is tagged. This behavior creates the problem of "CLP = 1 flooding." The CLP = 1 traffic, although conforming, is not eligible for QoS committments and it is not allocated any bandwidth. However, it tries to compete for the available resources. It is possible for some of the sources to send their complete traffic as CLP = 1 tagged up to PCR.

Proper handling of the CLP = 1 traffic becomes necessary so that it does not steal bandwidth away from services offering guarantees (such as ABR or GFR) but does get some fair share of available bandwidth. Futhermore, these tagged cells need to share the remaining resource fairly along with the bandwidth-on-demand services. If priority scheduling is used that gives higher priority to VBR service, and VBR.2 and VBR.3 are served at a higher priority than ABR, GFR, and UBR, the bandwidth-on-demand services can starve due to the VBR CLP = 1 flooding the available bandwidth. It is a philosophical discussion whether this CLP = 1 traffic should be given priority over UBR traffic (which in most cases is true, since VBR may be served as higher priority than UBR). However, CLP = 1 cells cannot affect the MCR guarantees of ABR and GFR. A weighted scheduling mechanism can solve this problem, by guaranteeing that each queue obtains some proportion of the available bandwidth.

Programming of the Weights

The programming of the weights of the fair-share schedulers in the case of per-group queuing can impact efficiency. As seen in this chapter, all the fair-share schedulers use some sort of weights (either per-connection weights or per-connection guaranteed rates) to guarantee bandwidth to each queue. When using per-VC/VP queuing, the weight is programmed at connection setup and is proportional to the traffic descriptors. When fair-share scheduling is used for a per-group queuing structure, an aggregate weight needs to be programmed. There are two possible paradigms:

Static weight: Program the weight when configuring the system. This guarantees a certain bandwidth to the given group queue, irrespective of how many connections are using it and the load on the queue.

Dynamic weight: Change the weight when connections are added or removed from the queue or when load increases or decreases. The weight is based on aggregate weights of all connections using a given queue.

When static weight setup is used, a portion of the link bandwidth is kept available for a given group, irrespective of the load on the queue. For example, consider the scenario in which grouping is based on service category (see Fig. 5.3). Assume that the ABR queue is given a weight of two and the UBR queue a weight of one. At a given instant, ten ABR connections and one UBR connection share the available bandwidth. The single UBR connection can use one third of the bandwidth, while each ABR connection obtains two thirtieths of the bandwidth. This creates a fairness problem among groups. With the dynamic weight setup, the efficiency of the scheduler depends on how often the weights are changed-on every connection setup or over a time interval, say, every few seconds. However, the weights are reprogrammed for each group, depending on the number of connections and the load. Therefore, the fairness problem among groups is minimized with significant increase in complexity. When using hierarchical scheduling, the weight recalculation is limited to a few subgroups or queues. The weight setup also has an impact on call blocking and network efficiency. Static weights may result in higher call blocking as the CAC takes into account the weight in assessing the bandwidth available for a given type of service. If the weight is static, connections may be rejected even if there is bandwidth available.

Review

The key to efficient multiservice platform performance in ATM networks is to provide appropriate queuing and scheduling mechanisms at various contention points in ATM networks. This chapter has focused on some of these mechanisms. Though comprehensive, this chapter's intention is to introduce the reader to the complex field of queuing and scheduling. Fair-share scheduling and per-VC queuing is necessary to provide guaranteed QoS. Generally, an ATM switch consists of a switching core and peripheral devices. The per-VC queuing can be limited to peripheral devices whereby traffic can be shaped (or controlled) into and out of the switching core. Pushing congestion to the ingress peripheral devices by appropriate control can reduce the complexity of the core. Which scheduling algorithm to choose depends on implementation complexity and economics. As a general rule, the bandwidth scheduler must take care of

1. The tradeoff between cost and efficiency
2. CLP flooding
3. CLP transparency support
4. Fair allocation of bandwidth to connections
5. Fair allocation of bandwidth to service classes
6. Delay guarantees to real-time services

It may be more efficient to use a combination of scheduling mechanisms. For example, at a low level of hierarchy traffic shapers are used for real-time services, while a WFQ scheme is used between non-real-time services. A priority queue can be used between the traffic shapers and the WFQ at a higher level of hierarchy.

It should be noted that main trade-off lies between simplicity of implementation and achieving fairness. Priority scheduling is simple to implement but does not yield fairness in dividing the available bandwidth, while weighted scheduling is more complex but can divide the available bandwidth in a fair and flexible manner between the queues. However, it should also be noted that fairness cannot be measured instantaneously. Therefore, a scheme that achieves long-term fairness is likely sufficient. Regardless of how well fairness is achieved, the queuing and scheduling mechanism at a contention point should provide the contracted QoS objectives of the connections.

References

[AD89] Ahmadi, H., and Denzel, W. "A Survey of Modern High-Performance Switching Techniques," *IEEE Journal on Selected Areas in Communications*, vol. 7, no. 7 (September 1989), 1091–1103.

[BK93] Banerjea, A., and Keshav, S. "Queuing Delays in Rate Controlled ATM Networks" *Proceedings of IEEE Infocom '93*, San Francisco (April 1993).

[BZ96] Bennet, J.C.R., and Zhang, H. "WF^{2}Q: Worst-Case Fair Weighted Queuing," *Proceedings of IEEE Infocom '96*, San Francisco (March 1996), 120–128.

[BZ97] Bennet, J.C.R., and Zhang, H. "Hierarchical Packet Fair Queuing Algorithms," *IEEE/ACM Transactions on Networking*, vol. 5, no. 5 (October 1997), 675–689.

[DKS89] Demers, A., Keshav, S., and Shenker, S. "Analysis and Simulation of Fair Queuing Algorithm," *ACM SIGCOMM Computer Communication Review*, vol 19, no. 4 (September 1989), 1–12.

[Eng88] Eng, K. "A Photonic Knock-out Switch for High-Speed Packet Networks," *IEEE Journal on Selected Areas in Communications*, vol. 6 (August 1988), 1107–1116.

[FP95] Figueira, N.J., and Pasquale, J. "An Upper Bound on Delay for the Virtual Clock Service Discipline," *IEEE/ACM Transcation on Networking*, vol. 3, no. 4 (August 1995), 399–408.

[FV90] Ferrari, D., and Verma, D.C. "A Scheme for Real-Time Channel Establishment in Wide-Area Networks," *IEEE Journal on Selected Areas in Communications*, vol. 8, no. 3 (April 1990), 368–379.

[Gar96] Garrett, M.W. "A Service Architecture for ATM: From Applications to Scheduling," *IEEE Network Magazine*, (May/June 1996), 6–14.

[GGPS96] Georgiadis, L., Guerin, R., Peris, V., and Sivarajan, K.N. "Efficient Network QoS Provisioning Based on Per Node Traffic Shaping," *IEEE/ACM Transactions on Networking*, vol. 4, no. 4 (August 1996), 482–501.

[Gol90] Golestani, S.J. "A Stop-and-Go Queuing Framework for Congestion Management," *ACM SIG-COMM Computer Communications Review*, vol. 20, no. 4 (September 1990), 8–18.

[Gol94] Golestani, S.J. "A Self-Clocked Fair Queuing Scheme for Broadband Applications," *Proceedings of IEEE Infocom '94*, Toronto, (June 1994), 636–646.

[HK88] Hluchyj, M.G., and Karol, M.J. "Queuing in High-Performance Packet Switching," *IEEE Journal on Selected Areas in Communications*, vol. 6, no. 9 (December 1988), 1587–1597.

[HuK96] Hung, A., and Kesidis, G. "Bandwidth Scheduling for Wide-Area ATM Networks Using Virtual Finish Times," *IEEE/ACM Transactions on Networking*, vol. 4, no. 1 (February 1996), 49–54.

[JH87] Hui, J. "A Broadband Packet Switch for Integrated Transport," *IEEE Journal on Selected Areas in Communications*, vol. SAC-5, no. 8 (October 1987), 1264–1273.

[KKK90] Kalamanek, C.R., Kanakia, H., and Keshav, S. "Rate Controlled Servers for Very High-Speed Networks," *Proceedings of IEEE Globecom '90*, San Diego (December 1990), 300.3.1–300.3.9.

[KLE75] Kleinrock, L. *Queuing Systems, Volume 1-Theory*, New York: John Wiley, 1975.

[MLF92] Mukherjee, A., Landweber, L.H., and Faber, T. "Dynamic Time Windows and Generalized Virtual Clock: Combined Closed-Loop/Open-Loop Congestion Control," *Proceedings of IEEE Infocom '92*, Florence, Italy (1992).

[MLG97] McDonald, D., Liao, R., and Giroux, N. "Variation Fluctuation Smoothing for ATM Circuit Emulation Service," *Proceedings of ITC*, 15, Washington, DC (June 1997), 761–770.

[PG93] Parekh, A.K., and Gallager, R.G. "A Generalized Processor Sharing Approach to Flow Control in Integrated Services Networks: The Single Node Case," *IEEE/ACM Transactions on Networking*, vol. 1, no. 3 (June 1993), 344–357.

[PG94] Parekh, A.K., and Gallager, R.G. "A Generalized Processor Sharing Approach to Flow Control in Integrated Services Networks: The Multiple Node Case," *IEEE/ACM Transactions on Networking*, vol. 2, no. 2 (April 1994), 137–150.

[RBGW97] Rexford, J., Bonomi, F., Greenberg, A., and Wong, A. "Scalable Architectures for Integrated Traffic Shaoing and Link Scheduling in High-Speed ATM Switches," *IEEE Journal on Selected Areas in Communications*, vol. 15, no. 5 (June 1997), 938–950.

[Rob94] Roberts, J.W. "Virtual Spacing for Flexible Traffic Control," *International Journal of Communication Systems*, vol. 7 (1994).

[Sri92] Sriram, K. "Methodologies for Bandwidth Allocation, Transmission, Scheduling and Congestion Avoidance in Broadband ATM Networks," *Proceedings of IEEE Globecom '92*, Orlando, Florida (1992), 1545–1551.

[SV96] Shreedhar, M., and Varghese, G. "Efficient Fair Queuing Using Deficit Round-Robin," *IEEE/ACM Transactions on Networking*, vol. 4, no. 3 (June 1996), 375–385.

[SVa96-1] Stiliadis, D., and Varma, A. "Design and Analysis of Frame-Based Fair Queuing: A New Traffic Scheduling Algorithm for Packet Switched Networks," *Proceedings of IEEE Sigmetrics '96* (1996).

[SVa96-2] Stiliadis, D., and Varma, A. "Latency-Rate Servers: A General Model for Analysis of Traffic Scheduling Algorithms," *Proceedings of IEEE Infocom '96*, San Francisco (March 1996), 111–119.

[SVa97] Stiliadis, D., and Varma, A. "A General Methodology for Designing Efficient Traffic Scheduling and Shaping Algorithms," *Proceedings of IEEE Infocom '97*, Kobe, Japan (1997), 326–335.

[SVC97] Suri, S., Varghese, G., and Chandranmenon, G. "Leap Forward Virtual Clock: A New Fair Queuing Scheme with Guaranteed Delays and Throughput Fairness," *Proceedings of IEEE Infocom '97*, Kobe, Japan (1997), 557–565.

[Tob90] Tobagi, F.A. "Fast Packet Switch Architectures for Broadband Integrated Services Digital Networks," *Proceedings of the IEEE*, vol. 78, no.1 (January 1990), 133–167.

[VZF91] Verma, D.C., Zhang, H., and Ferrari, D. "Delay Jitter Control for Real-Time Communication in a Packet Switching Network," *Proceedings of Tricomm '91*, Chapel Hill, North Carolina (April 1991), 35–46.

[WL97] Wrege, D.E., and Liebeherr, J. "A Near-Optimal Packet Scheduler for QoS Networks," *Proceedings of IEEE Infocom '97*, Kobe, Japan (1997), 576–583.

[YO90] Oie, Y., Suda. T., Murata. M., Kolson, D., and Miyabara. H., "Survey of Switching Techniques in High-Speed Networks and their Performance Miyahara," *Proceedings of IEEE Infocom '90*, 1242–1251.

[ZF93] Zhang, H., and Ferrari, D. "Rate Controlled Static-Priority Queuing," *Proceedings of IEEE Infocom '93*, San Francisco (April 1993).

[Zha90] Zhang, L. "Virtual Clock: A New Traffic Control Algorithm for Packet Switching Networks," *ACM SIGCOMM Computer Communication Reviews*, vol. 20, no. 4 (September 1990), 19–29.

[Zha95] Zhang, H. "Service Disciplines for Guaranteed Performance Service in Packet Switching Networks," *Proceedings of the IEEE*, vol. 83, no. 10 (October 1995), 1374–1396.

[ZK91] Zhang, H., and Keshav, S. "Comparison of Rate-Based Service Disciplines," *Proceedings of ACM Sigcomm '91*, Zurich, Switzerland, (September 1991), 113–121.

ABR Flow Control

The available bit rate (ABR) service specifies a flow control mechanism that (a) allows the traffic sources to adapt to the bandwidth dynamically available in the network and (b) attempts to avoid congestion [TM4.0]. Using ABR service thereby minimizes the possibility of losing data within the boundaries of the ATM network. The flow control specified as part of the ABR service category requires the use of "in-band" *resource management* (RM) cells to carry information about the sources and to obtain feedback from the switches (or network). The control loop requires the active participation of the source, the destination, and the switch elements of the network. This participation is defined as a set of rules for *source behavior*, *switch behavior*, and *destination behavior*. This chapter describes the ABR component behavior and describes some specific implementations and their relative performance.

ABR Service

The ABR service employs a reactive control mechanism that dynamically adjusts the rate of transmission of an ABR source. This dynamic control is based on congestion feedback obtained from the network; the congestion feedback is translated into an allowed cell rate (ACR) for each source. Every source transmits periodic resource management (RM) cells, called *forward RM* (FRM) cells, along with the data cells. The source sends a RM cell after every ($Nrm - 1$) data cells. In other words, ($Nrm - 1$) is the maximum number of cells a source may send for each forward RM cell. The default value of Nrm is 32. The RM cells along with the data cells may traverse a network of switches before reaching the destination. The destination turns around the RM cells as *backward RM* (BRM) cells, which are inserted in the backward direction of the connection. Each switch writes information about its congestion status onto the BRM cells, which carry the network (or switch) information back to the source. The information fed back to the source depends on the mode of the ABR loop (i.e., binary or explicit-rate mode). The RM cells contain many fields (see Table 6.1) to support these operations. Some of the RM cell fields include rate information of the source, such as the current cell rate (CCR) and minimum cell rate (MCR) of the connection. Upon receipt of the BRM cells, the source acts appropriately to control its rate of transmission (ACR). Figure 6.1 depicts such a unidirectional flow model of an ABR control loop. A similar loop will flow in the reverse direction for bidirectional operation.

Each entity (source, switch, or destination) in the model has a specified role [TM4.0]. The protocol also uses a concept of *virtual source* (VS) and *virtual destination* (VD), which are functions that can replicate the behavior of the source and destination *within the network*. The ABR control loop can operate under two modes or combination of them [TM 4.0]:

Binary Mode: In binary mode, a *switch* marks the EFCI (explicit forward congestion indication) bit in the data cell header to indicate impending congestion status. The *destination* saves and translates the EFCI information into bits such as congestion indication (CI) or no increase (NI), which are marked in the corresponding BRM cell. Upon receipt of the BRM cell, the *source* examines these bits and takes appropriate action. The actions could be to increase, decrease, or not change the transmission rate. In a variant of this method called the *relative rate marking*, the switch sets the CI/NI bits in the BRM cell. The EFCI setting mode is included because it is backward compatible with switches that conform to previous standards [UNI3.1].

Explicit Rate (ER) Mode: In the explicit rate mode, a *switch* computes a local fair share for the connection and marks the rate at which the source is allowed to transmit in the ER field of the BRM cell. The switch writes into this field only if the bandwidth it can offer is lower than what is already marked in the BRM cell (BER). The *source*, upon reception of the BRM cell, extracts the ER field and increases or decreases the transmission rate to the ER value using the rules of source behavior [TM4.0].

Figure 6.1. ABR flow model.

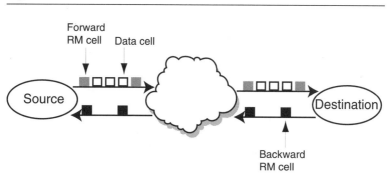

To comply with the TM4.0 specification, an ABR source and destination need to support both binary and explicit-rate modes. A switch can support one of the two modes. When detecting congestion, a switch can also generate a backward RM cell in order to convey the congestion status faster to the source, without having to wait for a RM cell that is part of the control loop. The additional RM cells imply extra overhead and have lower priority (CLP = 1). By convention, a CLP = 0 stream is referred to as *in-rate* cells while a CLP = 1 stream is referred to as *out-of-rate*. The source can also send extra lower-priority (out-of-rate) forward RM cells in an attempt to increase its rate.

The ABR service does not include a formal conformance definition [TM4.0]. However, verification that the source complies with the defined rules can be done by applying a dynamic GCRA (D-GCRA) or by using a virtual source (discussed later in this chapter). The D-GCRA is similar to a GCRA (Chap. 3), but the monitored rate is modified based on the receipt of BRM cells after some time delay to account for the propagation and processing of the BRM cells by the source.

Many applications (wireless, xDSL, and inverse multiplexing) that are subject to bandwidth variations can benefit from using the ABR service. Applications that seek to maximize the use of the bandwidth to carry only "good" data (data unlikely to get discarded in the ATM network) are potential users of the ABR service.

This chapter describes the ABR protocol, cell format, and control loop parameters. It discusses the binary mode and its performance limitations and provides a comprehensive review of the various explicit mode algorithms that can be implemented.

ABR RM Cell Format

Table 6.1 shows the format of the resource management cells in ABR service. The table describes some of the RM cell fields. Details on the size and position can be found in [TM4.0].

Control Loop Parameters

An ABR connection uses the PCR and MCR traffic descriptors as described in Chap. 2. The PCR indicates the highest cell rate that the application needs, and the MCR is the minimum bandwidth that is guaranteed. That is, if the source sends cells at MCR, it does not need to react to the flow control information in order to achieve a minimal cell loss. The network dynamically distributes the available bandwidth among the contending connections, and each ABR connection is allowed to send at the allowed cell rate (ACR), where $MCR \leq ACR \leq PCR$. The ABR control loop uses many other service parameters, which are described in Table 6.2. Default values and signaling aspects are discussed in [TM4.0] and [SIG4.0].

The "Informative Appendix I" in [TM4.0] shows an end-system pseudo-code that describes how some of these variables are used in the ABR control loop. The usage of some of these parameters is described in the following sections.

Table 6.1. Some fields of the ABR resource management cell format. Source: Modified from The ATM Forum Technical Committee. *Traffic Management Specification*, version 4.0, af-tm-0056.000 (April 1996), ATM Forum http://www.atmforum.com/. Copyright © 1996 the ATM Forum. Used with permission.

Name	Description
Header	Header: the first five bytes of a RM cell are the standard ATM header with PTI = 110 (binary) for a VCC, and additionally VCI = 6 for a VPC. The CLP bit is 0 if the RM cell is in-rate, and 1 if it is out-of-rate.
ID	Protocol identifier: identifies the service using the RM cell. ID = 1 for ABR service.
DIR	Direction: indicates which direction of data flow is associated with the RM cell. A forward RM cell indicated by DIR = 0 is associated with data cells flowing in the same direction. A backward RM cell indicated by DIR = 1 is associated with data cells flowing in the opposite direction. DIR is changed from 0 to 1 when the destination turns around the RM cell.
BN	BECN cell: indicates whether the RM cell is a Backward Explicit Congestion Notification (BECN) cell BN = 1 indicates a BECN RM cell generated by a destination or a switch. BN = 0 indicates that the RM cell was turned around at the destination.
CI	Congestion indication: allows a network element to indicate that there is congestion in the network. When a source receives a backward RM cell with CI = 1, it decreases its ACR. When turning around a forward RM cell, a destination will set CI = 1 to indicate that the previous received data cell had the EFCI state set.
NI	No increase: prevents a source from increasing its ACR. A network element can set NI to 1 to indicate impending congestion.
ER	Explicit rate: Limits the source ACR to a value that the network elements and the destination can sustain.
CCR	Current cell rate: Set by the source to its current ACR.
MCR	Minimum cell rate of the connection.
CRC-10	CRC used to verify the accuracy of the content.

Table 6.2. ABR service parameters. Source: Modified from The ATM Forum Technical Committee. *Traffic Management Specification*, version 4.0, af-tm-0056.000 (April 1996), ATM Forum http://www.atmforum.com/. Copyright © 1996 the ATM Forum. Used with permission.

Acronym	Name	Description
ICR	initial cell rate	Rate at which a source should send initially and after an idle period.
RIF	rate increase factor	Controls the amount by which the cell transmission rate may increase upon receipt of a RM cell.
Nrm	number of data cells per RM cells	Maximum number of cells a source may send for each forward RM cell.
Mrm		Controls allocations of bandwidth between forward RM cells, backward RM cells, and data cells.
RDF	rate decrease factor	Controls the decrease in the cell transmission rate.
ACR	allowed cell rate	Current rate at which a source is allowed to send.
CRM	missing RM-cell count	Limits the number of forward RM cells that may be sent in the absence of received backward RM cells.
ADTF	ACR decrease time factor	Time permitted between sending RM cells before the rate is decreased to ICR.
Trm	time between RM cell.	Provides an upper bound on the time between forward RM cells for an active source.
FRTT	fixed round-trip time	Sum of the fixed processing and propagation delays from the source to a destination and back.
TBE	transient buffer exposure	Number of cells that the network would like to limit the source to sending during startup periods, before the first RM cell returns.
CDF	cutoff decrease factor	Controls the decrease in ACR associated with CRM.
TCR	tagged cell rate	Limits the rate at which a source may send out-of-rate forward RM cells.

Control Loop Performance Metrics

The performance of the ABR control loop needs to be evaluated against the following criteria:

- Fairness
- Efficiency
- Stability
- Robustness

The performance of the control loop can be impacted by the parameter settings and the proprietary techniques employed by the node to set the EFCI/CI/NI bits or to calculate the ER values and the accuracy of the source and destination implementations.

Fairness

The ABR control loop attempts to allocate a fair share of bandwidth to contending connections. Consider a network of multiple-switching elements. The network is populated by a number of connections. The goal is to allocate bandwidth at each link so that the link is fully utilized while simultaneously achieving a fair distribution of bandwidth among connections. The fair share is defined as follows: With all sources active, let *the desired bandwidth allocation* for connection i be e_i, the achieved distribution be a_i and $y_i = a_i/e_i$. Then the fairness for a set of n VCs can be quantified by the fairness index, *FI* as [Jai96]:

$$FI = \frac{\left(\sum y_i\right)^2}{\left(n \times \sum y_i^2\right)} \tag{6.1}$$

The *desired bandwidth allocation* is determined by the fairness criteria. An example of a fairness criterion is *max-min* fairness [BG87]. The max-min fairness can be intuitively understood as the distribution of bandwidth among connections such that each connection receives an *end-to-end* bandwidth allocation that is equal to its fair share at the point in its path through the network where the resources are most scarce. The fair share in the context of max-min is defined as equal share; that is, the available bandwidth is equally divided among the competing connections at a queuing point. Many ER algorithms proposed in the literature for ABR traffic try to achieve the Max-Min fairness. However, in the context of MCR guarantees for ABR, other fairness policies can be defined. Various definitions (or policies) of fair-share distributions [TM.4.0] are *equal share, MCR proportional, weight proportional, MCR + equal share, MCR + MCR proportional, MCR + weight proportional*, and the like. The following text describes an iterative algorithm to determine a fair distribution of bandwidth in a network with a given fairness policy.

For each link j, reduce the *available* link bandwidth LR_j, by an amount equal to the total guaranteed bandwidth of all connections carried on the link. The *available* bandwidth is defined as the link bandwidth left after discounting the bandwidth used by the connections in order to meet their QoS objectives (e.g., PCR of CBR). Assign a weight, W_{ij}, to each connection i, and for each link j that the connection traverses. The weight is assigned according to any bandwidth distribution method. In the context of ABR, since MCR is guaranteed to each connection, the policies of *MCR + equal share, MCR + MCR proportional, MCR + weight proportional* are more appropriate. If a connection does not utilize a particular link, then W_{ij} is equal to zero. Perform the following steps:

1. Let S represent the set of all connections in the network that have not been allocated bandwidth. Calculate the available bandwidth B_{ij} for each connection at each link by the formula

$$B_{ij} = \min\left\{ PCR_{ij}, LR_j \times \left(\frac{W_{ij}}{\sum_{i \in S} W_{ij}} \right) \right\}.$$

2. Determine the pair *(n,m)* as $(n, m) = \{(i, j) | \min(B_{ij}) \forall i, j\}$, where n is the connection and m is the link.
3. Let A_i represent the bandwidth allocated to connection i, and set $A_n = B_{nm}$.
4. Reduce by the value A_n the available bandwidth, LR_j on all links j that are utilized by connection n. Remove n from the set S (i.e., it has now been allocated bandwidth). Proceed to Step 1 unless the set S is empty.

The number of iterations is equal to the number of connections in the network. When the iterations are complete, the set of values $\{A_i, i = 1,2, \ldots\}$ represents the fairly distributed bandwidth allocation to connections in the network according to the policies equal share, MCR proportional, and weight proportional. For policies MCR + equal Share, MCR + MCR proportional, MCR + weight proportional, the set $\{MCR_i + A_i, i = 1, 2, \ldots\}$ represents the fairly allocated bandwidth, where MCR_i is the guaranteed minimum cell rate of the connection. In the latter case, LR_j need to be discounted by the sum of MCR_i of the connections using the specified link.

Efficiency

Efficiency is given by the actual throughput achieved across an entity divided by the maximum achievable throughput for that entity. An entity in this context may refer to a single switching element or to a section of the network. The maximum achievable throughput in an ABR ER network is given by the sum of the ACRs of all connections divided by the available bandwidth, where their bandwidth is allocated according to a given fairness criterion. The efficiency is also measured in terms of how quickly the bandwidth dynamically unused by CBR and VBR can be used and released. Another key aspect of the control loop is the flexibility to apply different policies when allocating the available bandwidth.

For data applications (see Chap. 9), another measure of efficiency is termed "goodput." This is defined as the ratio of the *achieved* throughput to the maximum achievable throughput. The achieved throughput only refers to the amount of "good data," which is the actual amount of packets successfully received by the receiver (e.g., a TCP receiver). Retransmissions, or duplicate packets received at the receiver, are not counted as good data.

The time required to converge to a fair allocation of bandwidth is an important performance criterion for an ABR network. The convergence time will impact how quickly sources that are becoming active can acquire their share of the bandwidth, and therefore impact the end-to-end delay as perceived at the application level. On the other hand, sudden large decreases in ACR or frequent large variations in ACR may have adverse effects on higher layer protocols (e.g. TCP; see Chap. 9). Therefore, the convergence time needs to be carefully traded off with a low variance in the ACR value.

Stability

Stability is measured by the rate at which the control loop converges to a steady-state distribution of bandwidth after a perturbation (e.g., after a VBR source becomes active and sends a burst of data at the PCR). An unstable control loop does not converge to a steady-state distribution.

Robustness

A robust control loop exhibits fairness, efficiency, and stability under a variety of traffic scenarios. The robustness is measured by the ability of the network to achieve minimum cell loss. As in any control system, the controllability of a given variable depends on the delays involved in the system. In ATM networks, sources are away from switching elements. Therefore, the queuing and propagation delays determine how fast the ACR of a source can be controlled. In large-delay environments, it is possible to see large oscillations in ACR. This can cause cell loss to occur when smaller buffers are used. Thus, delay plays a very important role in ACR convergence and the ability to control the cell loss. The use of virtual source/destination addresses this issue.

As described before, the ABR control loop involves the cooperation of the sources, destination receivers, and switching elements. Each of these entities requires the "rules" of behavior for this co-operation. It is important to describe them before looking into the control algorithms, which try to achieve the required fairness criteria and bandwidth allocation.

Source/Destination Behavior

Source Behavior

The required behavior for the ABR source is described below. Further operational details and rules are provided in [TM4.0, Sec. 5.10.4]. The source is responsible for:

- Inserting a RM cell every (*Nrm*-1) data cells. These RM cells are included as part of the ACR. There are other exceptional cases for which RM cells need to be sent to deal with low-rate sources. The CCR field of the RM cell contains the current ACR. The data cells are sent with EFCI = 0.
- The source can send low-priority (CLP = 1) out-of-rate FRM cells in order to attempt to increase its rate more quickly. The rate at which the source sends these low-priority RM cells is limited to TCR.
- The source performs appropriate scheduling and shaping of the cells (Chap. 5) and congestion control (Chap. 7) to limit the rate to ACR.
- Adjusting the shaping rate (ACR) according to the information contained in the returning RM cell. The final value of ACR is then set as the minimum of the ACR and ER. The ACR is maintained between the MCR and the PCR (i.e., the rate should never exceed PCR). When the source starts up or has been idle for longer than ADTF, the ACR is set to ICR. Table 6.3 describes some of the rules for adjusting the ACR.

Table 6.3. ACR adjustment rules.

Event	Resulting ACR
(1) Source starts up	ACR = ICR
(2) BRM cell received with CI = 0 and NI = 0	max(MCR, min(ER, PCR, ACR + RIF × PCR))
(3) BRM cell received with CI = 1	max(MCR,min(ER,ACR-ACR × RDF))
(4) BRM cell received with NI = 1	ACR unchanged
(5) ADTF time is less than the time since the last RM cell sent	ACR = ICR
(6) Missing RM cell count reaches CRM	max(MCR,min(ER,ACR-ACR × CDF))

Destination Behavior

The ABR destination is responsible for:

- Keeping track of the *congestion state* of a connection. The congestion state can, for example, be the value of the EFCI bit of the last data cell received, or the average of the EFCI values received in the last N data cells. When this state is inserted into the BRM cell, it is reset.
- Upon reception of a FRM cell, the destination transmits (or turns around the FRM cell) a BRM cell (with DIR = 1) in the direction of the source.
- A destination may independently generate a backward RM cell without having received a forward RM cell. The rate of these backward RM cells (including both in-rate and out-of-rate) is limited to ten cells/second, per connection. When a destination generates a RM cell it sets either CI = 1 or NI = 1, it sets BN = 1, and DIR = 1.
- The content of the BRM cell is the same as FRM, except that CI field includes the congestion state of the connection. The destination may also indicate its congestion status by setting CI = 1 or NI = 1. Alternately, the destination can indicate a local fair-share of bandwidth by setting $ER_{BRM} - \min$ (local ER, ER_{FRM}).

Virtual Source and Destination Behavior

A virtual source/virtual destination (VS/VD) function replicates the source/destination (S/D) behavior within the network. VS/VD can be an important part of an ABR control loop. When a connection traverses a large number of hops, or long haul links with large propagation delays, the delay for the feedback, conveyed by the RM cells, becomes significant. The feedback delay impacts the time required for the source to react to the content of the RM cell. This delay can cause transient buffer buildup and even congestion if the RM cell indicates to lower the source rate. It can also cause temporary underutilization, if the RM cell indicates to increase the source rate. By incorporating the virtual-source (VS) or virtual-destination (VD) behavior into intermediate switching elements, the end-to-end ABR flow control loop is segmented into smaller loops, thereby reducing feedback delays in each subloop. This is depicted in Fig. 6.2 using a bidirectional traffic flow.

A VS/VD performs the ABR source and destination functions at the ingress or egress of a switching element. In this example, the ABR loop is segmented into two ABR control loops. ABR Loop 1 extends from the ABR source to the ingress of the switch and is referred to as the upstream loop. ABR Loop 2 reaches from the ingress of the switch to the ABR destination and is referred to as the downstream loop. Each subloop works independently; however, to maintain fairness and prevent congestion at the virtual source, the subloops need to be coupled to convey the feedback information end-to-end. There are three methods of coupling the subloops:

Figure 6.2.   VS/VD example.

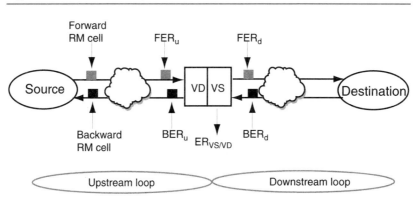

1. **No Coupling:** The virtual source indicates, in the backward RM cells going to the upstream loop, sufficient information to keep its buffers from congesting, that is, $BER_u = min(FER_u, ER_{VS/VD})$. However, no information from the downstream loop is directly used for the feedback.
2. **Loose Coupling:** The feedback information from the downstream loop is included in the upstream backward RM cell as a function of local congestion ($ER_{VS/VD}$) at the VS. A function can be used to weight the amount of local and downstream congestion, that is, $BER_u = min(FER_u, f(ER_{VS/VD}, BER_d))$.
3. **Tight Coupling:** The feedback information from downstream received by th VS and local congestion are combined with backward RM cells sent in the upstream loop as $BER_u = min(ER_{VS/VD}, BER_d, FER_u)$.

Here FER_u and BER_u are the ER marking in the FRM and BRM cells of the upstream loop and FER_d and BER_d are for the downstream loop.

Each of the coupling methods has different effects on the end-to-end control loop behavior and on the rate of convergence. The coupling employed between the two ABR loops allows the loops to interact such that upstream loops can further prevent congestion from occurring in the downstream loops. By having the feedback reach the actual source of traffic, the buffering requirement reduces and the end-to-end ABR connection can converge to the rate of the bottleneck along the path. Further analysis on the coupling mechanisms is provided later in this chapter.

Since the VS replicates the source actions, traffic exiting a VS will conform to the expected behavior regardless of the behavior in the upstream loop. If the upstream loop also conforms to the feedback, the VS will be transparent. If the upstream loop does not respond to the feedback the VS will firewall the misbehavior and act equivalently to a policing function. If the upstream loop behavior deviates largely from the expected behavior (an extreme example is an upstream loop that does not react at all to the feedback information), then the VS will congest and apply appropriate congestion control mechanisms (see Chap. 7). Even in this case, the downstream loop achieves the expected ABR performance. Using a VS to police ABR traffic is more effective and easier to engineer than implementing a strict dynamic policer that automatically discards non-conforming traffic based on assumptions of feedback delay.

Switch Behavior

The switch behavior constitutes the most important part of the ABR control loop. As discussed in Chap. 5, a switch may consist of multiple queuing points. Therefore, the switch has to monitor each of the queuing points and provide appropriate feedback to the source in order to avoid congestion. The monitoring and feedback methods are proprietary and generally are customized to a given queuing structure and scheduling function. The following are key points of ABR switch behavior [TM4.0]:

1. A switch must implement a feedback method, either binary or explicit, as discussed later in this chapter.
2. In order to convey feedback without having received RM cells from a source, a switch may generate BRM cells at a rate no greater than ten cells/second for each connection. These switch generated BRM cells should have either CI = 1 or NI = 1 and the BN bit is set to 1.
3. A switch may transmit RM cells out of sequence with respect to data cells, but sequence integrity among RM cells of a connection should be maintained. Due to this, it is possible for the switches to process RM cells separately and techniques such as RM-cell acceleration are possible. This technique is discussed later in the chapter.
4. A switch can reduce the ACR of a connection to the actual cell transmission of the source. This technique, also referred to as "use-it-or-lose-it," is discussed later in this chapter.

As discussed previously, the ABR control loop can operate in two modes, binary mode and explicit-rate mode, depending on how the switch marks its congestion information in the RM cells. Since the performance of the ABR loop is primarily determined by the feedback mode, the remainder of this chapter focuses on the performance of the ABR control loop when each of these methods is used.

Binary Mode ABR

This section discusses the binary feedback mode and provides some performance comparisons. A switch operating in binary mode uses the EFCI, CI, and NI bits of RM cells to mark its internal congestion. Depending on the mode, only some of these bits may be used. The main advantage of the binary mode ABR is that it can be simple to implement and may not need complex RM cell processing as well as rate monitoring functions. When the node detects impending congestion (e.g., a queue size exceeds a given threshold, or the queue size grows at a rate greater than a given threshold), the node provides binary feedback in one of the following ways (other combinations are also possible):

Simple EFCI: The node sets the EFCI bit in the *data cell.* Simple EFCI setting is available in all switches that are compliant to older standards [UNI3.1]. Switches participate in the flow control without having to handle or process RM cells. The participation of the *destination* in translating this EFCI information into CI and/or NI is necessary to convey the information back to the source.

Backward Marking of the CI Bit: The node sets the CI bit of the RM cell going in the backward direction of the connection. The EFCI bit in the forward direction and the NI bit are untouched.

EFCI and Backward Marking of the CI Bit: The node sets the CI bit of the RM cell going in the backward direction of the connection and the EFCI bit in the forward data cell. The NI bit is ignored. The method results in more aggressive response to impending congestion, since one action will trigger two rate decreases.

EFCI and Backward Marking of the NI Bit: The node sets the NI bit of the RM cell going in the backward direction of the connection and the EFCI bit in the forward-data cell.

The last two methods are conservative and are discussed here for comparison purposes (see App. B).

Performance Considerations of Binary Mode ABR

This section discusses some performance aspects of the binary mode.

Fairness

A *beat-down* phenomenon occurs when some connections go through multiple hops, while others go through fewer hops. The multiple-hops connections are more likely to have their EFCI bit marked and are therefore required to reduce their rate more aggressively. It can be shown that some applications can be beaten down to their MCR indefinitely, while other connections use most of the bandwidth.

This problem can be resolved by implementing per-VC accounting (Chap. 7) to selectively mark the EFCI bit of the connections with cell rates higher than a given threshold (this method is referred to as *intelligent marking*). By using different marking thresholds for each connection, a weighted fairness policy can be achieved using intelligent marking.

Intelligent network design (where every connection is routed through the same number of hops) can resolve beat-down in the majority of cases. Using separate queues to isolate multihop connections from those making few hops can also alleviate the problem.

Stability and Efficiency

Because the feedback is binary (uses only one bit), a number of backward RM cells are required in order for a source to converge to the currently available bandwidth. Recall that receipt of a backward RM cell with CI bit set causes a source to reduce its rate by *ACR* × *RDF*. Since the backward RM cells sent are a function of number of data cells sent, the sources may take a long time to converge to the rate available at the bottleneck. By the time convergence is reached, the available bandwidth might have already changed. This oscillatory behavior is more evident in cases of priority scheduling when there is a significant load of bursty high-priority traffic. Slow convergence results in less efficient utilization of available bandwidth and may cause cell loss. The convergence rate can be improved by indicating the congestion status directly in the backward RM cells (marking the CI bit) and/or by giving priority to the backward RM cells. But these solutions require handling the RM cells in the switch and significantly increase the complexity of the binary ABR implementation. Intelligent marking reduces some of the oscillatory behavior, as it triggers rate changes only on selected sources.

The performance of the binary ABR scheme is also affected by a whole set of other parameters. For example, a large ramp-up value (RIF) means that the source increases its rate at a much faster pace, which implies either greater cell loss or large buffers requirements. On the other hand, slower ramp up leads to potential underutilization, since the bandwidth is not completely used by the sources.

Connections that are idle for some period of time can start transmitting their next burst of data at no greater than ICR (initial cell rate) and can ramp up their transmission rate, based on the positive feedback in the RM cells. If a queue has small buffer size, ICR needs to be low to prevent buffer overflow when a few sources become active simultaneously. If sufficient buffering is available, then ICR can be large and the convergence problem is less of an issue. For large-file transfers, ICR has less impact on the application performance since the ramp-up time is negligible compared to the total file-transfer time. If intelligent marking is used, the ramp-up time is reduced, because the source ramping up will not be subject to rate reduction until it approaches its fair share of the available bandwidth.

When connections are required to throttle down their rates at the same time, a certain time elapses until all connections converge back to their fair share of bandwidth. This phenomenon may translate into temporary underutilization of the link. This issue is resolved with intelligent marking, where it is possible to selectively throttle down only some of the sources.

The method for detecting impending congestion can also impact performance. When small amount of buffers is available, it may not be possible to configure a marking threshold that will protect the queue from overflowing even under small feedback delays. A congestion measure based on queue growth leads to better performance under a very dynamic load environment (see Chap. 7).

Appendix B provides a performance comparison of various Binary ABR implementations. It illustrates that cell loss, low goodput, slow reaction to switch congestion, and rate oscillations leading to slow convergence all result from different binary ABR implementation. Of course, it is always possible to select different parameters to obtain completely different results.

Explicit Rate Mode ABR

In explicit rate (ER) mode, the switch indicates to the source the rate at which it should be sending cells to obtain its fair share of the bandwidth. Upon receipt of the backward RM cell, the source automatically adjusts to the lowest rate allowed in its path. The implementation of the explicit rate mode of ABR (ER-ABR) can *theoretically* address all the problems associated with the binary mode ABR. One fundamental difference between the two modes is that, in the explicit-rate mode, each queuing point in the network processes the RM cells and computes an explicit rate for each connection. This increased performance is achieved with higher complexity and cost.

Schemes can be designed such that the explicit rate is an accurate approximation of the fair share of a connection using the bandwidth available on the link at a given instant, allowing the quickest possible convergence to the available bandwidth. This also implies a significant reduction in the buffering requirements and increased link utilization. Some complex schemes can achieve as much as 97 percent utilization (maximum possible because of RM cell overhead, assuming $Nrm = 32$) with a buffer size less than 1000 cells. But these schemes are much more complex and costly to implement than the binary ABR with intelligent marking scheme. Therefore, cost of buffering versus cost of implementation must be considered.

The benefits of ER-ABR can be measured in terms of the achieved utilization of the available bandwidth and fairness in distributing this bandwidth to the connections. The ER-marking scheme alone does not guarantee connection isolation. The VS/VD and per-VC buffer management are also required. Furthermore, many of the proposed schemes make use of the current cell rate (CCR) field declared by the source. However, this value cannot be trusted in a public network environment, and rate measurement need to be incorporated with the ER calculation.

The performance gains of an ER implementation are fully dependent on how the ER algorithm is designed. Approximations such as rate granularity, frequency of updating the available bandwidth, and fair-share calculations of the connection can lead to a worse performance than the binary ABR with intelligent marking. Also, the utilization of the available bandwidth may be limited by rate granularity and rate mismatch between the ER scheme and the actual ABR source. Such approximations may also lead to cell loss. By inserting the explicit rate into the backward direction of the VC, the delay in the feedback loop can be effectively shortened. However, the stability of the feedback loop may still depend on the feedback delay.

The implementation complexity varies greatly with the switch architecture. The explicit-rate computation needs to be performed at every queuing point in the switch. However, it can be done independently. It is also possible to use different ER algorithms at each of the queueing points. The ER performance is fully achieved when *all* the queuing points in the path implement an ER scheme. The resulting performance of the path can be limited by the scheme that performs the worst along the path or by the performance of the scheme on the most highly utilized queues.

In order to discuss different ER algorithms, a generic queuing point is considered. The ER value is computed based on a set of measurements of the queue behavior. The possible measurement variables and locations at a queuing point are illustrated in Fig. 6.3. This is subsequently referred to as the "basic ER-queuing block." There are two levels at which traffic measurements may be taken: the group level and the VC level. The group referred to here is the group of ABR

Figure 6.3.   Basic ER queuing block.

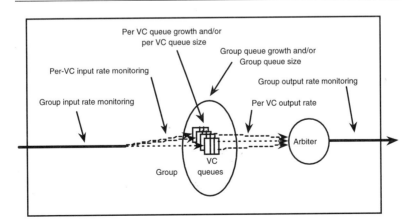

VCs traversing the given queuing point for which an ER needs to be calculated. Depending on the queuing point being considered, measurements at either of the two levels can be used. The various measurements are described in the "System Measurements" section later.

A simple application of the basic ER-queuing block is the modeling of a line card ER module, which is depicted in Fig. 6.4. In this figure it is assumed that the access rate is the rate at which the port is operating, and the switch internal rate is the rate at which a switch can send cells to the line card. Here only the VC-level abstraction is needed.

An example representation of a multiplexer (MUX) within an ATM switch with N inputs routed by the switching fabric on M different paths demonstrates that M such blocks be defined. Figure 6.5 illustrates such a MUX model. Connections from each of the N inputs can traverse any of the M different paths. However, they all use the same outgoing link, which is connected to a switch core in order to reach the output ports. The switch core routes the individual connections on M different paths to the corresponding outputs. Depending on the path congestion and the loading within the switch, the available bandwidth for each of the paths will vary. Therefore, the ER blocks in the MUX can appropriately distribute the available bandwidth among the groups first and then distribute bandwidth fairly among the contending connections within a group. Thus, both levels of abstraction can be used within a given model. Notice that each group input and output rates are variable and they may vary greatly from group to group. The two levels of abstraction provide different fairness measures for the connections. The model shown in Fig. 6.5 is primarily fair with respect to different paths, and secondarily to the connections using a path. However, if only one ER block is used, it achieves only the VC-level fairness, ignoring the group-level fairness.

An ER algorithm is designed using the following elements:

• Real-time system measurements
• Fair share policy
• Bandwidth sharing strategy

Figure 6.4. A line-card model.

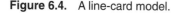

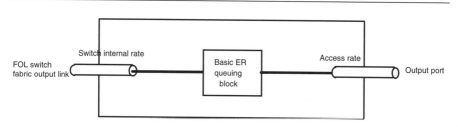

Figure 6.5. A MUX model.

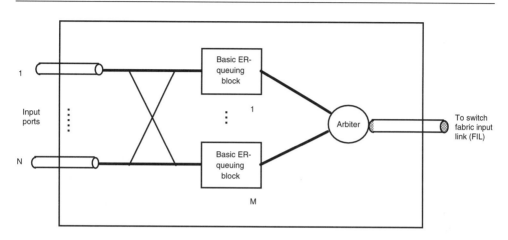

The ER block uses these elements to periodically compute an explicit rate for each connection. The resulting ER value is inserted in the backward RM cell only if it further reduces the ER already marked in the passing backward RM cell. The ER value cannot be set lower than the negotiated MCR. This periodicity at which the ER is computed has an impact on the stability of the ER algorithm. These issues are discussed later in the chapter.

System Measurements

The following measurements or calculations can be implemented on a basic-ER queuing block. Depending on the implementation, it may be more or less complex to perform these measurements. Depending on what is measured on a block, a different ER algorithm can be designed. The measurement variables in the basic ER-queuing block are:

Output Group Rate: The output group rate measures the bandwidth available to a group of ABR VCs. The measurement point is at the egress of the basic ER-queuing block. This can generally be performed by measuring the bandwidth consumed by the high-priority traffic (or guaranteed services such as CBR, VBR, etc.) and subtracting this amount from the link rate. A proportion of BW can also be removed for use by GFR and UBR traffic.

Input Group Rate: The input group rate measures the aggregate input rate of a group of ABR VCs. The measurement point is at the ingress of the basic ER-queuing block.

Group Queue Growth: The group queue growth is the rate at which the size of a queue shared by a group of ABR VCs is changing. Any two of the group queue growth rate, output group rate, and input group rate may be used to calculate the value of the third.

Input VC Rate: The input VC rate measures the input rate of a VC within a group. One can obtain this measurement either through rate monitoring or by extracting the value from the CCR field of the forward RM (FRM) cell. Using the CCR field is simpler, but false advertising may lead to cell loss. The CCR field can be used within a network protected at the edges by VS/VD functions.

Output VC Rate: The output VC rate measures the ouput rate of each VC within a group. The measurement is located at the egress of the basic ER-queuing block.

VC Queue Growth: The VC queue growth rate measures the rate at which a VC queue size is changing. Any two of the VC queue growth, output VC rate, and input VC rate may be used to calculate the value of the third. A per-VC queuing architecture or per-VC accounting is needed for this purpose.

Number of Active VCs: The number of active VCs measures the number of VCs that exhibited a rate of arrival not significantly less than the minimum cell rate (MCR) over the last time period.

Group Queue Size: The group queue size is the aggregate queue size of a group at a given instant.

VC Queue Size: The VC queue size of a given VC at a given instant.

Requested Explicit Rate: The requested explicit rate is set by the source in the ER field of the forward RM cell. It represents the maximum rate at which a cell stream may be transmitted to the switch. This value may be subsequently reduced by any switch.

Fair Share Policy

Using the system measurements described above, one can estimate the available bandwidth (BW_{ABR}) for the ABR traffic at a queuing point. This available bandwidth is distributed among the competing ABR connections. We refer to this term as the *local fair share* of the connection. This local fair share can be calculated using one of many policies [TM4.0], such as:

1. **Max-Min or Equal Share**, where BW_{ABR} is distributed equally among the contending active connections
2. **MCR(Weight) Proportional**, where the allocation is MCR(weight) weighted from BW_{ABR}
3. **MCR + Equal Share,** where the sum of MCRs (ΣMCR_i) is first subtracted from BW_{ABR}, and the remaining bandwidth is distributed as equal share among contending active connections.

4. **MCR + MCR Proportional**, where the sum of MCRs (ΣMCR_i) is first subtracted from BW_{ABR}, and the remaining bandwidth is distributed in MCR-proportional fashion among contending active connections

5. **MCR + Weight Proportional**, where the sum of MCRs (ΣMCR_i) is first subtracted from BW_{ABR}, and the remaining bandwidth is distributed weight-proportionally among contending active connections.

6. **Maximum of MCR or Max-Min**, where a connection's allocation is maximum of *MCR* or max-min shares.

Since ABR connection can also have a guaranteed minimum bandwidth (MCR), the local fair share of a connection can generally be calculated as

$$FS_i = MCR_i + BE_i \tag{6.2}$$

Here FS_i is the local fair share allocation to the connection i, BE_i is the fair-share bandwidth measure, and MCR_i is the minimum cell rate of connection. The fair-share bandwidth measure describes the bandwidth allocated to a VC in the local fair share calculation from the BW_{ABR}. The value of BE_i is not necessarily the same for each VC. In order to define a generic calculation for BE_i that is independent of the local fair share calculation, a local fair share factor LF_i is defined so that

$$BE_i = LF_i \times BW_{ABR} \tag{6.3}$$

The value of BW_{ABR} can be determined, for example, using the following expression:

$$BW_{ABR} = \left(\rho \times LR - BW_{CBR,VBR} - \left(\sum_{i \in ABR,GFR} MCR_i \right) \right) \tag{6.4}$$

Here LR is the link rate, $BW_{CBR,VBR}$ is the bandwidth required by CBR and VBR connections, $\rho \in [0,1]$ represents the target link utilization, and MCR_i is the minimum cell rate of ABR or GFR connection. The $BW_{CBR,VBR}$ can be calculated using traffic descriptors (i.e., effective bandwidth) or by monitoring the output rate of the CBR and VBR connections. The local fair share factor LF_i for each connection depends on the selected fair share policy. Some examples are shown below:

For MCR plus equal share scheme, for each i, LF_i is given by $LF_i = 1/N_{VCs}$, where N_{VCs} is the number of active VCs. As defined earlier, an active VC is the one that, in the previous monitoring interval, transmitted more than its *MCR*.

For MCR proportional, LF_i can be calculated as

$$LF_i = MCR_i \Big/ \sum_{k \in S_{active}} MCR_k$$

where S_{active} is the set of all active VCs.

For MCR plus weight proportional, LF_i is given by

$$LF_i = W_i \Big/ \sum_{k \in S_{\text{active}}} W_k$$

where S_{active} is the set of all active VCs and W_i is the weight of connection.

Bandwidth-Sharing Strategy

When a connection traverses many queuing points, the local fair share of a given connection can be different at each of the queuing points. Due to the nature of ABR flow control, a connection can only use the minimum of these local fair share calculations, referred to as the *global fair share* of the connection. That is, if a connection traverses through N queuing points, then the *global fair share* is defined as $\min(LF_{Q1}, LF_{Q2}, \ldots, LF_{QN})$, where LF_{Qj} is the local fair share allotted to the connection at queuing point j. Ideally, for an efficient network operation, a connection need not be given more than this global fair share at all queuing points the connection is traversing. Therefore, a queuing point generally serves two sets of connections: one set which is bottlenecked elsewhere in the network, and the second set which is bottlenecked at this queuing point. For efficient network operation, since the set of connections bottlenecked elsewhere do not use their total local fair-share bandwidth, the difference can, be allocated to the set of connections bottlenecked locally. Therefore, the two following scenarios for sharing bandwidth are possible.

Method 1: Bandwidth Conservation

With this method, if a connection does not need its local fair share, the remaining bandwidth is not taken away from that connection for redistribution to other connections. This method may not use the network efficiently, but the connection's fair share is available in case it needs it. As a result, the connection can suddenly start transmitting at a higher rate (up to the fair share if the source rate was constrained previously) without requiring other connections to reduce their rate and without causing any congestion, or incurring cell loss.

Method 2: Bandwidth Redistribution

With this method, if a connection is not using its local fair share (as determined by input rate monitoring, CCR field content, or forward ER marking), the remaining bandwidth is taken away from that connection and distributed to others. This approach is also called a "Use-it-or-Lose-it" policy. When fair share is calculated using only the equal share, this leads to "max-min fairness" across the network. However, the connection from which the bandwidth is taken should also be given a chance to retrieve its fair share. This can be done by one of three methods:

Slow Ramp-up: In this method, the connections from which fair share bandwidth is taken away can be given periodic chances to catch up via increasing their current share by a small fraction. The switch monitors the rate of the VC to determine if that VC utilizes additional bandwidth. This method of bandwidth readjustment exhibits the desirable property that the total fair-share bandwidth is equal to the available bandwidth at all times (no overbooking).

Overbooking: With the overbooking method, bandwidth that is not fully used by some of the VCs in a group is distributed in equal share to *all* VCs (including the ones not using their local fair share). As a result, the available bandwidth estimation is overbooked; that is, the sum of the advertised local fair-share bandwidths can be much larger than BW_{ABR}. The premise of this method is that, if a set of connections are not using their fair share of bandwidth, then in the short term, allocating more bandwidth to that set of connections will not affect their utilization level. When the connection starts using the available bandwidth, the congestion point detects an increased utilization level and adjusts the fair shares accordingly.

Consider, for example, a congestion point with a link rate of 100 Mb/s. Assume there are two connections with PCR = 100 Mb/s traversing through this queuing point. Also assume an equal share fairness policy. Then each connection should get a fair share of 100/2 = 50 Mb/s. Assume connection 1 is bottlenecked at 20 Mb/s somewhere else in the network. The remaining 30 Mb/s should be given to connection 2. The overbooking methods (see some of the ER algorithms discussed later) estimate the ABR available bandwidth as 160 Mb/s, thus giving 160/2 = 80 Mb/s to each connection. Therefore, connection 2 can now transmit at 80 Mb/s. Connection 1 still transmits at 20 Mb/s, which is its bottlenecked rate somewhere else in the network. However, if the bottleneck is relieved for this connection, there is a possibility that all of a sudden connection 1 can transmit at 80 Mb/s, causing congestion. The ER algorithm then reacts appropriately, reducing the ER of each connection to 50 Mbls.

Forward ER Marking: When ER marking is performed only in the backward RM cells, the downstream queuing points in a network along the path of a VC do not get any information about the queuing points upstream. Therefore, with the forward ER-marking method, the source and each switch along the transmission path mark the ER field in the forward RM cell. Then all switches in the transmission path have knowledge of the end-to-end bottleneck rate for each VC by reading and marking both the forward and backward RM cells. As a result, the bandwidth allocated to a VC in each switch can converge very quickly to the bottleneck rate for the VC. This scheme works only if all switches participate in forward ER marking, which is not currently required in the standards.

Generic Types of ER Algorithms

Based on the parameters measured on the system, very generic types of ER algorithms can be defined as in Table 6.4. The kind of fairness each of these algorithms achieves depends on the set of available measurements. Many other ER algorithms can be devised as variants of these basic methods. The section following Table 6.4 presents some of the ER algorithms, subsumable under these generic types.

Table 6.4a. Generic ER type 1.

Required Information	• CCR • Group queue size
Description	• The VC input rate (ACR) is extracted from the CCR (current cell rate) field of the forward RM cell. The size of the VC queue is read and compared with one or more predefined thresholds. The congestion level, determined by the highest-value threshold that is exceeded, is used to determine a factor, that multiplies the value read from the CCR field. The result is the ER value written into the backward RM cell.
Fairness	• None

Table 6.4b. Generic ER type 2.

Required Information	• Output group rate • Number of active VCs
Description	• The output group rate provides a measure of the bandwidth available to ABR connections. This available bandwidth is used in conjunction with the number of active VCs to distribute bandwidth among the VCs using any given fair share policy. Bandwidth redistribution is not possible since the arrival rates of VCs are unknown.
Fairness	• Any chosen fair share policy. • Based on bandwidth conservation strategy

(Continued)

Table 6.4c. Generic ER type 3.

Required Information	• Output group rate • VC queue size • Number of active VCs
Description	• The output group rate provides a measure of the bandwidth available to ABR connections. The bandwidth available to ABR is used in conjunction with the number of active VCs to distribute bandwidth among the VCs using any given fair share policy. The VC queue size is used in conjunction with one or more thresholds to bias the fair share bandwidth toward connections with lower queue occupancy. This causes the switch to be aggressive during periods of light loading and conservative during periods of congestion. Bandwidth redistribution is not possible because the actual rate of arrival for each VC is unknown.
Fairness	• Any chosen fair share policy. • Based on bandwidth conservation strategy

Table 6.4d. Generic ER type 4.

Required Information	• Input group rate • Output group rate • Number of active VCs
Description	• The input group rate provides a measure of the aggregate utilization by all ABR VCs in the group. The output group rate provides a measure of the bandwidth available to all ABR VCs in that group. The difference between these two measurements is underutilized/overallocated bandwidth. By distributing a factor of the underutilized bandwidth among all active VCs, a convergence towards global fairness can be achieved. The consequence however, is that the sum of the ACR of all ABR connections exceeds the available bandwidth (i.e., the switch is overbooked). When an underutilized VC is suddenly able to send at the given ACR, the switch will enter a period of congestion, during which the arrival rate is greater than the available service rate. The switch then re-calculates the fair share using the output group rate and the number of active VCs.
Fairness	• Any chosen fair share policy. • Based on bandwidth redistribution with overbooking

(Continued)

Table 6.4e.   Generic ER type 5.

Required Information	• Forward ER marking • Output group rate • Number of active VCs
Description	• The output group rate provides a measure of the bandwidth available to ABR connections. Each switch along the transmission path reads the ER field in the forward RM cell. The ER field contains the bottleneck bandwidth between the source and the switch. The switch then calculates the bandwidth that it can allocate to the VC. If the calculated bandwidth is less than the value presently in the ER field, the switch writes the new ER into the forward RM cell. The backward RM cell contains the end-to-end bottleneck rate. The switch then performs bandwidth redistribution and arrives at new ACR values for each VC.
Fairness	• Any chosen fair share policy. • Based on bandwidth redistribution with ramp-up

Table 6.4f.   Generic ER type 6.

Required Information	• Input VC rate • Output group rate • Number of active VCs
Description	• The output group rate is used to evaluate the fair share per group. This is divided among the active connections on that group as per chosen policy, as a fair-share for the connections. The per-VC bandwidth usage is known from the input per-VC input rate measurement. Thus, if a connection is using less than its fair share, then the current measured rate becomes its fair-share and the remaining bandwidth is distributed among the other connections. Since this method employs a "use-it-or-lose-it" behavior, the VCs that have lost their fair share should be given a chance to retrieve it. This can be achieved by the "slow ramp-up" method.
Fairness	• Any chosen fair share policy. • Based on bandwidth redistribution with ramp-up

(Continued)

Table 6.4g.   Generic ER type 7.

Required Information	• Group queue size
Description	• This algorithm tries to maintain a target group queue size by recursively multiplying the offered bandwidth with a multiplication factor (>1.0). The initial value of this offered bandwidth can be a link rate. If the queue grows beyond a threshold, the offered bandwidth is recursively decreased by another multiplication factor (< 1.0). This offered bandwidth is used to evaluate the fair-share per group. This is divided among the active connections on that group as per chosen policy, as a fair share for the connections. If a VC does not utilize itís fair share bandwidth, the global queue would not reach the target value and the offered bandwidth is increased, which is taken up by the VCs that need the most, thus achieving global fairness.
Fairness	• Any chosen fair share policy. • Based on bandwidth redistribution with overbooking

ER Algorithms

Based on the generic methodology listed in Table 6.4, a few explicit-rate (ER) algorithms are discussed below. Performance comparison is provided in Appendix B. The ER algorithms are:

Congestion Bias (CB), which belongs to generic algorithm 7 [DGL97].

Bandwidth Tracking (BT), which belongs to generic algorithm 4. Two different variations, BT-1 and BT-2, are discussed.

Detailed Rate Accounting (DRA), which belongs to generic algorithm 6 [KVR96].

The ER algorithms discussed use the following variables and terminology:

OBW available bandwidth "estimator" for the purpose of ER calculations. Note that this is an estimator and not a measured value. Mostly used by the overbooking methods.

ECR_i explicit cell rate calculated for connection i, which captures the cell rate that the network element can support.

BER_i contents of the explicit-rate field in the backward RM cell.

OCR_i offered cell rate for connection i, which captures the local bottleneck cell rate (or local fair share) for the VC.

RCR_i required-cells rate for connection i, which estimates the current maximum cell rate that can be supported end to end.

PCR_i peak cell rate of connection i.

QL_j queue threshold for an ABR connection.

QD group queue size of ABR connections.

AR aggregate input rate for all ABR connections, less the sum of MCR for all connections presently active.

LR output link rate on which connections are contending.

BW_{ABR} bandwidth available for distribution among ABR VCs beyond their MCR.

LF_i local fair share factor for connection i, using any given fair-share policy as discussed previously in this chapter.

An explicit-rate algorithm calculates an offered cell rate (OCR_i) for each ABR connection. When the backward RM cell passes through the switch, the ER field in the backward RM cell is marked according to the following equation:

$$BER_{out} = \min (BER_{in}, OCR_i) \tag{6.5}$$

Here, BER_{in} is the ER field marked in the incoming BRM cell and BER_{out} is the ER field when it leaves the switch

Congestion Bias (CB) Algorithm [DGL97]

This algorithm estimates the output bandwidth available (OBW) to ABR connections by *recursively* multiplying the OBW with a bias factor β. The bias factor is dependent on the depth of the aggregate ABR queue (QD). This algorithm is only triggered at the end of the control interval.

At the end of the interval, the variable $OBW(k)$ represents the total offered bandwidth in excess of the MCR-guaranteed bandwidth at iteration k, and is given by

$$OBW(k) = \beta \times OBW(k - 1) \tag{6.6}$$

Here β, for example, is given by

$$\beta = \begin{cases} 1 - \alpha & \text{if } QD > QL_2 \\ 1.0 & \text{if } QL_1 \leq QD \leq QL_2 \\ 1 + \alpha & \text{if } QD < QL_1 \end{cases} \tag{6.7}$$

Any initial value for OBW is suitable, though the time to converge to the steady-state value may depend on it. The factor β is only dependent on group queue size and thresholds. QL_1 and QL_2 are two thresholds ($QL_1 < QL_2 <$ maximum buffer size) and QD is the current group queue size. The OCR_i for connection i is given by

$$OCR_i = \min [PCR_i, (MCR_i + (LF_i \times OBW(k)))] \tag{6.8}$$

Note that there is a "dead-band" region ($\beta = 1$) where the bandwidth is neither increased nor decreased; α is a small constant, such as 0.01 or 0.05. The bias factor β permits an aggressive rate allocation when the switch is experiencing low utilization and a conservative allocation during congestion.

Bandwidth Tracking (BT)-1

The BT-1 algorithm tracks the output bandwidth available to ABR connections with the measured aggregate input rate for all ABR connections, without the need for maintaining the active VC state. The algorithm is only triggered at the end of a control interval.

At the end of the control interval, the aggregate input rate (AR) is subtracted from the current aggregate bandwidth available to ABR connections BW_{ABR}, to give the proportional error. The variable $OBW(k)$ represents the total offered bandwidth in excess of the MCR-guaranteed bandwidth at iteration k and is given by the following algorithm:

$$OBW(k) = OBW(k - 1) + (BW_{ABR} - AR) \tag{6.9}$$

When the input rate reaches a value equal to the bandwidth available to ABR, the value of $OBW(k)$ stabilizes. Since the algorithm does not monitor individual VC rates, it cannot identify the connections that are not utilizing their allocated bandwidth. Thus, all connections are scaled in proportion to their weights with respect to the same offered bandwidth. The OCR_i for connection i, is given by

$$OCR_i = \min[PCR_i, (MCR_i + (LF_i \times OBW(k))]$$

Bandwidth Tracking (BT)-2

This is a modification to BT-1. The difference between the algorithms is the way OBW is computed. The estimator $OBW(k)$ represents the total offered bandwidth in excess of total guaranteed MCR bandwidth. At the end of the control interval, set the total offered bandwidth as

$$OBW(k) = \left(\frac{BW_{ABR}}{AR}\right) \times OBW(k - 1) \tag{6.10}$$

The OCR_i for connection i is given by:

$$OCR_i = \min[PCR_i, (MCR_i + (LF_i \times OBW(k))]$$

Detailed Rate Accounting (DRA) [KVR96]

The DRA algorithm explicitly calculates the bandwidth allocated to each VC by considering the local bandwidth available to ABR and the end-to-end bottleneck link rate for each connection. The explicit cell rate calculation is performed in accordance with the method described in [KVR96]. The variable $BF(k)$ represents the free bandwidth not used by connections that are locally constricted. This free bandwidth is redistributed among connections that are bottlenecked at other points in the end-to-end path. The algorithm maintains connections into two sets: S_b, the bottlenecked set and S_s, the satisfied set. A bottlenecked connection is one whose rate is constrained by the switch. A satisfied connection is one whose rate is not constrained by the switch under consideration.

The algoithm responds to the following events: When there is a change in bandwidth available to ABR, the free bandwidth is updated according to the following expression, where FS_i is calculated according to Eq. (6.2).

$$BF(k) = \sum_{i \in S_s} (FS_i - ECR_i)$$

When there is a change in the active VC state, the value of LF_i is calculated as per the fair share policy. Execute above calculation when a change in the bandwidth available to ABR occurs.

When a forward RM cell is received, the connection under consideration is placed into the set of bottlenecked connections, and the appropriate bandwidth is subtracted from the free bandwidth measure (recall that the free bandwidth measure is the total bandwidth underutilized by satisfied connections). If the connection is presently in the satisfied set,

$$\text{if } (VC_i \in S_s) \qquad \{BF(k) = BF(k - 1) - FS_i + ECR_i\}$$

Determine the bandwidth that may be offered to the connection,

$$OCR_i = \min(PCR_i, FS_i + BF(k) \times LF_i)$$

The offered cell rate OCR_i may be calculated to be less than FS_i, but it is mandated to ensure that at least fair share is offered to the connection. Thus, $OCR_i = \max(OCR_i, FS_i)$.

Add the connection to either the bottlenecked set or the satisfied set, update the explicit cell rate ECR_i, and adjust the free bandwidth measure. If the offered cell rate OCR_i exceeds the required cell rate RCR_i, then the connection is satisfied:

$$\text{if}(OCR_i \geq RCR_i) \qquad \{ECR_i = RCR_i; \quad BF = BF(k - 1) + FS_i - ECR_i; \quad VC_i \in S_s\}$$

If the offered cell rate is less than the required cell rate, then the connection is bottlenecked:

$$\text{if } (OCR_i < RCR_i) \qquad \{ECR_i = OCR_i; VC_i \in S_b\}$$

The required cell rate RCR_i can be obtained from input VC rate measurements, ER marking of the backward RM cell or CCR field. That is, $RCR_i = \min (BER_{in}, CCR_i)$, for example.

Other ER Algorithms

Since it is impossible to discuss all possible ER algorithms in great detail, a short review of some published ER algorithms is presented here. An initial survey of recent trends in rate-based flow control schemes can be found in [Jai95]. A rate-based flow control framework is presented in [BF95].

One of the initial works on an ER algorithm is [CCJ95]. The algorithm achieves max-min fairness by maintaining two sets, the restricted set and the unrestricted set, similar to DRA. The algorithm uses these sets, along with the number of connections in each set, to compute an advertised rate. A connection belongs to the unrestricted set if the cell arrival rate of that connection is higher than the advertised rate; otherwise it belongs to the restricted set. The algorithm achieves max-min fair share since the advertised rate is computed as equal-share bandwidth among members of the unrestricted set.

A general-rate-allocation-policy-based ER algorithm is described in [HTP97]. Considering the MCR/PCR constraints of each ABR connection, a *MCRadd* policy is described. The algorithm keeps track of CCR for each VC to monitor the current rate of transmission. The algorithm maintains a set of restricted VCs and an unrestricted set of VCs through a consistent marking technique similar to DRA.

The explicit-rate indication for congestion avoidance (ERICA) [TM4.0] achieves max-min fair share among contending connections. This algorithm uses rate measurements to determine a load factor on each link. Using the CCR and the load factor, the VC's share is computed as a CCR/load factor. The algorithm also evaluates a fair share of the connection as the ratio of ABR capacity to the number of active connections. Then, the connection's ER is evaluated as the maximum of the VC's share and the fair share. The algorithm is further modified as ERICA+ by incorporating queuing delays as well as queue congestion information.

An ABR feedback control tracking algorithm called Uniform Tracking (UT) is proposed in [FLL97]. This algorithm tracks the effective number of sources through an effective fair share estimate and the aggregate ABR arrival rate. This effective number is in turn used to estimate the equal fair share for connections. The UT algorithm is extended by Su et al. [SVW97] by considering the queue congestion information. The original UT algorithm is based on rates and does not take into account the queue lengths. Since it tries to match the rates, if a queue gets congested, it may take a very long time before it can deplete its queue. Therefore, [SVW97] considers a drift function based on the difference between the current queue depth and a target queue depth.

One of the major concerns with the ABR flow control is its response to the dynamic changes in available bandwidth. That is, when the bandwidth available to ABR reduces (say, due to burst arrivals on high-priority traffic or similar dynamic changes in bandwidth) it takes a certain amount of time before the correct fair share is computed and the information reaches the source. During this period, the aggregate ABR arrival rate may be higher than the available capacity, which causes congestion to build and queue length to grow. Therefore, the queue length information should be built into the ER computation. Another scheme that manages the queue buildup at a switch is proposed in [MR97].

A Smith-predictor-based algorithm is proposed by Mascolo et al. [MCG96]. The source rates are adjusted according to the VC queue levels at intermediate nodes along the path of a VC. A simple proportional control and a Smith predictor are used in the queuing model. The resulting mechanism is capable of filling in quickly the unused bandwidth and thus achieves high utilization. The simple proportional controller is used to maintain a target queue depth.

A rate-control algorithm based on EFCI setting is proposed by Yin and Hluchyj [YH94]. When congestion occurs at a queuing point, the EFCI bit is set for calls passing through that point. Destination returns this congestion information to the source end-system. The source reacts to this congestion information by either additive increase of its rate or multiplicative decrease.

The effect of multiloop delays and the presence of high-priority traffic are considered by Zhao and Li [ZL96] in proposing an ABR feedback control scheme. A generic prediction control method is applied to the control model for control stability and reduction of control loop oscillations. The ABR traffic is adapted to the low-frequency variations of the high-priority traffic. The resulting scheme achieves high link utilization with small buffer requirements.

Some ABR Issues

As described earlier, the feedback delay involved in conveying the network congestion information back to the source plays a very important role. For small-delay networks, accelerating the backward RM cell can reduce the feedback delay. For large networks, the use of VS/VD to segment the network into multiple loops is essential. These issues are addressed in the following sections.

Accelerating the BRM Information

The key for stable operation of the control loop is that the feedback information from the network should reach the source as soon as possible. In other words, the feedback delay should be small for faster convergence to the fair share. There are two ways to "accelerate" the information.

The first method is applicable when ABR is served as low-priority traffic at a queuing point. In this case, RM cells get behind the data cells. During arrivals of high-priority traffic bursts, the low-priority ABR queue may not be served, thus delaying the ABR feedback. A switch need not maintain cell sequence integrity between data cells and RM cells; however, the sequence should be maintained within individual streams. Therefore, RM cells can be served in a different queue of higher priority, thus accelerating the RM cell flow. However, this method requires assigning bandwidth to RM cell flow and also causes RM cell clumping. High-priority traffic generally has well-defined traffic parameters and is admitted using connection admission control procedures. Therefore, if carred with high-priority traffic, the RM cell flow has to be properly characterized and assigned a virtual bandwidth. This can be a difficult task and can lead to inefficient utilization of link bandwidth.

With the second technique, the *ER* field of the next text departing backward RM cell is marked with $BER_{out} = \min(BER_{in}, OCR_i)$ where BER_{in} is the value of the ER field in the most recently received RM cell as shown in Fig. 6.6. This functionally is similar to giving RM cells highest priority through the switch. However, this has added advantages that the RM cell stream is not disturbed with respect to the data cells and a separate CAC procedure is not needed for RM cells. This implementation avoids the problem of RM cell clumping.

The ER information acceleration reduces the feedback delay to the ABR source considerably, because the queuing delay through the buffer has been eliminated. This is a huge saving, considering that the queuing delay of switches with big buffers may dominate the feedback delay to the ABR source. When the feedback delay is minimized, the control loop has better response in terms of accessing available bandwidth and reacting to congestion.

Figure 6.6. ER information acceleration example.

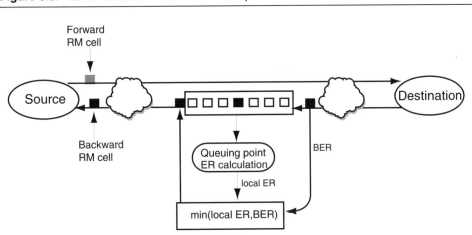

VS/VD Coupling

VS/VD behavior divides an ABR connection into two or more separately controlled ABR segments (see Fig. 6.2). The ATM Forum does not specify a coupling mechanism between adjacent segments (i.e., the sharing of information between the VD of the upstream loop and the VS of the downstream loop), so, it is, therefore implementation specific. The coupling is discussed earlier in this chapter; some performance considerations of the different options are discussed here.

Figure 6.7 provides a functional description of the VS/VD architecture. It is assumed that the ER algorithms run as background processes to compute the offered bandwidth. At the arrival of an FRM cell, appropriate *OCR* (Offered Cell Rate) of the connection is computed. *OCR* indicates the local congestion information ($ER_{VS/VD}$) at the VS point. The VD point turns around these RM cells and marks the ER field as a function of (*OCR, BER, and FER*), where *BER* is the backward explicit rate coupled from the backward RM cell and *FER* is the forward ER marked in the FRM cell. At the arrival of a BRM cell, the BER coupler extracts the *BER*, drops the BRM cell, and determines the rate (allowed cell rate) at which the connection is to be shaped. The allowed cell rate (*ACR*) can be determined as follows. First, the connection's explicit cell rate (*ECR*) is determined as *ECR = min (OCR,BER)*. Then the shaping rate (*ACR*) is either increased or decreased from it's current shaping rate to this *ECR*, using the source behavior rules.

A tight coupling scheme between the loops achieves network-wide fairness faster as the bottleneck information is coupled immediately. However, with tight coupling, any transient perturbation in one loop propagates to another, causing oscillatory behavior. As described in the

Figure 6.7. VS/VD architecture (unidirectional flow).

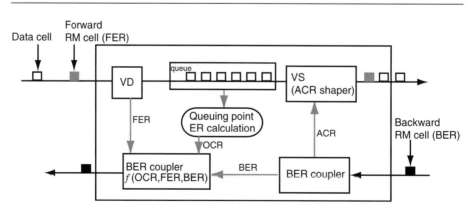

VS/VD section earlier in the chapter, a no-coupling method only uses the local congestion ($ER_{VS/VD}$) at the VS point. Therefore, the ER algorithms that use queue congestion information in deriving the $ER_{VS/VD}$ would achive network-level fairness. A VS shapes a connection to its bottleneck rate. If there is a large rate mismatch between the loops, the queue builds up and the ER algorithm reduces the allowed cell rate for the connection. If the ER scheme does not incorporate such a queue congestion measure, there is no way (other than using explicit coupling of BER information between loops) to match the rates between the loops and the no-coupling method may not achive network-wide fairness. Therefore, a compromise between the two methods is to employ loose coupling with an appropriate coupling function.

[KJJ98] presents the design considerations for VS/VD in ABR networks using the ERICA algorithm.

Point to Multipoint ABR

The support of point-to-multipoint ABR connections is not a requirement for standard ABR compliance. However, the support of this type of traffic may be of interest. For point-to-multipoint connection setup, a separate connection setup from a source to the multiple destinations is not necessary. By setting up multiple connections, bandwidth assignment and resource reservation are needed for each such branch, thereby using a lot of network resources. Instead, branch points can be used within the network (see Fig. 6.8) that copy (multicast) the cells of a given connection onto multiple branches.

Figure 6.8. ABR point-to-multipoint operation.

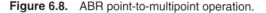
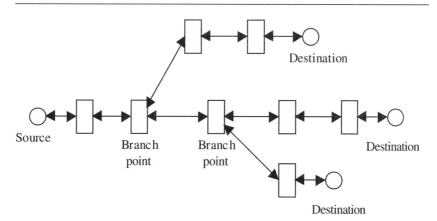

A source is located at the root of the point-to-multipoint tree and destinations are at each of the leaves. A branch point is located at an intersection of two or more branches and performs the "copy" function. Located on each branch of the tree may be one or more VS/VDs, as well as one or more branch points.

Implementing ER schemes for point-to-multipoint traffic can be complex. The first issue is related to the ER consolidation algorithms that should be executed at each of the branch points. Note that the ER loops are split one-into-many at a branch point. Thus, when BRM cells arrive on the down-stream loops, the ER information should be consolidated and fed into the upstream loop. That is, if there are *N* branches, then the consolidation algorithm should absorb the *N* BRM cells that arrive on *N* branches and pass the information in one BRM cell in the upstream loop. The second issue is related to the ER information itself. That is, the source should be throttled back to the "slowest" of the leaves. Thus, the global fair-share bandwidth of a connection should not be more than the smallest of all the allowed fair shares in the multipoint branches. These two issues should be considered for proper implementation of point-to-multi-point ABR. Since a branch point consists of multiple downstream branches, which may go through different paths and congestion points in a switch, it also needs to perform separate ER calculations for each of the downstream loops. Branch point behavior may be implemented together with the VS/VD function.

Engineering the ABR Parameters

The ABR control loop has many parameters (e.g., *ICR, RIF, RDF, Nrm, CRM, Trm,* etc.). For stable operation of this control loop, these parameters should be set properly to achieve high network utilization. This section looks at some of these variables and their settings.

Open-Loop State

An ABR connection will be in a closed-loop state when the source is receiving feedback from the network (i.e., receiving BRM cells), else it can be considered to be in an open-loop state. The ABR flow control mechanism enters into an open-loop state at connection startup, as well as after long periods of inactivity. The open loop state lasts for a maximum of one RTT (round trip time). It begins when the source sends the first cell and lasts until the first RM cell is received by the source. That is, the ABR loop is considered to be in an open-loop state until the ABR source receives the first BRM cell. During this time, the connection sends data at ICR. The ICR is dependent on ABR source parameters *FRTT* and *TBE*. The *TBE* defines the maximum number of cells that can be sent into the network before the source receives feedback; *TBE* is also seen as the maximum number of cells (worst case) that a switch element must be capable of buffering before the ABR control loop for the connection is established. If the connection traverses multiple hops, the queuing element with the smallest buffering resources in the path should be used to determine the *TBE* value. At connection setup, the ICR value is set to

$$ICR = \min(ICR_{user}, TBE/FRTT) \qquad (6.11)$$

Here, ICR_{user} is the ICR set at the source by the user. The *FRTT* is the fixed-round-trip-time portion of the RTT. It is important to select a proper value of *TBE* in order to minimize cell loss during the open-loop state.

The ABR source behavior contains (see Table 6-3, Event 5) a rule that handles situations when ABR connections experience long periods of inactivity. As when a connection is first set up, the ABR loop also enters an open-loop state after long periods of inactivity. Network resources must be protected when a connection begins to send traffic again because, in the worst case, the last recorded value of ACR could be PCR, possibly leading to congestion when the connection resumes sending traffic. To prevent this, if a connection becomes active after an idle period of the *ADTF* (ACR decrease time factor), the ACR value is reset to ICR. The value of *ADTF* should be related to the expected traffic characteristics and network type (LAN or WAN).

RIF and *RDF*

With a binary mode ABR loop, the queue length at the bottleneck switch tends to oscillate around the EFCI threshold (see Fig. 6.9). As the *FRTT* increases, the magnitude of the oscillations also increase unless strict control of the ABR loop is maintained. The magnitude of the overshoot above the EFCI threshold must be controlled to minimize cell loss and the *RDF* and *RIF* values must be set taking into account the FRTT of the connection. One solution is to segment an ABR connection into several independent loops (VS/VD) in which the FRTT delay for each ABR segment is not a significant contributor to the magnitude of oscillations. For example, with a short FRTT (e.g., LAN) there is more flexibility in setting values for *RDF* and

Figure 6.9. Queue occupancy oscillations.

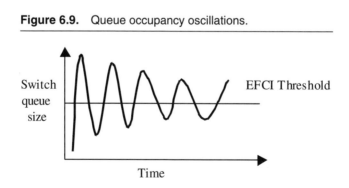

RIF to control the oscillation overshoot and minimize cell loss. Another solution is to include the end-to-end delay into the function and have less flexibility for the selection of the *RDF* and *RIF* values.

The *RIF* and *RDF* parameters largely control the binary ABR loop. When the network is not congested, ACR increases linearly (see Event 2 in Table 6.3); when impending congestion is detected, ACR decreases exponentially (see Event 3 in Table 6.3). Setting *RIF* aggressively allows the source to increase ACR toward PCR quickly. However in some cases cell loss may occur because the source is too aggressive. But if *RIF* is small, the ABR loop may not be able to access available bandwidth quickly enough to utilize the bottleneck link fully. The same can be said for *RDF*, where a large value of *RDF* may contribute to a conservative source, while a small *RDF* may contribute to cell loss because the source is unable to reduce its ACR quickly enough in response to rate decrease feedback. It is clear that there is a certain trade-off to be made in order to maximize the performance. If all network elements support ER, then RIF and RDF can be set to default values of one and 1/32768 respectively.

Choosing *CRM*

An important ABR parameter is *CRM*. One of the source behavior rules (Event 6 of Table 6.3) is intended to protect the network against broken links and extreme congestion. The *CRM* is the number of outstanding FRM cells sent from the source without receiving a BRM cell. When this source behavior rule is triggered, ACR of the ABR connection decreases exponentially by a factor of CDF as depicted in Table 6.3. The *CRM* is defined at the source as

$$CRM = \left(\frac{TBE}{Nrm}\right) \tag{6.12}$$

Because *CRM* is dependent on *TBE*, the correct behavior of this ABR mechanism depends on the accurate knowledge of available resources in the network. Generally speaking, *CRM* has a value that is related to ICR because ICR is also related to *TBE* (see Eq. 6.11). Certain conditions, for example, a small *TBE* in a WAN configuration, increase the chances of triggering this source behavior rule, which is based on CRM. The effect of inadvertently triggering this rule on an ABR connection cannot be underestimated. If it is triggered when the connection is in the closed-loop state, the ABR source behavior may be very inefficient.

This section illustrates how the source behavior rule based on *CRM* (Event 6 in Table 6.3) can be improperly triggered and how it can be avoided. Let us consider a worst-case example (see Fig. 6.10).

Assume that the source is sending cells at MCR at time t_1. The source then receives feedback that allows it to increase its rate to PCR at time t_2. The source then receives congestion

Figure 6.10. ACR oscillation diagram.

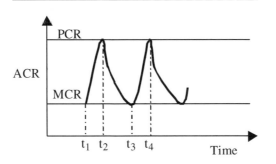

feedback and ACR is reduced to MCR again at time t_3. Again, ACR is allowed to increase to PCR at time t_4. At time t_4 the source is sending cells at PCR, and let's assume that the RM cells sent at time t_1 are now beginning to arrive at the source. Therefore, the RM cells are being received with interarrival times of

$$Max \text{ period of arriving RM cells} = \left(\frac{\text{MCR}}{Nrm}\right)^{-1}$$

and when RM cells are sent at PCR, the interarrival time is

$$Min \text{ period of RM cells sent} = \left(\frac{\text{PCR}}{Nrm}\right)^{-1}$$

For the source behavior, which is based on *CRM* (Event 6 of Table 6.3), not to be triggered, the following inequality must be satisfied:

$$CRM = \left(\frac{\left(\frac{\text{MCR}}{Nrm}\right)^{-1}}{\left(\frac{\text{PCR}}{Nrm}\right)^{-1}}\right) \geq \frac{TBE}{Nrm} \tag{6.13}$$

For example, let $Nrm = 32$ cells, PCR = 353 000 cells/sec (OC3), MCR = PCR/20 = 17642 cells/sec. Then the formula simplifies to

$$20 \geq \left(\frac{TBE}{32}\right) \tag{6.14}$$

Therefore, the minimum value of *CRM* in this example is 20 to avoid triggering this source behavior rule. The minimum value of *TBE* would then be 640 cells. Inadvertently triggering this source behavior rule will cause the ACR value to be decreased without an explicit indication from the network. This may cause underutilization of the ABR connection. It is therefore important that the *CRM* and *TBE* values be correctly set to avoid the above implications, especially in WANs.

Effect of Large Delays

Large delays in the network may also cause Event 6 (Table 6-3) of the source behavior rule to be triggered improperly unless the CRM value is appropriately set. A large CRM value is required to avoid the ACR decrease associated with this rule. Because CRM is dependent on TBE, a large TBE value is required as well.

The EFCI threshold is also affected by large delays. With short RTTs (e.g., LAN), a more aggressive EFCI threshold is acceptable to provide high utilization. An aggressive EFCI threshold must also assume that the RDF and RIF values will be able to control the queue size at the switch to minimize cell loss. In WANs, the EFCI threshold must be set to a more conservative value (such as 25 percent of the available buffer size) to minimize cell loss as well as provide adequate performance.

When RTT increases, such as in WANs, the ability of the source to control an ABR connection is reduced because the feedback received at the source is out of date. It is difficult to maximize performance for an ABR connection when the feedback is outdated. One solution to this problem is the use of Virtual Source/Virtual Destination (VS/VD).

Nrm and *Trm*

The *Nrm* determines the number of data cells separating the FRM cells. As *Nrm* decreases, more FRM cells are injected into the data stream and more feedback is received by the source. However, the trade-off for higher feedback is a decrease in network efficiency, because the FRM cells consume bandwidth from data cells. As *Nrm* increases, fewer FRM cells are injected into the cell stream. As a result, fewer updates of network conditions are received back at the source, but the network efficiency may increase because of the reduction in overhead. This may not be acceptable in a network where the amount of available bandwidth for ABR connections changes significantly and frequently. In this case, frequent feedback would be required to maintain control of the ABR loop and maintain adequate performance. The *Trm* is the maximum amount of time between FRM cells on active connections; *Trm* is a precautionary measure that prevents deadlock and maintains minimum FRM cell flow for active ABR connections.

Minimizing the Cell Loss

An important parameter to minimize the cell loss is the maximum queue length for an ABR connection. A formula that estimates the queue length for ABR connections is proposed in [OMS98] and was verified using simulations. The equation is given by

$$Q_{\max} = Q_H + \frac{N_{VC}}{RDF} \sqrt{\frac{2Nrm \times Q_H \times RIF \times \text{PCR}}{BW}}$$

$$- \frac{Nrm \times N_{VC}}{RDF} \log \left(1 + \sqrt{\frac{2Q_H \times RIF \times \text{PCR}}{BW \times Nrm}} + \frac{FRTT \times RIF \times \text{PCR}}{Nrm} \right)$$

$$+ FRTT \left(\sqrt{\frac{2BW \times Q_H \times RIF \times \text{PCR}}{Nrm}} + \frac{N_{VC} \times RIF \times \text{PCR}}{RDF} \right)$$

$$+ \frac{FRTT^2 \times BW \times RIF \times \text{PCR}}{Nrm}$$

$$(6.15)$$

where:

Q_H is the EFCI threshold at a queue;

BW is the bandwidth available at the bottleneck;

N_{VC} is the number of active ABR connections;

$FRTT$ is the fixed round trip time.

ER-Only Networks

Besides some of the ABR-engineering parameters discussed above, the performance of the ER algorithms depends on the control interval and the techniques used in rate/congestion monitoring schemes.

The ER algorithms perform the computation of available bandwidth (and hence the offered bandwidth) based on a periodic control interval. This control interval is generated by the system every few milliseconds. If the control interval is too short, the system will be very dynamic (reacts to even small changes) and can show oscillatory behavior. On the other hand, if the control interval is too long, the system may not use the resources efficiently, since it may take a very long time to reach convergence towards fair share. Therefore, the performance of the control loop depends on appropriate engineering of the control interval.

The ER algorithms in general are based on measurements of system parameters. Using instantaneous variables of these parameters can cause a system to be too dynamic and the control loop may not be able to reach stability. Therefore, usage of filters to smooth the measurements is also essential to achieve good performance. For example, when computing the available bandwidth, the low-frequency variations of high-priority traffic need to be considered [LCH95]. Thus, the filter performance can also affect the overall network utilization and the control loop behavior.

Review

This chapter presents the ABR flow control mechanism. The key elements of this flow control are the set of "behavior" rules that the sources, switching elements, and destinations follow. One key behavior of the switching elements is that they need to indicate a fair-share of the available bandwidth to each connection via cells called "resource management" cells, which are sent back to the source. Upon receipt of these cells (BRM cells), the source adjusts the transmission rate as per network feedback. Two modes of providing feedback information are defined: binary mode and explicit-rate mode. With the binary mode the feedback information consists of a few bits and the source adjusts its rate based on these bits and other parameters. With the explicit rate mode, the network provides the source with a specific rate at which to send.

The explicit-rate mode involves monitoring the system parameters, such as available rates, cell arrival rates for each connection, and/or queue depth information. This chapter presented a general methodology that can be used for calculating fair ER values. Many ER algorithms can be devised based on this methodology and further extensions are possible. Four explicit-rate (ER) algorithms are considered in detail: congestion bias (CB), bandwidth tracking (BT-1, BT-2), and detailed rate accounting (DRA). The performance of some of these algorithms is presented in Appendix B.

The use of VS/VD can be essential for achieving good performance in large delay networks. This chapter also discussed some issues related to the segmentation of control loops.

Proper engineering of various ABR control loop parameters is essential for efficient network operation to maximize the network utilization and to reduce the incurred cell loss.

References

[BF95] Bonomi, F., and Fendick, K. "The Rate-Based Flow Control Framework for the Available Bit Rate ATM Service," *IEEE Network* (March/April 1995), 25–39.

[BG87] Bertsekas, D., and Gallager, R. *Data Networks*, 2nd ed. Englewood Cliffs, NJ: Prentice Hall, 1987.

[CCJ95] Charny, A., Clark, D.D., and Jain, R. "Congestion Control with Explicit Rate Indication," *Proceedings of IEEE ICC '95*, Seattle (June 1995), 1954–1963.

[DGL97] Davis, T., Ganti, S., and Lee, D. "Recursive Congestion-Based Dynamic Fair-Share Bandwidth Allocation Algorithm," Patent Pending, 1997.

[FLL97] Fulton, C., Li, S.Q., and Lim, C.S. "An ABR Feedback Control Scheme with Tracking," *Proceedings of IEEE Infocom '97*, Kobe, Japan (April 1997), 805–814.

[HTP97] Hou, Y.T., Tzeng, H.Y., and Panwar, S.S. "A Rate Allocation Policy with MCR/PCR Support and Distributed ABR Implementation Using Explicit Rate Feedback," *Proceedings of IEEE International conference on Multimedia Computing and Systems '97*, Ottawa, Canada (June 1997), 20–27.

[Jai95] Jain, R. "Congestion Control and Traffic Management in ATM Networks: Recent Advances and a Survey," *Computer Network and ISDN Systems*, vol. 28, no. 13 (1996), 1723–1738.

[KJJ98] Kalyanaraman, S., Jain, R., Jiang, J., Goyal, R., and Fahmy, S. "Design Considerations for the Virtual Source/Virtual Destination (VS/VD) Feature in the ABR Service of ATM Networks," to appear in *Computer Networks* and *ISDN Journal* (1998).

[KVR96] Kalampoukas, L., Verma, A., and Ramakrishnan, K.K. "Dynamics of an Explicit Rate Allocation Algorithm for Available Bit-Rate (ABR) Services in ATM Networks," technical report UCSC-CRl-95-54, University of California, Santa Cruz (February 1996).

[LCH95] Li, S., Chong, S., and Hwang, C. "Link Capacity Allocation and Network Control by Filtered Input rate in High-Speed Networks," *IEEE/ACM Transactions on Networking*, vol. 3, no.1 (February 1995), 10–25.

[MCG96] Mascolo, S., Cavendish, D., and Gerla, M. "ATM Rate-Based Congestion Control Using a Smith Predictor: an EPRCA Implementation," *Proceedings of IEEE INFOCOM '96*, San Francisco (1996), 569–576.

[MR97] Ma, Q., and Ramakrishnan, K.K. "Queue Management for Explicit Rate-Based Congestion Control," *Proceedings of ACM Sigmetrics '97*, Seattle (June 1997), 39–51.

[OMS98] Ohsaki, H., Murata, M., Suzuki, H., Ikeda, C., and Miyahara, H. "Parameter Tuning of a Rate-based Congestion Control Algorithm for ABR Networks," *International Journal of Communication Systems*, vol. 11, no. 2 (February 1998), 103–128.

[SIG4.0] The ATM Forum Technical Committee. *User-Network Interface Signaling Specification*, version 4.0, 1996.

[SVW97] Su, C.F., DeVeciana, G., and Walrand, J. "Explicit Rate Flow Control for ABR Services in ATM Networks" (1997), Submitted for publication http://www.ece.utexas.edu/~gustavo/.

[TM4.0] The ATM Forum Technical Committee. *Traffic Management Specification*, version 4.0, af-tm-0056.000 (April 1996), ATM Forum http://www.atmforum.com/.

[UNI3.1] The ATM Forum Technical Committee. *User-Network Interface Specification,* version 3.1, 1994.

[YH94] Yin, N., Hluchyj, M.G., "On Closed-Loop Rate Control for ATM Cell Relay Networks," *Proceedings of IEEE INFOCOM '94*, Toronto (1994), 99–108.

Congestion Control

The support of multiple services on a single network requires the use of sophisticated CAC functions, complex scheduling, and flow control mechanisms. Nevertheless, these functions do not necessarily prevent queuing points from becoming congested and exceeding their capacity. In order to provide a stable queuing system, the average traffic load that arrives to a queue should be less than the service rate—the rate at which the traffic can be extracted from it. The instantaneous traffic load (or burst) can be greater than the instantaneous service rate, as long as there is enough buffer space to temporarily store the cells. With a greater rate mismatch, a larger buffer is required to handle a given length of burst. If the buffer is not large enough, it overflows and cells are discarded. The frequency at which the overflow occurs depends on the load and the mix of services supported. For example, a network with many active GFR and UBR connections is more likely to encounter overflow than a network that supports only CBR and ABR traffic.

In order to deal with buffer overflow conditions without affecting the QoS objectives, *congestion control* mechanisms need to be implemented at all the contention points. The congestion control functions decide which cells to drop when the buffer occupancy is such that QoS objectives of the connections may be jeopardized. The objectives of the congestion control functions are to

1. Make efficient use of the buffering resources.
2. Distribute the buffering resources fairly between the contending connections.
3. Prevent connections from affecting the QoS of each other.
4. For VBR CLP-significant service, prevent cells with CLP = 1 from affecting the QoS of cells with CLP = 0.
5. Minimize the delivery of *partial* AAL-5 frames.

In the case of CBR and CLP-transparent VBR services (Chap. 3), congestion is less likely to occur unless the CAC function allows overbooking. It may be sufficient simply to discard cells when the buffer occupancy reaches a predetermined threshold. In the case of real-time services, this predetermined threshold can be calculated based on the maximum delay tolerance.

For CLP-significant VBR service, the cells with CLP = 1 can be transmitted without rate restriction and are not allocated resources. It is important to ensure that they do not affect the QoS of the cells with CLP = 0, while allowing as many cells as possible with CLP = 1 to access the network.

In the case of ABR traffic, the network delay in conveying the congestion information feedback from the network can cause a time lag for the sources to react and adjust their rate accordingly. This can cause congestion of the buffers. If congestion occurs, it is important to ensure fair access to the buffering resources in order to maintain the fairness achieved by the ABR fair-share bandwidth allocation (Chap. 6).

The GFR and UBR services are designed to send as much traffic as necessary to the network and let the network distribute the buffering resources among the contending connections. The GFR and UBR connections generally could use as much buffer space as available. For these services, it is critical to decide intelligently when to drop cells or entire AAL-5 frames in order to provide fair access to the buffering resources among the connections.

As discussed below, it is efficient to share the buffering resources among different services in order to maximize the buffer usage. However, such sharing requires the congestion control functions to ensure that the traffic from one service (e.g., UBR cells) does not affect the traffic of other services.

It is well known that, as the offered traffic load increases, the throughput of the network decreases sharply after a critical occupancy level [Kam81] is reached. Therefore, it is important to limit the offered load to control the congestion. One way of limiting the offered load is by applying *preventive control mechanisms* to ensure that the network does not reach unacceptable load levels. Preventive control methods such as CAC, traffic policing, traffic shaping, and ABR flow control may succeed in preventing the buffer overflow; however, they cannot prevent CLP = 1 cells, GFR traffic, and UBR traffic from overflowing the buffers. In order to deal with this type of traffic, the buffer space needs to be carefully partitioned and appropriate discard mechanisms implemented. This chapter discusses various ways to implement such mechanisms.

Congestion control involves three essential elements:

1. *Buffer partitioning*, which defines the amount of buffer space available to a given queue and the ways in which total available buffering resources are shared among a set of queues.
2. *Occupancy measure*, which defines how the occupancy of the queue is measured. The occupancy measure along with the buffer partitioning defines the *congestion level* of a queue.
3. *Discard policy*, which determines whether to discard or queue the cell, based on the congestion level. When dealing with AAL-5 frames, the discard policy may also depend on whether previous cells of the current frame have been discarded.

These steps are shown in Fig. 7.1.

Figure 7.1.   Elements of congestion control.

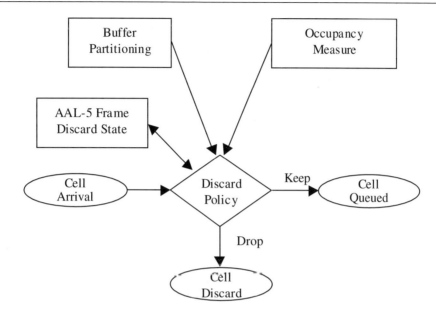

A buffer-partitioning policy along with the occupancy measure is used to detect the congestion level. Depending on whether the service is cell based or frame based (such as AAL-5), a decision is made as per the discard policy either to accept an incoming cell or not. This chapter first discusses a general overview of the buffer-partitioning policies. It is essential to understand the buffer organization mechanism to design proper cell discard mechanisms. Later sections discuss different occupancy measures and discard policies.

Buffer-Partitioning Policies

An overview of ATM switch architectures is presented in Chap. 5, which discussed the necessity of queuing structures in an ATM switch. As shown, the queue structures can be organized as per-Group or per-VC. In either case, a set of queues is needed at a contention point, and each queue needs access to some amount of buffer space.

The goal of the buffer partitioning is to use the available buffer space efficiently while providing isolation between traffic going to different queues. Efficiency is achieved by sharing the pool of buffer resources among as many queues as possible. Some of the buffer-partitioning schemes offer isolation naturally, while others need to be coupled with a more intelligent discard policy in order to prevent one queue from taking over the available buffers and starving others. A lowest level of efficiency is achieved when each queue has a dedicated set of buffer space that cannot be used by any other queue (complete partitioning) when they are unoccupied. A higher level of efficiency is achieved when multiple queues at a contention point share a subset of the buffer pool (complete sharing). A further level of efficiency and related complexity is achieved when many queues at many contention points share a subset of the buffer pool. The complexity of buffer partitioning increases as the number of queuing points sharing the buffer increases because providing isolation becomes more complex. The following discussion [Kau81, KK80] applies to single level of buffer partitions, although it can be easily applied to multiple levels. Assume that there are a set of N queues sharing a buffer space B; that is, $Q = \{Q_1, Q_2, \ldots, Q_N\}$. Let B_i represent the maximum buffer limit each queue can use and q_i represent the actual buffer occupancy of a given queue. The possible buffer partitions can be organized as per one of the policies discussed below [KK80].

Complete Partitioning

In complete partitioning, the available buffering resource is divided among the queues such that each queue gets its own buffer space. That is,

$$B_1 + B_2 + \cdots + B_N = B$$

$$B_j \cap B_k = \Phi \quad \forall (j,k) \in \{1,2,\cdots,N\} \text{ and } j \neq k \tag{7.1}$$

$$q_1 + q_2 + \cdots + q_N \leq B$$

Thus, the buffering resource is completely partitioned among the queues and no two queues can use or share the same buffer space. Since each queue gets its own buffer space, isolating the queue from the others is easy. However, this method does not make efficient use of the buffer. If a queue does not use its allocated buffer space, the space cannot be used by any other queue.

Complete Sharing

In complete sharing, the available buffering resource is fully shared among the queues. That is,

$$B_1 = B_2 = \cdots = B_N = B$$

$$B_j \cap B_k = B \quad \forall (j,k) \in \{1,2,\cdots,N\} \text{ and } j \neq k \tag{7.2}$$

$$q_1 + q_2 + \cdots + q_N \leq B$$

Thus, the buffer is completely shared among the queues and any queue can use the total resource space. Since each queue does not get a reserved buffer space, isolation between the queues becomes difficult. The QoS of a queue can be affected by the traffic in other queues. However, this method makes very efficient use of buffers, since any queue has access to the complete available buffer resource. Some congestion control techniques described further in this chapter can provide isolation even with a complete sharing policy.

Sharing with Minimum Allocation

A sharing policy that reserves a minimum buffer space for each queue while remaining buffering resources are completely shared among the queues provides a compromise between the above two methods. If L_i is the minimum guaranteed buffer space for each queue,

$$B_1 = B_2 = \cdots = B_N = (B - \sum_{i=1}^{N} L_i)$$

$$B_j \cap B_k = (B - \sum_{i=1}^{N} L_i) \quad \forall (j,k) \in \{1,2,\cdots,N\} \text{ and } j \neq k \tag{7.3}$$

$$q_1 + q_2 + \cdots + q_N \leq B$$

Again, as with the complete-sharing policy, this scheme suffers some level of isolation problem because the shared buffer space can be unfairly utilized by the queues. However, since this scheme allocates a minimum buffering space to each queue, it does provide some level of isolation.

Sharing with Maximum Queue Length

This sharing policy allows complete sharing of the buffer space among the queues. However, each queue is limited by a maximum buffer size, which means that cells belonging to streams using a queue will be dropped if the queue size reaches a given maximum limit, even though there may be space available in the system. With this policy, each queue is not allowed to take more space than its maximum buffer limit. Let M_i be the maximum buffer limit for each queue:

$$B_1 = M_1; B_2 = M_2; \cdots; B_N = M_N$$

$$B_1 + B_2 + \cdots + B_N \geq B$$

$$B_j \cap B_k \neq \Phi \quad \forall (j,k) \in \{1,2,\cdots,N\} \text{ and } j \neq k \tag{7.4}$$

$$q_1 + q_2 + \cdots + q_N \leq B$$

By using the maximum queue length, a queue cannot take more than this share from the common pool of buffer. Thus, this scheme protects the system from unfair use of buffer space but is less efficient. If $M_i = B$ the scheme is equivalent to complete sharing. If $\sum M_i = B$ the scheme is equivalent to complete partitioning. Otherwise the scheme can provide some isolation since no queue can use the full buffer.

Sharing with a Maximum Queue Length and Minimum Allocation

This is a combination of the above two methods and achieves the benefits of both. This scheme limits the maximum shared space that a queue can occupy and reserves a minimum buffer space for each queue.

Other Sharing Methods

Only the basic methods of buffer sharing are discussed above. Proposed and studied in the literature [CGK94, CGGK95, WM95, BCH97 and RRK96] are many other possible variations that combine both buffer-sharing and discard policies such as pushout (discussed later). It is also possible to divide the buffer space into hierarchies, each having a different buffer-sharing policy. For example, a buffer space can be divided first among the output ports and then among the queues of each output port. One can use complete partitioning of memory between output ports while using a complete-sharing policy among the queues for a given port. On the other hand, the memory can be shared among queues of the same group type between different output ports, while partitioning the memory between the groups. In the former case, isolation is achieved between ports, while in the latter, isolation is achieved between groups.

Occupancy Measure

The occupancy measure is a metric that provides an instantaneous or filtered estimation of the utilization of the buffer pool at different levels (e.g., per VC count, per queue, or per aggregate queue in the case of sharing). This metric indirectly provides the amount of buffer that is still available in the pool. This information is used along with the buffer-partitioning limits and fairness policies in order to perform discard decisions on arriving cells.

The occupancy measure is implemented at every contention point in the switch. Depending on the buffer-sharing policy, monitoring of aggregate and/or individual queue sizes may be needed. For example, if complete partitioning is used between the queues, then an occupancy measure of individual queue sizes is sufficient. On the other hand, if complete sharing is used between the queues, then both individual as well as aggregate occupancy (i.e., total buffer space occupied by all queues) measures are needed.

In order to achieve per-VC fairness in buffer allocation, the occupancy measure can also be applied at the VC level. Often referred to as *per-VC accounting*, this technique may be used to isolate connections while allowing maximum use of the buffer pool [KV95]. Some degree of fairness can be achieved by keeping track of the per-VC usage count of the buffer. The per-VC usage count is a measure indicating how the buffer is being used by each individual VC. So a per-VC account would keep track of how many buffers each VC currently uses. By setting soft thresholds on the per-VC counts, cells can be dropped only for the connections that exceed their buffer usage limit. Therefore, buffers can be fairly allocated to connections even when per-VC queuing is not employed. Depending on how many connections are active (based on periodic monitoring), the soft thresholds can be programmed for optimum performance.

The occupancy measures can include one or more of the following:

1. Instantaneous queue size
2. Queue growth

Queue Size

The queue size can be used as a measure of occupancy. In this case, the instantaneous value of the current queue depth, or the cell count of a given VC (in case of per-VC accounting strategy), is used as an occupancy measure. Due to the bursty nature of ATM traffic, this occupancy measure tends to be highly variable and does not capture the trends in the buffer utilization. This behavior forces the discard policies to be conservative and can lead to unnecessary discards.

Queue Growth

Queue growth is an alternative occupancy measure that measures the rate of increase and decrease of the queue size (or the VC count). Regular periodic estimation of this measure is necessary, and the length of the measurement interval (defined as a monitoring period) is the key to providing a stable and meaningful measure. This measurement can be used to predict whether the queue will overflow in the next monitoring period. Since it is a filtered and stable measure, it does not result in the conservative cell discards that result from using instantaneous queue size.

Discard Policies

When each cell is received at a queuing point, a decision needs to be made whether to queue or discard the cell. This decision is based on a combination of one or more of the following factors:

1. Priority of the cell (CLP bit) for CLP-significant services, or priority of the service class if traffic from service classes is mixed in the same buffer
2. Occupancy measures combined with the limits of the buffer partition
3. Frame discard status for AAL-5 services

Alternatively, more complex and efficient implementation consists of queueing all incoming cells when any buffer space is available. When the buffer pool is depleted, a decision is made as to which of the cells in the queue should be removed (or *"pushed out"*) [RRK96, STM94, CH96] in order to accommodate the arriving cell. If none of the queued cells are judged less important than the arriving one, then the arriving cell is discarded.

An alternative discard scheme, *front-dropping*, is proposed in [YH93] to discard the cell at the head of the queue when an incoming cell causes buffer overflow. Though complex to implement, this method improves overall loss performance for time-constrained traffic.

As discussed later, there are advantages in some cases to discarding multiple contiguous cells of the same connection when one cell is discarded. In this case, some arriving cells may be discarded regardless of the occupancy measure or the priority of the cell.

Low-Priority Discard

Some ATM services use the CLP bit to differentiate the priority of cells within the same connection (Chaps. 2 and 3). In order to maintain the cell sequence integrity, all cells of the same connections are queued together in a FIFO manner. The low-priority cells therefore share the same queue and buffer pool as the high-priority cells. In order to prevent degradation of the CLR for the CLP = 0 cells, incoming low-priority (CLP = 1) cells are discarded when the occupancy measure reaches a given level. This scheme is generally referred to in the literature as "partial

Figure 7.2.   Low-priority discard mechanism.

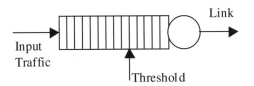

buffer sharing." A threshold is established in order to guarantee sufficient room in the buffer pool for the CLP = 0 cells that could arrive in the future (see Fig. 7.2.). For example, if the occupancy measure is the queue size, the policy is to discard any CLP = 1 cells arriving if the queue size exceeds, for example, 60 percent of the total pool. When it is below the threshold, the CLP = 1 cell is queued. The value of the threshold also impacts the efficient use of the buffer pool. If it is set too low, the low-priority cells cannot benefit from the available buffering, even if there are no high-priority cells. If the level is set too high, the CAC has to allocate more resources (Chap. 4) for the CLP = 0 cells, since the only guaranteed buffer size is the total buffer pool minus the discard level. In this example, it would be 40 percent of the buffer pool.

Service-Class-Based Discard

As discussed in Chap. 2, a network can offer different levels of QoS for a given service category. For example, the network can offer two types of CBR services, class 1 (C1) with CLR = 10^{-10} and class 2 (C2) with CLR = 10^{-5}. Both classes can share the same queue while a discard policy differentiates the classes. If the occupancy measure is above a given threshold upon arrival of a C2 cell, the cell is discarded, leaving room for potentially incoming C1 cells, which have a more stringent CLR requirement. If the service class is CBR or VBR (CLP transparent), this method can provide two or more guaranteed QoS classes using a single queue. If the service class supports bandwidth-on-demand services or CLP-significant traffic, then this model offers relative differentiation between the two classes. For example, [Yeg92] developed an exact analysis for such an implementation using the *MMPP/G/1/N* queuing system.

Partial buffer sharing is used to share a given buffer space among a set of service classes with different QoS objectives. In this scheme, each class i is set a discarding threshold Th_i. At arrival of a class i cell, the decision to discard is made if the occupancy measure is larger than the threshold Th_i. If classes are indexed with decreasing priority (i.e., $i = 0$ indicates highest priority), then $Th_i > Th_{i+1}$. The highest-priority class has access to the whole buffering resource.

In both low-priority discard or the service-class-based discard, pushout as well as pushout with partial buffer-sharing schemes are also possible. In the pushout scheme, low-priority cells are admitted as long as there is room in the buffer. When the buffer is full, however, a low-priority cell is pushed out to make room for a higher-priority cell. The pushout with partial buffering uses a discard threshold on low-priority cells. Upon arrival of a high-priority cell when the buffer is beyond the threshold, a low-priority cell is pushed out. See [RRK96] for a Markov-Modulated Bernoulli Process (MMBP) used to derive cell-blocking probabilities for these two types of partial buffer schemes using two priority classes. Further extensions, such as threshold-based push-out and probability-based pushout [STM94] are also possible.

Fair-Share-Based Discard

Even if an arriving cell is not lower priority and the buffer pool does not support different service classes, a cell may be discarded in order to ensure that the buffer pool is shared fairly among contending connections. This prevents one user from tying up an unfair amount of buffer space and denying access to others. Fairness can be based on many policies (equal-share, proportional-to-the-allocated-bandwidth, etc.) that can be used to divide the available buffer pool. When a cell arrives, if the allocated share for the connection is exceeded, the cell is discarded. Alternatively, a pushout scheme is also possible whereby, if a cell arrives to a full buffer, it can push out a cell of a connection that is using more than its fair share of buffer space. The allocated share varies dynamically as connections become active or inactive. The fair-share-based discard scheme allows much more efficient buffer usage than a scheme with a fixed threshold that does not consider the dynamics of the connection's behavior.

A per-VC accounting scheme can be used to keep track of the VC-count-usage measure of the buffer. As explained in the "Occupancy Measure" section, the per-VC accounting scheme can set per-VC thresholds on the buffer usage. Many schemes for setting per-VC thresholds are possible. One example is to set the per-VC thresholds proportional to the MCR. That is, the threshold for connection i is set as

$$\text{Threshold}_i = (MCR_i / \textstyle\sum_i MCR_i) \times \text{buffer size} \tag{7.5}$$

For increased efficiency, instead of performing the summation over all connections, only the active set of connections is considered. In this case, per-VC queuing provides better fairness than per-VC accounting in terms of access to bandwidth (see Chap. 5). Fairness in terms of access to buffers is comparable, and depends on the buffer partitioning policy.

A dynamic threshold (DT) scheme is proposed by [CH98] whereby each queue limits its queue length to some function of the unused buffer space. The DT scheme uses a control threshold whose value is determined by monitoring the total amount of unused buffer space. The control threshold can be thought of as the queue limit that each queue with sufficient traffic flow can get. At time t, let the control threshold be defined as $T(t)$. Let $Q(t)$ be the sum of all queue lengths and $Q_i(t)$ be the length of queue i. If $Q(t)$ is the total occupancy of the shared memory, then an arriving cell for queue i is dropped at time t if $Q_i(t) \geq T(t)$. The control threshold $T(t)$ is determined as $T(t) = f(B - Q(t))$. The DT scheme uses a simple function for control threshold as $T(t) = \alpha \times (B - Q(t))$. Here $Q(t) = \sum_i Q_i(t)$. The overall performance of the DT scheme is somewhere between that of static thresholds and pushout schemes.

Discarding AAL-5 Frames

For packet- (or frame-) based application (e.g., support of IP), the ATM reference model uses an ATM adaptation layer (AAL) [TM4.0, I.371] that converts packets into cells at the source side and vice versa at the destination. The AAL layer is divided into a SAR (Segmentation And

Reassembly) layer and a convergence sublayer (CS). The CS is further divided into the service-specific convergence sublayer (SSCS) and the common-part convergence sublayer (CPCS). For the various types of AAL layers and their segmentation and re-assembly processes, readers are referred to [AA93]. One of the AAL protocols used for transport of data services is the AAL-5, which divides the packet into 48 bytes of payload to transport as an ATM cell [AA93] by adding padding if necessary. The header of the last cell has the third bit of the payload type indicator (PTI) field set to "1", which indicates that it is at the end-of-packet (EOP) position. This bit is known as ATM-layer-user-to-ATM-layer-user (AUU) parameter. Therefore, by checking the header of each cell, a node can recognize the last cell of an AAL-5 packet.

A cell can be either lost inside the network due to the transmission errors (such as bit errors) or discarded due to congestion control. In general, the destination cannot reconstruct an AAL-5 packet when cells are missing and therefore discards the packet (and remaining cells). The whole packet is retransmitted again by the source in this case. For example, a transmission-control-protocol (TCP) [Kes97] segment is broken into multiple cells when carried over ATM networks. The loss of a single cell causes retransmission of the whole TCP segment again by the upper-layer protocols. Therefore, for AAL-5 connections, if one cell of the AAL-5 packet is discarded in the network, it is useless to carry the remainder cells of the packet to the destination. The network resources can be conserved and overall efficiency can be increased by dropping the complete AAL-5 packet within the ATM switch when any given cell needs to be discarded. Four techniques can be employed to achieve this goal:

1. Hysterisis-based discard
2. Partial packet discard (PPD) or tail dropping (TD)
3. Early packet discard (EPD)
4. Random early discard (RED)

Note that preference for frame discard treatment (i.e., which method to use) can be signaled at connection setup. Dropping cells without any regard to the AAL-5 delineation can cause severe performance problems. In Fig. 7.1, this cell discard is achieved when the AAL-5 frame discard state is set as "inactive." This simple dropping policy can randomly discard cells from many successive frames. As an extreme example, if a cell is dropped from every frame, then the effective throughput (or "goodput") can be very small, as the destination cannot re-construct any of the frames, even though the network did carry many of the cells. Simulations show that the effective throughput or goodput can be as low as 34 percent [RF95] for large packet lengths when cell-based discard is employed. On the other hand, the goodput can be higher than 90 percent if the AAL-5-based discard is performed. The actual performance figures depend on the traffic mix and the system configuration. As the packet length increases, the effective throughput decreases due to a higher probability of cell discard and the corresponding retransmissions. The TCP window size also has effect on the throughput, with a decrease in throughput as the window size increases. For a given packet size, the effective throughput can be increased with an increase in the buffer size. Any discard mechanism that considers the AAL-5 structure performs better.

Hysterisis

A simple approach to attempting to discard complete packets is to use hysterisis in the discard policy. Two occupancy levels (L1, L2) are defined such that L1 > L2. When the occupancy measure reaches L1, the incoming cells are discarded. Once that state is reached, all incoming cells continue to be discarded until the occupancy measure drops below L2. This technique allows dropping multiple cells contiguously, as opposed to the single-level technique, which tends to oscillate around the level and drop cells in a more random fashion. This implementation does not guarantee that complete packets are dropped or that multiple packets in a row are not discarded at the destination. However, if there are only a few connections, then it can provide better goodput than a one-level discard policy. The advantage of this technique is the simplicity of implementation and the fact that it does not require per connection context and AAL-5 awareness.

Partial Packet Discard (PPD) or Tail Dropping (TD)

The partial packet discard (PPD) scheme [AA93] is triggered after the discard policy has made a decision to discard a cell of a given connection. Since it is useless to transmit the remaining cells, a PPD state is enabled for that connection and all the remaining cells of the frame *except for the last cell* are dropped, regardless of the occupancy measures or the cells' priority. The per connection PPD-enabled state is maintained until the end of the frame. The first cell of the next frame is subject to the discard policy, just like any other cell. Note that the cell with AUU = 1, the end-of-packet (EOP) cell, cannot be dropped because it provides the delineation between two consecutive frames. If the last cell is dropped, the destination merges the two frames, identifies the merged frames as in error, and drops both frames.

Simulation results are presented in [RF95] for TCP traffic. Considerable improvement is observed with PPD as opposed to simple discard. For example, with a 100-Kbyte buffer and a TCP packet length of 9180 bytes and 64-Kbyte windows, the effective throughput observed in simple discard is about 60 percent versus 80 percent with PPD. As PPD only discards the remaining cells of the frame, the overall improvement in performance can be limited, since some amount of useless cells (the front of the packet) are still transmitted.

Assuming an Interrupted Bernoulli Process (IBP), [KKTO96] analytically derived the packet loss probability in a system that applies PPD on packets. An approximate analytical model is also developed in [Kam96] for a PPD scheme where the sources are characterized by a two-state on-off process with geometric distributions. The mean delay of successful packets and the blocking probability are derived.

Early Packet Discard (EPD)

The PPD scheme only discards the tail of the packet when a cell is discarded. The head portion of the packet still goes through and uselessly consumes network resources. To improve the performance, [RF95] proposed the EPD scheme. The EPD scheme uses the occupancy measure to proactively decide to drop an entire packet before any cell discard occurs. For example, when the first cell of an AAL-5 packet arrives and the occupancy measure is at or above a given threshold, that cell is discarded and the EPD state for that connection is enabled.

Every cell arriving on that connection, up to and including the last cell of the packet, is discarded regardless of the occupancy measure. The EPD state is reset after the last cell is discarded. If all the cells are dropped, it is not necessary to keep the last cell, since the delineation is provided by the previous packet. The occupancy level has to be established such that there is enough room in the remainder of the buffer to wait for the beginning of the next packet before the discard is triggered.

From the simulation results of [RF95], with a 100-Kbyte buffer, a TCP packet length of 9180 bytes, and 64-Kbyte windows, the effective throughput for an EPD scheme is about 98 percent. The EPD threshold is set to half of the buffer size in this example. The EPD threshold also has an impact on the performance. For example, [KKTO96] extended the EPD method to variable thresholds determined by the number of accepted packets, assuming geometrically distributed packet lengths. It is shown that EPD outperforms PPD when packet sizes are fixed, but not necessarily when packet lengths vary. Analytical results are derived for both EPD as well as modified EPD, assuming Interrupted Bernoulli Process (IBP) arrival process.

A network simulation model with four switches, eight end-nodes, and ten TCP sessions is used to study the EPD performance in [KV95]. The EPD threshold is chosen to be $\max\{0.8,(B - 3 \times SS)/B\}$, where B is the buffer size and SS is the TCP segment size. The lower value of the threshold is limited to 80 percent of the buffer size by this method. As before, these simulations also indicated an increased effective throughput with an increase in buffer size and better performance with EPD as opposed to simple discard. The fairness achieved also varied considerably with buffer size. The mean packet delays are a function of packet and buffer sizes. For large packet sizes and small buffer size, the packet retransmissions cause increased mean packet delays. Selection of EPD threshold also plays an important role. It is found in [KV95] that a static threshold comprising, say, 80 percent of the buffer length may reserve too much space for large buffers and not enough for small buffer sizes.

If the EPD method does not employ any per-VC measures, it can cause unfairness among connections. Therefore, the per-VC accounting mechanism can be combined with EPD to achieve some degree of per-VC fairness. In this case, the first cell of a packet for a given connection is dropped if the current queue size is greater than the EPD threshold and the per-VC queue occupancy is greater than the per-VC threshold.

Random Early Discard (RED)

For packet-switched (e.g., IP) networks, random early detection (RED) gateways are proposed in [FJ93] for congestion avoidance. A similar concept can be adopted in ATM switches. In this case, different occupancy levels are defined, $L_1 < L_2 < \cdots < L_n$. When the occupancy measure reaches L_1 and the first cell of a packet arrives, that cell and the remainder of the packet is dropped with probability P_1. When the occupancy measure reaches L_2 and the first cell of a packet arrives, that cell and the remainder of the packet is dropped with probability P_2, and so on, where $P_1 < P_2 < \cdots P_n = 100$ percent. When the occupancy measure reaches L_n, all the arriving cells are dropped.

This random scheme has the advantage of increasing the fairness without requiring per-VC occupancy measures. That is, a connection that sends a lot of traffic has a higher chance of having its packets dropped than a connection that sends less packets.

Review and Future Directions

This chapter focused on the congestion control techniques for contention points in ATM networks. The congestion control function within a switch encompasses the combination of buffer partition, occupancy measure, and discard policy. The ATM switches use a fixed amount of cell storage, which can be shared by various queuing points. The buffer partition policies define how the buffer space is accessed by the queues and provide limits on how much access to the buffer pool each queue has. Various occupancy measures can be used to evaluate the load and discard cells in order to prevent QoS degradation. The occupancy measure can be applied at the VC, queue, and aggregate levels. More sophisticated discard policies may be necessary when congestion is frequent (e.g., for uncontrolled services like GFR and UBR) in order to ensure fair access to the buffering resources and to isolate connections from each other. Improved fairness requires occupancy measures at the VC level, along with dynamic limits on the queue size.

One future direction for congestion control may be *prediction-based policies*, which try to predict whether congestion is about to occur. In reacting to the congestion level derived from the prediction, the congestion function prevents services or connections from losing their QoS. A few examples of possible congestion function reactions are:

1. Dynamically changing the buffer allocation or threshold,
2. Dynamically adjusting the service rate (e.g., changing the weights of a weighted fair scheduling),
3. Dynamically changing the service priority of the queues.

Instead of using queue size or queue growth functions, "rate monitoring" functions can also be used for occupancy measure. It is shown in [LH93], [LCH95] that queue congestion is indicated by the low-frequency traffic behavior. The input traffic to a queuing system is divided into high- and low-frequency components. The high-frequency component is effectively absorbed by the finite buffer provided at each node. However, the low-frequency variation in the network traffic can cause queue congestion if enough service capacity is not available. The low-frequency component of the input traffic is captured by using a low-pass filter at the input to the queue. [LCH95] shows that the low-frequency component stays intact when the traffic travels through a set of queuing points. Therefore, by monitoring the filtered input traffic, one can overlook the queuing process in the low-frequency band and use the rate measurement as a congestion indicator. It is also possible to estimate the available link capacity by incorporating a rate-monitoring function at the output of the queue. The rate measurements are used to determine the congestion level by setting thresholds on the input rates.

Note that for the prediction-based policies, the queue-growth and/or rate-monitoring functions need to be performed periodically for the queues involved at a queuing point. The performance of the system depends on the interval of this monitoring (or control) period. The schemes based on queue growth or rate monitoring are expensive due to additional overhead involved in implementing the periodic monitoring functions and the filtering algorithms. For fast and effective congestion control schemes, prediction becomes necessary. The nodes should be able to avoid the congestion situation via prediction. A multiagent control system with a prediction function is described in [GB96]. The scheme, called the "Predictive Agents in a Threshold-based Algorithm for Control" (PATRAC) is proposed in [GB96] and implements a cooperative congestion control scheme.

References

[AA93] Armitage, G.J., and Adams, K.M. "Packet Reassemby During Cell Loss," *IEEE Network Magazine* (September 1993), 26–34.

[BCH97] Basak, D., Choudhury, A.K., and Hahne, E.L. "Sharing Memory in Banyan-Based ATM Switches," *IEEE Journal on Selected Areas in Communications*, vol. 15, no. 5 (June 1997), 881–891.

[CGGK95] Cidon, I., Georgiadis, L., Guerin, R., and Khamisy, A. "Optimal Buffer Sharing," *IEEE Journal on Selected Areas in Communications*, vol. 13, no. 7 (September 1995), 1229–1240.

[CGK94] Cidon, I., Guerin, R., and Khamisy, A. "On Protective Buffer Policies," *IEEE/ACM Transactions on Networking*, vol. 2, no. 3 (June 1994), 240–246.

[CH98] Choudhury, A.K., and Hahne, E.L. "Dynamic Queue Length Thresholds in a Shared Memory ATM Switch," *IEEE/ACM Transactions on Networking*, vol. 6, no. 2 (April 1998), 130–140.

[FJ93] Floyd, S., and Jacobson, V. "Random Early Detection Gateways for Congestion Avoidance," *IEEE/ACM Transactions on Networking*, vol. 1, no. 4 (August 1993), 397–413.

[GB96] Gaiti, D., and Boukhatem, N. "Cooperative Congestion Control Schemes in ATM Networks," *IEEE Communications Magazine*, vol. 34, no. 11 (November 1996), 102–110.

[I.371] ITU-Telecommunication Standardization Sector. *Traffic Control and Congestion Control in B-ISDN*, recommendation I.371 (May 1996).

[Kam81] Kamoun, F. "A Drop and Throttle Flow Control Policy for Computer Networks," *IEEE Transactions on Communications*, vol. COM-29, no. 4 (April 1981), 444–452.

[Kam96] Kamal, A.E. "Performance Modeling of Partial Packet Discarding Using the End-of-Packet Indicator in AAL Type 5," *IEEE/ACM Transactions on Networking*, vol. 4, no. 6 (December 1996), 929–940.

[Kau81] Kaufman, J.S. "Blocking in a Shared Resource Environment," *IEEE Transactions on Communications*, vol. COM-29, no. 10 (October 1981), 1474–1481.

[Kes97] Kessler, G.C. *An Overview of TCP/IP Protocols and the Internet.* http://www.hill.com/library/tcpip.html.

[KK80] Kamoun, F., and Klienrock, L. "Analysis of Shared Finite Storage in a Computer Network Node Environment Under General Traffic Conditions," *IEEE Transactions on Communications*, vol. COM-28, no. 7 (July 1980), 992–1003.

[KKTO96] Kawahara, K., Kitajima, K., Takine, T., and Oie, Y. "Performance Evaluation of Selective Cell Discard Schemes in ATM Networks," *Proceedings of IEEE Infocom '96*, San Francisco, CA (March 1996), 1054–1061.

[KV95] Kalampoukas, L., and Verma, A. "Performance of TCP over Multi-Hop ATM Networks: A Comparative Study of ATM-Layer Congestion Control Schemes," *Proceedings of IEEE ICC '95*, Seattle, WA (June 1995), 1472–1477.

[LCH95] Li, S.Q., Chong, S., and Hwang, C. "Link Capacity Allocation and Network Control by Filtered Input Rate in High-Speed Networks," *IEEE/ACM Transactions on Networking*, vol. 3, no. 1 (February 1995), 10–25.

[LH93] Li, S.Q., and Hwang, C. "Queue Response to Input Correlation Functions: Continuous Spectral Analysis," *IEEE/ACM Transactions on Networking*, vol. 1, no. 6 (December 1993).

[RF95] Romanow, A., and Floyd, S. "Dynamics of TCP Traffic over ATM Networks," *IEEE Journal on Selected Areas in Communications*, vol. 13, no. 4 (May 1995), 633–641.

[RRK96] Ramesh, S., Rosenberg, C., and Kumar, A. "Revenue Maximization in ATM Networks Using the CLP Capability and Buffer Priority Management," *IEEE/ACM Transactions on Networking*, vol. 4, no. 6 (December 1996), 941–950.

[STM94] Suri, S., Tipper, D., and Meempat, G. "A Comparative Evaluation of Space Prioirity Strategies in ATM Networks," *Proceedings of IEEE Infocom '94*, Toronto (June 1994), 516–523.

[THP94] Tassiulas, L., Hung, Y., and Panwar, S. "Optimal Buffer Control During Congestion in an ATM Network Node," *IEEE/ACM Transactions on Networking*, vol. 2, no. 4 (August 1994), 374–386.

[TM4.0] The ATM Forum Technical Committee, *Traffic Management Specification*, version 4.0, af-tm-0056.000 (April 1996).

[WM95] Wu, G., and Mark, J.W. "A Buffer Allocation Scheme for ATM Networks: Complete Sharing Based on Virtual Partition," *IEEE/ACM Transactions on Networking*, vol. 3, no. 6 (December 1995), 660–670.

[Yeg92] Yegani, P. "Performance Models forATM Switching of Mixed Continuous-Bit-Rate and Bursty Traffic with Threshold-Based Discarding," *Proceedings of IEEE ICC '92* (1992), 1621–1627.

[YH93] Yin, N., and Hluchyj, M. "Implication of Dropping Packets from the Front of a Queue," *IEEE Transactions on Communications*, vol. 41, no. 6 (June 1993), 846–851.

Managing Frame Relay Traffic on ATM Networks

Frame Relay is a connection-oriented networking technology initially designed for narrow-band ISDN and is based on principles similar to ATM [Fla91]. Frame relay (FR) networks are widely deployed and their usage continues to grow rapidly. It is very common to carry traffic from private frame relay networks over high-speed flexible ATM backbones, because FR is currently only standardized for lower-speed interfaces (e.g., VDSI, DS3). Furthermore, the flexibility of ATM service offerings make the technology more applicable to large high-speed multiservice backbones.

FR and ATM share a subset of similar traffic management capabilities—namely, the concept of a traffic contract, conformance monitoring, selective discarding, and congestion feedback. In order to carry FR traffic over ATM networks efficiently, the traffic management capability of FR must be mapped appropriately. The mapping considers two reference configurations, *service interworking* and *network interworking*. Service interworking generally consists of one FR end-system communicating with an ATM end-system. The frame relay header is therefore removed when segmenting the frame into cells. Network interworking generally considers two FR end-systems communicating with each other through an ATM network. In this case, the FR header is preserved, carried as part of the cell payload and recovered at the reassembly point.

The boundary between the FR and ATM networks is referred to as an interworking function (FR/ATM IW). Correspondingly, the ATM/FR IW is the interworking function at the ATM-to-FR network boundary. Both IW functions are usually co-located in one bidirectional unit. The FR/ATM IW is responsible for segmenting the frames into cells and adding the appropriate ATM header information. It is also responsible for shaping the cells according to the ATM traffic descriptors. The segmentation function may not be capable of segmenting the frames as fast as the line rate. Therefore, the *segmentation rate* is the throughput of the segmentation function or the maximum speed at which back-to-back cells can be emitted. The ATM/FR IW function is responsible for reassembling the cells, removing the ATM headers, and re-creating the original frame. Both IW functions may map the priority and congestion notification information that is described later in this chapter.

Figure 8.1 depicts different scenarios of service and network interworking. End-systems A and C, D and C are communicating via service interworking while end-systems A and B, D and B are communicating via a network interworking configuration. The figure represents only traffic flowing from left to right. The interworking functions can be located inside the switch or in a separate unit.

When FR traffic is carried over an ATM network, it is important to map the traffic management capabilities in a way that makes most efficient use of the resources. This chapter describes how the FR traffic is managed on an ATM network to support the configurations illustrated in Fig. 8.1. First, a basic overview of frame relay is provided, focusing on the elements involved in the traffic management. The mapping of the FR connections to the appropriate ATM service category is discussed next. The mapping of the FR traffic descriptors onto ATM traffic descriptors is then described, followed by a discussion on how the priority and congestion control information is mapped at the interfaces.

Figure 8.1. Reference configurations for frame relay carried over ATM.

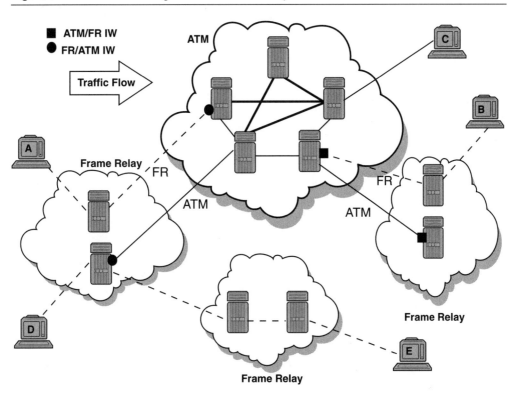

Overview of Frame Relay

The frame relay (FR) technology, like ATM, is connection oriented. Connections can be set up dynamically (SVC) via signaling or permanently (PVC) via a network management system. One key difference between FR and ATM is that the FR transfer unit, a frame, is of variable length for a given connection. The recommended maximum frame size is 4 Kbytes. Frame relay does not support the concept of virtual path (VP) or any hierarchy, and it does not yet offer different services and QoS levels. [Fla91,Mul91].

The header of the frame contains a priority bit referred to as the discard eligibility (DE) bit, which is the equivalent of the CLP bit in ATM. Two other bits, forward and backward congestion notification (FECN and BECN), are used to convey the congestion status of the network. Unlike ATM, FR does not standardize a flow control mechanism that uses the FECN and BECN information. It is therefore uncommon to find end-systems that react to it.

A frame relay connection characterizes its traffic requirement as committed information rate (CIR) and excess information rate (EIR). The CIR and EIR are defined as the number of bytes, B_c and B_e, respectively, that can be transmitted over a defined time period T. The CIR represents the bandwidth committed to a connection; that is, a connection sending at or below the CIR should have a very low number of frames discarded due to congestion. The connection can send traffic at a rate up to the sum of CIR and EIR. The portion of bandwidth between the CIR and EIR is provided on a "best-effort" basis with no commitment to deliver, and those frames have their discard eligibility bit set to "1" to indicate a lower priority. The portion in excess of the sum of CIR and EIR is usually discarded by the network.

Frame relay connections may be subject to a policing function very similar to ATM policing (Chap. 3). The policing function consists of a dual leaky bucket. At each frame arrival, the bucket is incremented by the number of bytes in the frame. The buckets continuously leak at a rate of CIR and EIR respectively. The bucket depths are limited to B_c and B_e, respectively. See [Fla91] for more details on the FR technology and [FRF] for details of the policing algorithm.

The Frame Relay Forum, along with the ITU-T [I.370] is responsible for specifying the interoperability aspects of the technology. These organizations are currently considering multiple service classes and QoS aspects.

Selecting the Appropriate ATM Service Category

Frame relay currently supports two types of services: a service offering bandwidth guarantees (i.e., CIR > 0, EIR ≥ 0) and a best-effort service (i.e., CIR = 0, EIR > 0). Work is progressing in the standardization groups for defining other types of frame relay services, including real-time services.

When interworking FR networks with ATM networks, FR services can be mapped onto equivalent ATM service categories. Frame relay connections map most naturally onto a VBR service, because the concepts of the CIR and EIR are similar to SCR and PCR. Both sets of traffic descriptors characterize the traffic (average and peak) using a dual leaky bucket framework. However, other ATM service categories can also be used. Low-delay FR service can be mapped to CBR or, more efficiently, to rt-VBR. Low-loss FR service is generally mapped to nrt-VBR,

GFR, or ABR. Best-effort service can be mapped to ABR, UBR, or GFR. The mapping of the FR traffic descriptors onto the ATM traffic descriptors is the key to ensure efficient mapping of the services.

Mapping the Traffic Descriptors

When defining how to map the traffic descriptors of FR onto ATM, one key consideration is the reversibility of the mapping. That is, if the connection is set up via SVC, in a network interworking scenario the ATM/FR IW unit has to be capable of re-creating the original FR parameters from the converted ATM parameters without any additional information.

Evaluating the Interworking Overhead

When mapping the traffic descriptors, it is important to take the protocol overhead into account [BICI]. Define $IOHR_{FR\text{-}ATM}$ as the overhead ratio used for converting between FR payload (bytes) and cells. This ratio when converting from FR to ATM ($IOHR_{FR\text{-}ATM}$) differs from the ATM-to-FR ($IOHR_{ATM\text{-}FR}$) ratio as follows:

$$IOHR_{FR\text{-}ATM} \text{ (cells/byte)} = \frac{\left\lceil \dfrac{n_{avg} + FRHS + AALH5}{48} \right\rceil}{N_{avg}}$$

$$IOHR_{ATM\text{-}FR} \text{ (bytes/cell)} = \frac{1}{IOHR_{FR\text{-}ATM}}$$

where

$AALH5$ is the AAL-5 trailer (8 bytes).

$FRHS$ is the frame relay header size (2 or 4 bytes); FRHS is set to zero in a service interworking configuration, since the header is not carried over the ATM network.

n_{avg} is the average user information (payload) in a frame (bytes/frame).

N_{avg} is the average information in a frame that is included in the definition of CIR and EIR (bytes/frame). In some networks, the frame overhead (FRHS and FROH) is included as part of the CIR and EIR specification (e.g., $N_{avg} = n_{avg}$) and other networks count only the user payload (e.g., $N_{avg} = n_{avg} + FRHS + FROH$), where FROH is the HDLC overhead (4 bytes of CRC-16 and flags).

If n_{avg} is not known, a small worst-case value (e.g., 128 bytes) can be used to prevent the FR/ATM shaping function to overflow.

The following sections propose approximate mapping of the traffic descriptors. The mapping does not consider the overhead due to the generation of partially filled cells. Therefore, the resulting ATM parameters may need to be inflated according to the variability in the frame size, assuming it is known.

FR over CBR

In some ATM networks, the CBR service may be the only service that can guarantee a low cell loss (e.g., VBR is not available). In this case, FR connections with CIR greater than zero are mapped onto the CBR service category. The CBR service may also be used when supporting FR connections that are sensitive to delay and jitter.

When mapping FR connections onto the CBR service, the CIR cannot be taken into account to achieve statistical gains. At the FR/ATM IW, the PCR can be derived from the CIR and EIR as follows.

$$(CIR+EIR) \times IOHR_{FR\text{-}ATM} \leq PCR_{0+1} \leq \min(\text{Line rate, Segmentation rate})$$

Unless the PCR is set to the segmentation rate, the FR/ATM IW is required to perform traffic shaping to ensure that the cells of one frame do not enter the ATM network at the line rate or at the segmentation rate. If traffic shaping is not available, then the PCR is set to the ATM access line rate, or it can be set lower and the CDVT can be engineered to account for the jitter. The CDVT can be calculated assuming the largest frame size. If the worst-case frame size translates into N cells, the CDVT can be calculated as follows:

$$CDVT = \frac{N}{PCR_{0+1}} - \frac{N}{\min(\text{Line rate, Segmentation rate})}$$

In case of CBR, CDVT can significantly impact the efficiency of the ATM network (Chap. 4). If the PCR is set lower than $(CIR + EIR) \times IOHR_{FR\text{-}ATM}$, then the interworking unit may get congested. The lower the shaping rate, the longer it takes to reassemble a frame at the other end (ATM/FR unit), but less bandwidth is required to be statically allocated by the ATM network.

The delay incurred by reducing the PCR is not as noticeable as the delay incurred by transmitting a file made up of multiple frames. In this case, the frames are generated at an average rate of CIR, so only the last frame would be delayed if traffic shaping is applied. That is, transmitting a file of N frames, where the total file size exceeds B_c, over a pure FR network (e.g., terminal A to terminal E in Fig. 8.1) takes

$$\frac{(N-1) \times FS}{(CIR + EIR)} + \frac{FS}{LR} \text{ units of time,}$$

where FS represents the frame size and LR the line rate. The same file transmission over an FR/ATM network (e.g., terminal A to terminal B in Fig. 8.1) takes

$$\frac{(N-1) \times FS}{(CIR + EIR)} + \frac{FS}{PCR} \text{ units of time.}$$

Therefore, the longer the file to be transmitted, the lower the impact of shaping the cells at a lower peak rate. Figure 8.2 demonstrates the diminishing return of sending frames at the line rate as a function of the number of frames in a file.

Figure 8.2. File transfer delay (units of time) as a function of the PCR for different file sizes expressed in number of frames (512 bytes) per file. It is assumed that the CIR = 20 units, and the line rate is 40 units.

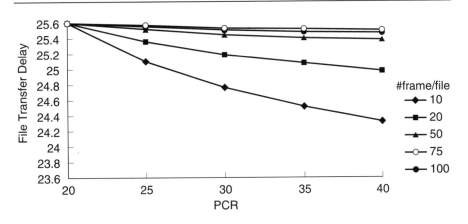

If the size of the file is smaller than the size of the B_c+B_e bucket, the impact of the shaping function is more noticeable because the frames can be sent back to back at the line rate in the frame relay side, but the cells are transmitted at a lower rate into the ATM network.

When mapping from ATM to FR, the CIR is set to $PCR_{0+1} \times IOHR_{ATM-FR}$.

FR over VBR

Generally, FR connections are mapped onto ATM VCs of the VBR service category under the VBR.3 conformance definition (Chap. 2) because of the commonality of the traffic descriptors, the significance of the discard priority, and the applicability of the tagging function. This section discusses mappings of the different traffic descriptors [FRF, BICI].

Since the CIR represents the average of committed traffic, it maps to the SCR of the CLP = 0 flow as follows:

$$SCR_0 = CIR \times IOHR_{FR-ATM}$$

The FR leaky bucket depth B_c maps to the ATM leaky bucket depth or burst tolerance BT. Therefore the MBS can be derived as follows:

$$BT \times SCR_0 = B_c \times IOHR_{FR-ATM}$$

$$(MBS_0-1) \times \left(\frac{1}{SCR_0} - \frac{1}{PCR_{0+1}}\right) \times SCR_0 = B_c \times IOHR_{FR-ATM}$$

$$MBS_0 = \frac{B_c \times IOHR_{FR-ATM}}{1 - \frac{SCR_0}{PCR_{0+1}}} + 1$$

As discussed for the CBR mapping case, the PCR can be derived as follows:

$$(CIR + EIR) \times IOHR_{FR\text{-}ATM} \leq PCR_{0+1} \leq min(\text{Line rate, Segmentation rate})$$

In this case, the PCR can be set higher with less impact on the statically allocated bandwidth, since an equivalent bandwidth will be derived. The curves in Fig. 8.2 can also exemplify the impact of the PCR on the file transfer delay. When mapping from ATM to FR, the traffic descriptors are converted as follows:

$$CIR = SCR_0 \times IOHR_{ATM\text{-}FR}$$

$$EIR = (PCR_{0+1} - SCR_0) \times IOHR_{ATM\text{-}FR}$$

$$B_c = (MBS_0 - 1) \times \frac{SCR_0}{PCR_{0+1}} \times IOHR_{ATM\text{-}FR}$$

If the ATM network does not offer VBR.3 conformance definition, VBR.1 can be used. In this case, the SCR and MBS also include the excess traffic. The mapping is derived as follows:

$$SCR_{0+1} = (CIR + EIR) \times IOHR_{FR\text{-}ATM}$$

$$BT \times SCR_{0+1} = (B_c + B_e) \times IOHR_{FR\text{-}ATM}$$

$$(MBS_{0+1} - 1) \times \left(\frac{1}{SCR_{0+1}} - \frac{1}{PCR_{0+1}} \right) \times SCR_{0+1} = (B_c + B_e) \times IOHR_{FR\text{-}ATM}$$

$$MBS_{0+1} = \frac{(B_c + B_e) \times IOHR_{FR\text{-}ATM}}{1 - \dfrac{SCR_{0+1}}{PCR_{0+1}}} + 1$$

In this case, PCR should be set higher than the SCR, as follows:

$$(CIR + EIR) \times IOHR_{FR\text{-}ATM} < PCR_{0+1} \leq min(\text{Line rate, Segmentation rate})$$

Using VBR.1 when mapping from ATM to FR, the signaling protocol cannot be recovered automatically as the original FR parameters from the VBR.1 traffic descriptors. With only the SCR of the CLP = 0+1 information, it is not possible to extract which proportion covers the committed traffic. Therefore, the worst-case assumption is that SCR_{0+1} represents only committed traffic, to ensure that all the committed traffic is included in the CIR of the downstream network.

$$CIR = SCR_{0+1} \times IOHR_{ATM\text{-}FR}$$

$$EIR = (PCR_{0+1} - SCR_{0+1}) \times IOHR_{ATM\text{-}FR}$$

$$B_c = (MBS_{0+1} - 1) \times \frac{SCR_{0+1}}{PCR_{0+1}} \times IOHR_{ATM\text{-}FR}$$

FR over ABR

Frame relay connections can be mapped onto ABR ATM VCs. In order to use this configuration, the FR/ATM and ATM/FR IW functions are required to implement the ABR source/destination behavior [TM4.0]. When using ABR, the MCR is set to $CIR \times IOHR_{FR\text{-}ATM}$ and the PCR can be set to the segmentation rate or the line rate without affecting the efficiency of the network. With such mapping, frames are transmitted as fast as the network can handle them but not slower than the committed rate.

Mapping from ATM to FR, the traffic descriptors are mapped as follows:

$$CIR = MCR \times IOHR_{ATM\text{-}FR}$$

$$EIR = (PCR_{0+1} - MCR) \times IOHR_{ATM\text{-}FR}$$

FR over GFR

GFR is a frame-based service and is therefore well suited to support FR. In this case, the traffic descriptors are derived almost as they would be for VBR. The key difference between GFR and VBR for supporting FR traffic is that the GFR service requires static allocation of a lower amount of bandwidth.

$$MCR = CIR \times IOHR_{FR\text{-}ATM}$$

The MFS is set to the largest frame size supported by the connection or the network. The FR leaky bucket depth B_c maps to the ATM leaky bucket depth or burst tolerance BT. Therefore the MBS can be derived as follows:

$$BT \times MCR = B_c \times IOHR_{FR\text{-}ATM}$$

$$(MBS_0 - 1) \times \left(\frac{1}{MCR} - \frac{1}{PCR_{0+1}} \right) \times MCR = B_c \times IOHR_{FR\text{-}ATM}$$

$$MBS_0 = \frac{B_c \times IOHR_{FR\text{-}ATM}}{1 - \dfrac{MCR}{PCR_{0+1}}} + 1$$

As discussed for the CBR-mapping case, the PCR can be derived as follows:

$$(CIR + EIR) \times IOHR_{FR\text{-}ATM} \leq PCR_{0+1} \leq \min(\text{Line rate}, \text{Segmentation rate})$$

When mapping from ATM to FR, the FR parameters are recovered as follows:

$$CIR = MCR \times IOHR_{ATM\text{-}FR}$$

$$EIR = (PCR_{0+1} - MCR) \times IOHR_{ATM\text{-}FR}$$

$$B_c = (MBS_0 - 1) \times \frac{MCR}{PCR_{0+1}} \times IOHR_{ATM\text{-}FR}$$

FR over UBR

Frame relay connections with a zero CIR can be mapped onto a UBR service category. The PCR can be set to any value between $EIR \times IOHR_{FR\text{-}ATM}$ and the minimum of the line rate and the segmentation rate. In this case, because there is no bandwidth allocation, the PCR does not affect the network capacity.

Mapping from ATM to FR, the EIR is calculated as $PCR \times IOHR_{ATM\text{-}FR}$.

Traffic Shaping at Interworking Units

Even if the FR traffic emitted by the source conforms to the FR traffic descriptor, the FR/ATM IW needs to perform traffic shaping to ensure that the ATM traffic conforms to the mapped ATM traffic descriptors. Similarly, at the ATM/FR IW function, traffic shaping needs to be performed to ensure that the reconstructed FR traffic behaves as per the FR traffic descriptor. If the traffic is not shaped at PCR, then the CDVT has to be set such that it allows a full frame to come out at the segmentation rate, which impacts efficiency (Chap. 4). Furthermore, there could be policing functions at the entry point to the ATM network or at the entry point to the downstream FR network; it is therefore important to ensure that segmentation/reassembly does not negatively impact the traffic behavior to make it non-conformant.

If the ABR service is used to carry FR traffic, the interworking function has to implement the source and destination behavior as defined in [TM4.0].

When using the UBR service, shaping is also required if the PCR is lower than the segmentation rate when the downstream ATM node performs policing.

Mapping Priority

In FR (as in ATM), the priority bit can be set by either the user or the network. When the bit is set by the user, it represents the lower importance of a frame relative to others. The user-set priority can be applied, for example, to carry embedded video encoding where acceptable quality is maintained if high-priority packets are received and higher quality is achieved if the lower-priority frames successfully reach the destination along with the high-priority packets. There may be economic incentives for lowering the priority of some of the packets. This approach makes sense for applications that do not retransmit a packet when it is discarded. The network can reduce the priority of a packet when it violates the negotiated traffic descriptors (Chap. 3). However, the network cannot increase the priority of a packet.

At the interface between a FR and ATM network it is optional to map the content of the priority field of a frame into the corresponding ATM cells. It is useful to preserve the user-set priority into the ATM network. However, in the case of network-set priority, the traffic behavior at the cell level is significantly different and the conformance needs to be reassessed in order to properly set the priority of the cells emitted by the FR/ATM IW function. Since the single-priority bit does not indicate whether it is user-set or network-set, it is safer to map the priority bit, unless it is known that there are no applications making use of the user-set priority capability.

When performing the mapping at the FR/ATM IW function, cells resulting from the segmentation of a frame that has its DE (discard eligibility) bit set also have their CLP bit set.

Conversely the ATM/FR IW function maps the CLP bit of the cells into the DE bit of the frame. In this case, many approaches can be adopted. The DE bit of the reconstructed frame could be set to one, if the majority, or all cells have their CLP bit set. This functionality is also optional and the network may not map the priority of the cells into the DE bit of the reassembled frame.

Mapping the Congestion Notification

The ATM congestion notification information is only used with the ABR service category (unless nonstandard proprietary flow control loops are implemented with the other service categories). Frame relay standards and interoperability specifications do not define how to react to the congestion notification; it is therefore uncommon to have an end-system react voluntarily. When mapping FR connections onto non-ABR service categories, the FECN bit of the frame can be mapped to the EFCI bit of the resulting cells at the FR/ATM IW. At the ATM/FR IW, the FECN bit of the reconstructed frame can be set if one or more of its cells had an EFCI bit set. Without ABR in the ATM network, there is no reverse flow in which the BECN bit can be mapped (the EFCI bit indicates only forward congestion); it is therefore not possible to close the FR control loop over the ATM network.

When using ABR, the congestion information can be mapped as depicted in Fig. 8.3. The FR/ATM IW function turns around the FECN information in the BECN bit of the returning frames. The upstream FR network is isolated in a control loop. The EFCI of the ABR loop is reset in order to create a new loop that is controlled by the FR/ATM IW function source behavior. The ATM/FR IW function behaves as per the ABR destination requirement and therefore maps the forward congestion (EFCI/ER) information onto the backward path (CI/NI/ER) of the

Figure 8.3. Mapping of the congestion information.

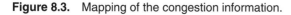

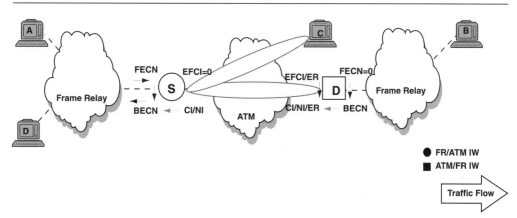

ATM loop. The ATM/FR IW does not need to map the EFCI forward to the next loop because it takes care of turning around the information.

The BECN information of the downstream loop can optionally be mapped into the backward path of the ATM loop (into the CI/NI bits). This mapping allows the extension of the ABR control loop to include the downstream FR network. In this case, the ABR source reacts to the congestion in the downstream FR network as well as in the ATM network. The FR/ATM IW can map the CI/NI information into the upstream BECN bit. If the FR end-systems react to the congestion information, this mapping would allow extension of the control loop end to end. The ATM/FR IW would in this case have to implement a proprietary reaction to the BECN bit from the FR network. The increase in the reassembly queue size would then trigger the ATM ABR control loop to slow down. If the FR end-system does not react, the ATM/FR IW can map the BECN into the CI/NI of the RM cell to convey the load status to the ATM virtual source.

Review

Frame relay networks are growing rapidly. These networks are also interfacing with the ATM multiservice backbone networks. Therefore, it is important to properly map the frame relay traffic descriptors onto the ATM traffic contract so that it can make efficient use of the resources in the ATM network. The similarity between the FR and ATM traffic descriptors and traffic management concepts permits one to define such a mapping and apply it automatically for switched connections. The frame relay priority and congestion indications can also be mapped onto the corresponding ATM cell priority and congestion indications.

References

[BICI] The ATM Forum Technical Committee. *B-ISDN Inter Carrier Interface Specification*. The ATM Forum, version 2.0, af-bici.0013.003 (December 1995).

[Fla91] Flanagan, W. *Frame, Packets and Cells in Broadband Networking*. New York: Telecom Library (1991).

[FRF91] The Frame Relay Forum. *User-To-Network Implementation Agreement*. The Frame Relay Forum (January 1991).

[I.370] ITU-Telecommunication Standardization Sector. *Congestion Management for ISDN Frame Relaying Bearer Service*, recommendation I.370 (1991).

[Mul91] Muller, N.J., Davidson, R.P. *The Guide to Frame Relay and Fast Packet Networking*. New York: Telecom Library (1991).

[TM4.0] The ATM Forum Technical Committee, *Traffic Management Specification*, version 4.0, af-tm-0056.000 (April 1996).

CHAPTER 9

Managing IP Traffic
on ATM Networks

The Internet Protocol (IP) suite was created as part of the ARPANET project, which started around 1978 [COM88]. Today, the vast majority of computers use IP-based protocols. Although IP technology is widespread and continuously expanding, it does not eliminate the need to deploy ATM networks, because [BEN98] ATM offers a standard set of traffic management mechanisms that can interoperate among different vendors to allow efficient support for different types of services (Chap. 2) and effectively guarantee a QoS to the connections. The ATM also provides a flow control mechanism that allows a network to avoid loss in the core and to maximize the usage of expensive links. For public network providers, it can therefore be more efficient to build a core network using ATM technology. However, in order to support many users, the network provider needs to provide interworking capability with the IP networks. This function deals with routing and addressing aspects, but the focus of this chapter is to discuss the role of the interworking function in providing the traffic management functionality to support IP when it is mapped onto an ATM network.

Figure 9.1 presents typical interworking scenarios and locations of interworking functions. The IP/ATM IW refers to the function that segments the IP packets into ATM cells and shapes the ATM cells into the ATM network as per the selected traffic contract (Chap. 3). The ATM/IP IW reassembles the ATM cells into IP packets.

The Internet Engineering Task Force (IETF) is the body responsible for defining interoperability specifications for the IP protocol. The IETF is currently working on adding QoS support for the protocol, but at this time there are no agreements on how the QoS will be supported nor on the specification of the related mechanisms (e.g., CAC, flow control).

This chapter discusses how to carry IP traffic over ATM networks efficiently. It focuses on the current implementation of IP networks (e.g., "best-effort" service). First, a high-level overview of the current IP protocol is provided with emphasis on the aspects relevant to traffic management. Different options for mapping IP traffic onto ATM service categories are described.

Figure 9.1.   Reference configurations.

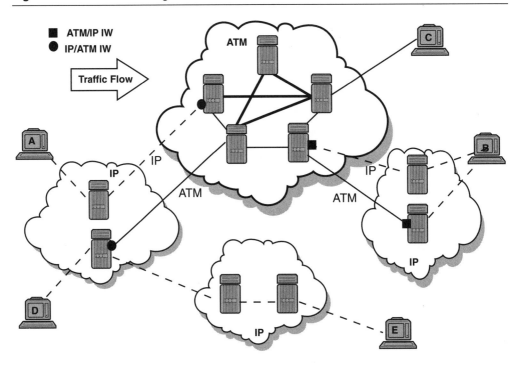

Overview of IP

IP is a connectionless protocol that currently supports a single best-effort quality of service, with no guaranteed QoS. The IP layer is responsible for the delivery of variable-size protocol data units (PDU). IP does not guarantee that the packets are delivered in the same order as when created.

IP supports many different higher-level protocols. The most commonly used are the transmission control protocol (TCP) and the user datagram protocol (UDP). These protocols are used by various applications, such as Telnet (terminal access), file transfer protocol (FTP), and WWW access [Kes97]. These applications vary widely in terms of their bandwidth, QoS requirements, and traffic characteristics.

Overview of TCP

The TCP uses an *end-to-end window-based* flow control protocol to regulate the flow of PDUs into the network. The TCP is connection oriented and generally uses IP to deliver the PDUs.

The protocol is managed by the end-systems, the traffic source, and the destination (e.g., *end-to-end*). The network does not take an active role in the flow control, other than by discarding packets.

Applications that require reliable delivery use TCP. Applications using TCP/IP are guaranteed to receive all the data in order, even though the network loses, misorders, or discards packets. The TCP protocol ensures that the lost packets are retransmitted prior to delivering them to the destination application. The reliable and ordered transmission is possible because of the use of acknowledgments (ACK) and sequence numbers [RFC793]. TCP cannot, however, control the delay for delivery of the packet.

The TCP control loop is managed primarily by the destination, which governs the amount of data that the source can send. The destination returns a *window* as part of the ACKs. The window indicates which sequence numbers of PDUs the source is allowed to send without receiving further acknowledgment. The window represents a number of octets that the source can send.

The feedback carried to the source is not based on any explicit information from the network other than the fact that a packet has been delivered. The destination realizes that a packet is missing with the help of the sequence numbers in the received IP packet and timers. It notifies the source that a given packet is missing. The source also uses timers to retransmit packets when no acknowledgment (or negative acknowledgment) is received. When the source figures that a packet is missing, it assumes that there is congestion in the network and reduces the window size to reduce the amount of traffic it offers to the network. The window size is increased by steps once positive acknowledgments are received from the destination indicating that the congestion may have been relieved. The window fluctuates around some value that implicitly represents the share of bandwidth available for this connection.

The loss of a packet may imply that the source must retransmit some number of packets (e.g., go back *N*). This behavior can seriously impact the performance and the efficiency of the network [Ahn93].

The performance of most implementations of TCP are affected if more than one packet is lost in a given window. In this situation, the TCP window shuts down to one and increases slowly, thus impacting the performance. Therefore, the network has to carefully select which packets to drop to prevent "beat-down" of some connections [Flo91]. Beat-down is a phenomenon that occurs because some connections that are going through more hops are more likely to have more than one packet dropped within the same window. These connections have their window size set to the minimum, while the other connections use more bandwidth.

The performance of TCP also depends largely on the round-trip time (RTT) of the packets in the network and on the buffers available [RFC1072]. The window size needs to be set large enough that a given connection is able to send the equivalent of at least *bandwidth* × *RTT* bytes in the network, where *bandwidth* is the rate of the bottleneck link in the path. If the window is smaller, the network bandwidth may be underutilized and the connection may experience longer transfer time than required. A much larger window does not provide increased benefit, since the acknowledgments should be coming back fast enough to make the window size oscillate around an optimum point. If the window size is large, the TCP connection can cause longer-lasting congestion. The TCP timers also affect the performance, as they determine how long the protocol waits before retransmitting a packet [RFC1323].

Overview of UDP

The user datagram protocol (UDP) also generally uses IP as the underlying protocol. UDP allows applications to send messages or files to other applications with minimum protocol overhead (e.g., no flow control). The protocol is transaction oriented (as opposed to connection oriented) and delivery or protection against duplicate packets is not guaranteed to the application [RFC768].

An application using UDP needs to be capable of realizing when PDUs are missing and ask the sending application for the missing information, if necessary. Some voice applications designed to run over the UDP protocol may not require the packets to be retransmitted. The network file system (NFS) is a higher-layer application that can use UDP/IP as underlying protocols. NFS is a file-system management application. The NFS has its own flow control protocol that sends multiple PDUs and, if one PDU is declared missing by the destination or if a timer expires, all the PDUs are retransmitted. It does not rely therefore on UDP for reliable and ordered delivery. When the group of PDUs successfully reaches the destination, the application sends another group. The NFS usually runs over UDP when the probability of loss is low; otherwise it uses TCP/IP.

Selecting the ATM Service Category

This section discusses different options for selecting the service category to carry the traffic from IP networks. The following performance goals need to be considered in order to carry IP traffic efficiently over an ATM network:

- Minimize the delay within the ATM network by maximizing the use of the available bandwidth.
- Maximize the "goodput."
- Maximize utilization of the network resources.
- Ensure consistent performance.
- Ensure some level of fairness to prevent beat-down.

An application using the IP network evaluates the performance based primarily on the end-to-end transfer delay for transferring a data entity (e.g., a file). A secondary measure is based on the "goodput." Goodput measures the amount of data that need not be retransmitted in order to reach the destination successfully, or:

$$\text{goodput} = \frac{\text{packets sent}}{\text{packets retransmitted} + \text{packets sent}}$$

where "packets sent" represents the number of original packets sent by the source, excluding the packets that were retransmissions of original packets. "Packets retransmitted" represents the number of packets that were sent more than once, excluding the original packet. The goodput therefore also measures the network efficiency.

It is not necessary to have 100 percent goodput in order to minimize the delay. For most applications and therefore end users, the fact that some packets are retransmitted during the file transfer is not an issue, as long as the resulting transfer time is acceptable. For TCP, the end-to-end delay can be even lower if selective packets are lost, thereby appropriately slowing down transmission, rather than buffering the packets in a large buffer and having the source stop the transmission while waiting for acknowledgments. In the case of UDP, (mainly NFS over UDP), lower goodput can translate to higher end-to-end transfer delay if retransmission is necessary.

In general, an end user is also looking for a *consistent* or *deterministic* performance, so that regardless of the time of day, the same file transfer requires a similar amount of time. The user also expects consistent behavior regardless of where the destination application is located (e.g., regardless of the round-trip time). Consistency is achieved by preventing beat-down and providing fair access to the available resources while allocating some minimum amount of bandwidth.

If congestion occurs in the network, the faster the TCP protocol is notified that a packet is discarded, the faster that connection slows down and helps reduce the intensity and duration of the congestion.

In general, it is difficult to characterize the IP traffic in terms of its behavior when carried over the ATM network, since traffic from many sources going to the same destination are generally carried over the same ATM VC [Dan91]. The aggregate traffic behavior is difficult to characterize, and traffic shaping becomes essential.

IP over CBR or rt-VBR

The CBR or rt-VBR service category may be used to carry voice or video applications that use IP. Such applications can generally characterize their bandwidth, and the IP/ATM IW function can shape to the corresponding traffic descriptors (Chaps. 2 and 3).

However, an IP/ATM IW could use the CBR service to carry all the data through the ATM network with minimal loss. The IP/ATM IW function needs to perform the traffic shaping at PCR and is likely to overflow and discard packets if the sending sources can transmit faster than the PCR of the ATM connection. In the case of TCP, the loss at the IP/ATM IW gets conveyed to the source, which eventually slows downs its transmission.

In the case of rt-VBR, an average rate and burstiness can be specified, allowing for statistical gains. However, these characteristics need to be specified at the connection setup. Since the traffic behavior of the TCP session is not known ahead of time and because there are usually many TCP sessions sharing one ATM VC, worst-case conservative assumptions need to be taken when setting up the traffic descriptors.

Because of its stringent QoS objectives and low statistical gains, the CBR and rt-VBR service may not be a cost-effective way to carry non-real-time IP traffic. The value of the PCR has direct impact on the file transfer delay and the efficiency. The use of CBR does not allow access to unused ATM network bandwidth on an as-needed basis, so the transfer delay cannot be optimized. It also does not maximize network utilization. The use of rt-VBR with VBR.2 or VBR.3 conformance definitions can allow for access to excess bandwidth by using the CLP bit.

However, the small buffers used to achieve the delay guarantee do not allow much storage for low-priority cells.

IP over nrt-VBR

The use of nrt-VBR raises efficiency concerns similar to those for CBR or rt-VBR. However, in this case larger bursts (MBS) can be efficiently supported, and the IP/ATM IW function can shape the traffic to a predefined PCR, SCR/MBS. The traffic is then carried in the ATM network at a committed loss rate. Again, since the traffic descriptors cannot be predetermined prior to transmission, it is likely that the traffic shaping at the IP/ATM IW results in packet loss. The higher the SCR/MBS and PCR compared to the source sending rate, the lower the likelihood of discarded traffic at the IP/ATM IW. However, the traffic descriptors directly impact the amount of bandwidth that is statically allocated in the ATM network (Chap. 4). The use of nrt-VBR with the VBR.2 and VBR.3 conformance definitions allows access to the unused bandwidth by tagging the traffic as low-priority cells. However, these cells are more likely to be discarded by the network, and the cell loss commitment does not apply to them. The IP packets corresponding to the discarded cells are eventually retransmitted.

IP over ABR

Using the ABR service prevents having to characterize the traffic descriptors and statically allocate the bandwidth in the ATM network. It also minimizes the loss in the ATM network and therefore maximizes the goodput and the network utilization in the ATM portion. However, it does not prevent the IP/ATM IW function from overflowing, because there is no connection between the ATM and IP flow control protocols. Therefore, the end-to-end goodput may not be maximized.

When compared to a pure IP network, the use of ABR service increases the delay before the source is notified that there is congestion. The result is an increased delay before the TCP flow control can react to the congestion by slowing down. Figure 9.2 demonstrates the delay for notifying the source in the case of an IP network. D_{up} represents the delay between the congestion point and the destination end-system. D_{up} includes the queuing, transmission, and propagation delays at each node, including the congested node. The delay between the destination and the source is represented by D. The big X depicts where the congestion occurs.

In the case of IP, the delay for the congestion feedback to reach the source is $D_{up}+D$. Figure 9.3 demonstrates the increased delay when using ABR in the core ATM network. In this case, D_{dn} represents the delay for the feedback to go from the congestion point up to the virtual source. This delay represents the delay incurred by the backward RM cell. D_{up} represents the delay from the congestion point to the end destination (IP).

When using ABR in the ATM network, the delay for the congestion feedback to the TCP source is increased to $2 \times D_{dn} + D_{up} + D$. The backward RM cell that flows from the congested switch reaches the VS point after a delay corresponding to D_{dn}. Then the loss of a packet that eventually occurs at the virtual source (VS) gets notified to the destination after a delay of

Figure 9.2. IP feedback.

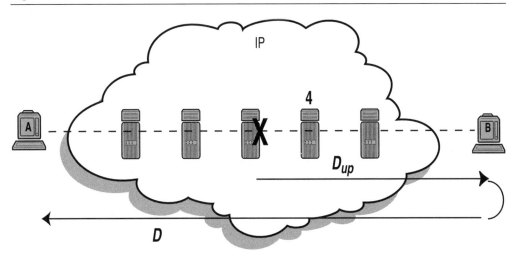

Figure 9.3. IP/ABR/ATM feedback delay.

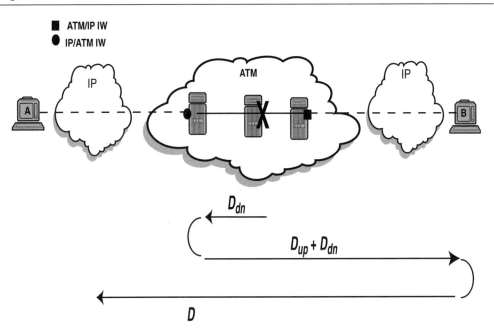

$D_{dn} + D_{up}$, and the destination then notifies the source after a delay of D units. The increased delay may be insignificant, depending on the propagation delay and the speed of the physical links. However, ABR does absorb transient congestion by spreading it across multiple upstream switches. If congestion is sporadic and of short duration, the added delay does not negatively impact the performance. In this case, the use of ABR achieves better end-to-end performance.

In the case of TCP, the two flow control mechanisms are not linked, and therefore the congestion at the IP/ATM IW cannot be conveyed directly to the IP layer. Congestion at the IP/ATM IW is conveyed to the TCP source after the notification of discarded packets has reached the IP destination and the ACK is sent back to the source. TCP assigns a retransmission timer with every unacknowledged packet. If the timer expires before reception of an ACK, TCP assumes that the packet was lost or corrupted, triggers appropriate flow control (e.g., reduce the window) and eventually retransmits the packet. The duration of the timer varies and is based on an estimation of the round trip time (RTT) calculated based on previous acknowledged packets. If the RTT suddenly increases by a significant amount, the timeout will expire before the ACK can reach the source, and TCP will determine that the packet is lost.

Using ABR to carry TCP can cause the RTT to suddenly increase, if the ER scheme is designed such that the ACR can drop by a large amount in two consecutive RM cells or greatly vary from one RM cell to another. In the case of binary ABR, large RDF values can also cause the RTT to increase sharply. However, it is possible to design ER mechanisms that bound the amount of ACR reduction per RM cell, preventing an adversely effect on TCP. When sufficient buffering is available, congestion-based ER schemes (e.g., congestion bias; see Chap. 6) also provide a more progressive (or "TCP friendly") ACR reduction. The progressive ACR reduction may impact the *convergence time* of the ABR loop, since it will take longer to reach the fair share distribution of the bandwidth.

Figure 9.4. IP/ABR direct feedback delay.

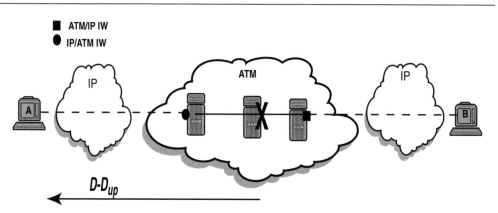

The ABR service, either ER based or binary with intelligent marking, combined with intelligent dropping (Chap. 7) at the IP/ATM IW ensures performance consistency and prevents beat-down because resources are allocated fairly in the network.

Overlapping the TCP and ABR control loops from the ATM network carries each packet only once and therefore the goodput of the ATM portion of the network is maximized. Furthermore, ABR is designed to minimize the buffering requirements in the ATM network and to push the congestion to the edge; therefore, larger buffers are required at the IP/ATM IW function. The overhead required to run ABR on each connection (a default of 6 percent of the bandwidth) and the complexity of deploying ABR (e.g., setting up parameters and VS/VD) also need to be considered [Van98, Kal96-1, Kal96-2].

Ultimately, the best optimization of both networks can be achieved by explicitly tying the ABR feedback directly with the TCP layer at the IP/ATM IW function. Evolving TCP to make it "rate knowledgeable" and using the ACR in the RTT estimation can also maximize the efficiency of both networks. Figure 9.4 demonstrates the impact on the feedback delay of tying the ABR feedback to the TCP layer. The performance of both networks and the end-to-end performance would be greatly improved [Kal98].

IP over GFR or UBR

The IP network provides a "best-effort" service that is equivalent to the ATM UBR service. However, in order to achieve comparable performance, the UBR service needs to be enhanced with the frame discard capability (Chap. 7). Without this capability, due to the random cell discard, the UBR service achieves far lower goodput and larger transfer delay [Tur95].

When the ATM network encounters congestion, packets are discarded and congestion is conveyed to the TCP layer in less than round-trip time, as depicted in Fig. 9.2. Although the congestion status is conveyed more quickly to the TCP layer than when using ABR (see Fig. 9.3), the packets that are discarded have already used resources in the upstream network elements and are retransmitted eventually.

Different fairness mechanisms (e.g., per-VC accounting) can be applied at the congestion point in order to increase the consistency of the performance (Chap. 7). Using GFR instead of UBR provides more consistent performance and increased throughput by guaranteeing a minimum amount of bandwidth in the core.

In order to provide good performance for TCP applications, the buffers need to be capable of holding packets equivalent to multiple TCP windows. In order not to lose *any* packets during congestion, the buffer size needs to equal the sum of the window sizes of the transmitting connections. However, this requirement results in an impractical buffer size and underutilization of the resources, since only a few connections are active at the same time. This buffer size requirement can be reduced by taking into account the probability of many sources sending data simultaneously. Also, a very large buffer may not optimize the end-to-end delay since the packets are waiting for transmission in the large buffer while the source is stopped, waiting for acknowledgments [Goy97-1, Goy97-2, Goy97-3, Rom95, Mol95, Ben98].

Review

The IP-based applications are continuously growing, so ATM network providers have to carry IP traffic efficiently. There has been intense debate regarding the best way to carry IP traffic over an ATM network. A multitude of simulation studies have been performed comparing TCP over ABR, UBR, and GFR. The performance depends on the configuration of the IW units and the nodes in terms of buffers and congestion control capabilities, and conclusions can vary widely. Simulations of a specific network and its capabilities are necessary in order to make the appropriate selection. However, some high-level observations can be used in the decision process. The use of ABR may increase the complexity of the core ATM network, but the network carries only data that is usable by the destination, while minimizing the buffering requirements in the ATM network. The IP/ATM IW function still requires significant buffering to handle potential congestion in the core network. The use of UBR with frame discard or GFR can achieve performance equivalent to an IP network without requiring the IP/ATM IW function to support large buffers. In this case, bandwidth upstream from the congestion point is used to carry packets that end up being retransmitted. Therefore, if the link bandwidth is very expensive (e.g., overseas links), the use of ABR may provide benefits that outweigh the increased complexity and cost of the increased buffer at the IW units.

In order to provide better support for IP applications, the ATM network has to apply congestion control in a fair manner and implement the frame discard capability (Chap. 7).

IP is moving toward supporting QoS "assurances" and is therefore designing traffic management concepts similar to those defined for ATM (e.g., policing, CAC, flow control). The IP/ATM IW function will map the IP QoS concepts into the ATM service categories.

References

[Ahn93] Ahn, J., Danzig, P.B., Liu, Z., Yan, L. *Evaluation of TCP Vegas: Emulation and Experiment.* Http://excalibur.usc.edu/research/vegas/doc/vegas.html (1993).

[Ben98] Bentall, M., Hobbs, C., and Turton, B.C. *ATM and Internet Protocol, a Convergence of Technology.* New York: John Wiley & Sons (1998).

[Com88] Comer, D. *Internetworking with TCP/IP—Principles, Protocols and Architecture.* Englewood Cliffs, NJ: Prentice Hall, 1988.

[Dan91] Danzig, P.B., Jamin, S. "TCPlib: a Library of TCP Internetwork Traffic Characteristics," technical report CS-SYS-91-01, Computer Science Department, University of Sourthen California (1991).

[Flo91] Floyd, S., Jacobson, V. "On traffic Phase Effects in Packet-Switched Gateways," *Computer Communication Review.* vol. 21. no. 2 (April 1991).

[Goy97-1] Goyal, R., Jain, R., Kalyanaraman, S., Fahmy, S., Kim, S.C. "Improving Performance of TCP over ATM/UBR Service," *Proceedings IEEE ICC '97*, Montreal (June 1997), 1042–1048.

[Goy97-2] Goyal, R., Jain, R., Kalyanaraman, S., Kota, S., Samudra, P. "Selective Acknowledgements and UBR+ Drop Policies to Improve TCP/UBR Performance over Terrestrial and Satellite Networks," *Proceedings of IC3N '97* (September 1997).

[Goy97-3] Goyal, R. "Improving the Performance of TCP over ATM-UBR Service," to appear in *Computer Communications*. Goyal@cis.ohio-state.edu.

[Kal96-1] Kalyanaraman, S., Jain, R., Fahmy, S., Goyal, R. "Buffer Requirements for TCP/IP over ABR," *Proceedings of IEEE ATM '96* (August 1996).

[Kal96-2] Kalyanaraman, S., Jain, R., Goyal, R., Fahmy, S., Kim, S.C. "Performance of TCP/IP Using ATM ABR or UBR Services over Satellite Networks," *IEEE Communication Society Workshop on Computer-Aided Modelling, Analysis and Design of Communication Links and Networks,* McLean, VA (October 20, 1996).

[Kal98] Kalampoukas, L., Varma, A., Ramakrishnan, K.K. "EWA: Explicit Window Adaptation for Improving TCP Performance," *Proceedings of IEEE Infocom '98*, San Francisco (April 1998), 242–251.

[Kes97] Kessler, G.C. *An Overview of TCP/IP Protocols and the Internet.* Http://www.hill.com/library/tcpip.html.

[Mol95] Moldeklev, K., Gunningberg, P. "How a Large ATM MTU Causes Deadlock in TCP Data Transfer," *IEEE/ACM Transactions on Networking*, vol. 3. no. 4 (August 1995), 409–522.

[RFC1072] *TCP Extensions over Long Delay Paths*, (IETF)-RFC 1072, Internet Engineering Task Force (October 1988).

[RFC1323] *TCP Extensions for High Performance*, (IETF)-RFC 1323, Internet Engineering Task Force (May 1992).

[RFC768] *User Datagram Protocol*, (IETF)-RFC 768, Internet Engineering Task Force (August 1980).

[RFC793] *Transmission Control Protocol*, (IETF)-RFC 793, Internet Engineering Task Force (September 1981).

[RoM95] Romanow, A., Floyd, S. "Dynamics of TCP traffic over ATM networks," *IEEE Journal on Selected Areas in Communications*, vol. 13, no. 4 (May 1995), 633–641.

[Tur95] Turner, J. *Maintaining High Throughput During Overload in ATM Switches*, research report WUCS-95-07, Washington University (April 1995).

[Van98] Vandalore, B., Kalyanaraman, S., Jain, R., Goyal, R., Fahmy, S. "Worst Case Buffer Requirements for TCP over ABR," *Proceedings of SICON '98*, Singapore (June 1998).

CHAPTER 10

Designing Scalable Networks

Designing efficient ATM networks can be challenging. The main challenge lies in ensuring that the design is scalable in terms of call processing capacity and connectivity, which means maximizing the connectivity while minimizing the call processing requirements and complexity. Scalable network design can seamlessly evolve to support increasing demand. This chapter provides an example of how an ATM core network can be designed to ensure scalability. It assumes that the network elements support specific capabilities, such as ABR.

The complexity of implementing all the required traffic management features is proportional to the number of entities (connections) managed and the speed at which they are handled (e.g., link rates).

Optimizing the core network efficiency means attempting to maximize the statistical gains of the high-speed links, by keeping the core links full of "good traffic." In other words, what is carried in the core network is useful to the destination; otherwise it is more efficient to discard it at the edge and let other connections use the network resources. This objective should be achieved while minimizing the probability of rejecting connections, ensuring fair access to bandwidth, and guaranteeing QoS. The efficiency of the core network needs to be evaluated while considering the overall network usage, with all services combined. It is very difficult to ensure high utilization of the links solely with statically allocated bandwidth, since applications rarely use their full traffic descriptors all the time. However, by making good use of the bandwidth-on-demand services, which can take advantage of the unused bandwidth, it is possible to have highly utilized links.

Scalability, complexity, and efficiency issues can be addressed by making efficient use of ATM's virtual path (VP) capability. By designing the core of the network with VP switches, the handling of large number of VCs is restricted to the edge of the network, while providing maximum connectivity.

Figure 10.1 illustrates an example of a network with a VP core and VCs aggregated onto VPs at the edge. The VP switches do not have to terminate the call processing of each single VC. The reduced amount of call processing maximizes fault recovery time by minimizing the rerout-

Figure 10.1.   VP core network and aggregation points. Source: Rosenberg, S., Aissaoui, M.,
Galway, K., and Giroux, N. "Functionality at the Edge: Designing a Scalable
Multi-service ATM Network," *IEEE Communications Magazine*, vol. 36, no. 5
(May 1998), © 1998 IEEE.

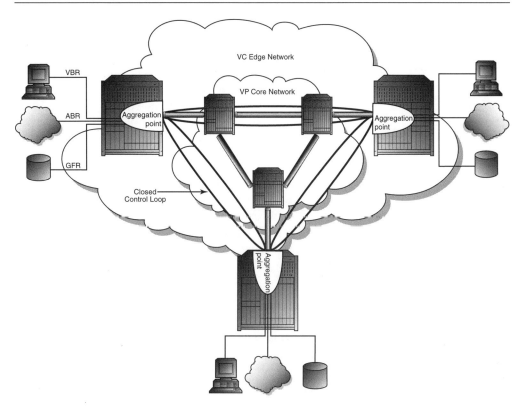

ing delays. Such architecture also simplifies network management, since the management information (e.g., statistics and alarms) is automatically consolidated.

The efficiency of the VP core network depends on which service categories are supported.
A simple approach is to provide a full mesh connectivity for VPs of each service class supported
at the VC level. However, there is no requirement to carry VCs on VPs of the same category.
The complexity of selecting the proper traffic descriptors for each VP at provisioning time, without prior knowledge of the mix of VCs that are dynamically set up and torn down in the VP, can
seriously affect the efficiency of the core network. The use of a smaller number of VP service
categories can further simplify the management of the core network. In fact there is no need to
carry more than two types of VPs in the core, a real-time and a non-real-time VP, as long as they
both provide some minimum bandwidth guarantees. Furthermore, by supporting this minimum
set of VPs, the core network does not need to be upgraded to support the ever-increasing list of
different service categories and protocols. The aggregation function (multiplexing the VCs onto

the VP) can also perform an interworking function (e.g., mapping the service categories and protocol behaviors).

This chapter provides an example how to efficiently assign service categories to the VPs in order to support the various types of service categories that can be offered at the VC level. By reducing the number of services supported, the design and engineering of the VP core network is simplified, allowing for increased connectivity.

The chapter is organized as follows: First, different options for selecting the real-time and non-real-time VP service categories are described. Then the benefits of using an ABR VP to carry all the non-real-time services is discussed, followed by a description of the functionality required at the edge of the VP core network to ensure that the required quality of service is achieved.

Real-Time Traffic

For real-time traffic, it is important to ensure that the mapping onto a VP does not affect the delay and jitter requirements of the individual VCs. Therefore, CBR and rt-VBR VCs can only be carried over a CBR VP in the core of the network without affecting the VC QoS. The nrt-VPs may incur too much delay and jitter, which would affect the underlying real-time VCs. The rt-VBR VCs can be aggregated onto rt-VBR VPs, but CBR VCs may suffer too much jitter if they are aggregated onto a rt-VBR VP. To ensure that the quality of service of the CBR VCs does not suffer because they are carried on a rt-VBR VP, the MBS of the VP needs to be large enough to account for simultaneous arrivals of cells from different VCs and to prevent delaying cells. The large MBS, combined with the fact that buffering is kept small to ensure that the delay requirements are met, means that the virtual bandwidth allocated to the rt-VBR VP is close to the PCR of the VP and that there are no statistical gains achieved. Table 10.1 demonstrates the sensible combinations of real-time VCs onto VPs.

The use of rt-VBR VP allows statistical gains among the VPs in the core. However, as discussed in Chap. 4, statistical gains are more significant when the number of connections is large. Since the number of VPs is relatively low, the gains may not be significant. Also, when a large number of VCs are aggregated onto a VP, it is likely that the bandwidth of the VP is constantly utilized, thus reducing further the potential to achieve statistical gains among different VPs. Therefore, the use of rt-VBR VPs may not increase the efficiency of the core network.

Table 10.1. Possible (✓) combinations of real-time VCs onto VPs.

	CBR VP	rt-VBR VP	nrt-VBR VP	ABR VP	GFR VP	UBR VP
CBR VC	✓	✓	✗	✗	✗	✗
rt-VBR VC	✓	✓	✗	✗	✗	✗

For real-time VPs, the traffic descriptors are defined when the VP is provisioned and the bandwidth is therefore statically allocated (see Chaps. 2 and 4). The VCs of different traffic descriptors are dynamically added and removed from the VP, thus the aggregate traffic characteristics are constantly changing. As a result, the VP needs to be shaped at the aggregation point in order to conform to the VP-level traffic characteristics. The VCs can be added to the VPs until the CAC determines that the VP bandwidth is exhausted. The traffic descriptor of the VP is selected to minimize the bandwidth statically allocated in the core network, while also minimizing the rejection of new connections and delay experienced by the VCs.

Non-Real-Time Traffic

In the case of non-real-time traffic, there can be several different choices of service categories. Table 10.2 demonstrates which types of VCs can be aggregated onto which types of VPs.

Non-real-time applications are bursty by nature and the characterization of their behavior is not a simple task. Thus, provisioning a VP to carry non-real-time VCs can be challenging when the aggregate behavior of a number of bursty sources is not well understood. Determining an adequate traffic descriptor for the VP is crucial for achieving network efficiency while ensuring the QoS objectives of the individual connections.

GFR and UBR VPs cannot be used to aggregate the traffic of nrt-VBR and ABR VCs, because those services offer no quality beyond the minimum guaranteed for the bandwidth used. Furthermore, the frame-discard capability is not available on VP switches. In order to aggregate all non-real-time VCs onto one type of VP, the CBR, VBR, and ABR service categories can be considered:

> **CBR VP** offers non-real-time VCs the highest possible QoS guarantees, far exceeding their requirements. However, this mapping does not permit any statistical gains among the VPs in the core. The bursty nature of ABR and UBR is not accommodated well by this static VP provisioning of bandwidth, as it restricts access to excess bandwidth available in the core. However, if the intensity of the traffic at the VP aggregation point is high and all the VPs in the core have equivalent amounts of traffic, this simple solution may be acceptable and efficient since there may not be much statistical gain to be achieved among the VPs in the core.

Table 10.2. Possible (✓) combinations of non-real-time VCs onto VPs.

	CBR VP	rt-VBR VP	nrt-VBR VP	ABR VP	GFR VP	UBR VP
nrt-VBR VC	✓	✓	✓	✓	✗	✗
ABR VC	✓	✓	✓	✓	✗	✗
GFR VC	✓	✓	✓	✓	✓	✗
UBR VC	✓	✓	✓	✓	✓	✓

rt-VBR VP also offers non-real-time VCs the highest possible QoS guarantees, far exceeding their requirements. Although the use of rt-VBR may allow some statistical gain among the VPs, it is generally limited by the small amount of buffering offered in the core for that type of service. The rt-VBR VP does not make use of the excess network bandwidth efficiently, other than through the use of the tagging function, which may conflict with the minimum bandwidth guarantees of the VCs.

nrt-VBR VP is more efficient than a real-time VP because some statistical multiplexing gain is possible in the core of the network due to large buffers available for this service category. However, it is a complex task to select the proper traffic descriptors for the VP to maximize the number of connections admitted while supporting as many VPs as possible and allowing ABR, GFR, and UBR VCs to maximize the use of the available core bandwidth. This problem becomes more difficult with the increased use of switched connections, which make the dynamics of the aggregate bandwidth characteristics even less predictable. Also, the nrt-VBR VP cannot optimally use the bandwidth dynamically available in the core to distribute it to its underlying bandwidth-on-demand VCs, other than by using the tagging function, which can conflict with the VC-level cell priority. Again, if the amount of statistical gain to be achieved among the VPs is small because of the high intensity of traffic being aggregated on each VP, then the traffic descriptors can be set to a large value, and this solution is acceptable.

ABR VP presents a unique set of characteristics that efficiently carry traffic of all non-real-time services. This solution can be used when the amount of traffic on each VP varies widely, and there could be a lot of statistical gain achieved at the VP level. It is discussed in more detail in the next section.

Using ABR VPs to Carry Non-Real-Time VCs

The ABR VP's control loop is terminated using VP sources and destinations, which can be available at VS/VD points. They can carry non-ABR traffic, as long as there are no real-time requirements. The aggregation point can also terminate or interwork with any other type of flow control methods (e.g., ITU-T ABT—see Appendix A). The ABR VP follows the rules defined for the ABR service category (Chap. 6), the source behavior is performed at the origin of the VP, and the destination behavior is performed at the VP termination point. The ABR VP control loop can be segmented by using VS/VD at any point in the network when the link propagation delay is too long.

The ABR VP is provisioned with a minimum cell rate (MCR), which represents the static bandwidth required for the network to achieve the QoS of the constituent VCs. The setting of this parameter is simple and can be done without prior knowledge of the network dynamics. The CAC generally allows connections to be added to the ABR VP until the sum of the MCRs of the GFR VCs added to the sum of the virtual bandwidths of the nrt-VBR VCs exceeds the MCR of the ABR VP. Since the aggregation point supports large buffer sizes, the virtual bandwidth of the VBR VC can reduce to its SCR, thereby maximizing the statistical gains.

The ABR VP is subject to the ABR flow control mechanism, allowing controlled access to unused bandwidth in the core network while preventing congestion and loss. With this capability the core network can carry traffic that successfully reaches its destination. The cell loss can therefore be controlled in order to meet the requirements of the underlying nrt-VBR VCs. With an explicit rate (ER)-based core network (Chap. 6), this efficiency can be achieved with minimum buffering in the core network, thus increasing the cost effectiveness of the solution. Depending on the ER algorithm implemented in the core nodes, the VP network can allocate the excess bandwidth according to a given fairness policy.

If the core network is designed with GFR VPs, the lack of frame-level discard requires buffer sizes orders of magnitude larger in each queuing point to achieve the same level of performance as observed in the ABR VP case [Ros98]. When carrying TCP-based applications, the buffering requirement for a GFR-based solution increases proportionally with the network round-trip delay, thus not providing a scalable solution. When carrying traffic from non-flow-controlled application (e.g., UDP), the buffering required in the core network elements to achieve a performance comparable to the ABR solution grows without limit as a function of the number of connections (Chap. 9).

This solution requires appropriate handling of the non-real-time VCs at the aggregation point at the edge of the network via proper scheduling and congestion control as discussed below. It does not require the end-systems to support ABR or to be made aware that the core network uses ABR.

VC Intelligence at the Edge

The rationale of the two-services VP core is to move the complexity associated with VC management to the edge of the network. At the edge, lower aggregate bandwidth allows for more cost-effective implementation of sophisticated per-VC intelligent traffic management functions.

The aggregation of non-real-time VCs into an ABR VP is performed at the edge of the core network. At the aggregation point, per-VC scheduling and congestion management are required to isolate different VCs of different service categories and provide fair access to the VP bandwidth. The aggregation function also needs to ensure that the QoS of the VCs is maintained even under the worst-case congestion in the network; that is, the VP obtains only its MCR. The aggregation point therefore needs to apply proper connection admission control (Chap. 4), scheduling (Chap. 5) and per-VC intelligent congestion control (Chap. 7). The implementation of these functions is similar to multiplexing traffic onto a link; however, it has to be capable of handling dynamically varying link rates resulting from the ABR VP allowed-cell-rate value.

Using this model, the congestion encountered in the core network is pushed to the edge without necessarily reaching the actual source of the traffic. Therefore, the aggregation point requires a large amount of buffering in order to be able to absorb the congestion of the core, while continuing to receive traffic from the applications without being able to convey the congestion status of the network to them. However, since the aggregation point is generally handling lower-speed interfaces, the large buffering requirement is still cost effective.

Review

This chapter discusses an example design of a scalable ATM network, achieved by provisioning the core network with two types of VPs, real-time and non-real-time. The utilization of the expensive, high-speed core network links can be maximized, while the available bandwidth is shared fairly and the QoS objectives are met. The VP-level ABR flow control, used for the non-real-time VP, pushes the congestion to the edge of the network and ensures that only traffic that reaches the destination enters the core network. The aggregation function at the edge ensures fairness, isolation, and QoS guarantees. Using CBR VPs to carry all the real-time traffic simplifies the provisioning of the core network but does not affect the capacity of the network, since the non-real-time VP using ABR attempts to use all available bandwidth.

Based on this design, high-capacity core switches can be designed to support only two services, real-time and non-real-time. The core VP switches can use simple weighted round robin (Chap. 5) between the two types of service and can implement an ABR explicit-rate calculation algorithm for the non-real-time traffic. The ER algorithm is performed on a relatively small number of VPs.

Aggregating all non-real-time connections onto a single ABR VP increases the statistical gain of the network core. The network core becomes simple because there is no need for sophisticated per-VC queuing, scheduling, and per-VC congestion management. This architecture reduces the complexity associated with managing the provisioned paths.

Non-real-time applications such as TCP are very bursty and their performance degrades with larger delays. For example, TCP over UBR requires extremely large amounts of buffers in the core as the network round-trip time increases. This problem is controlled with the use of ABR VPs, that minimizes queue buildup in the core. For very large delays, the ABR control loop for the VP can be segmented into smaller loops by adding VS/VD functions in the core.

With a VP-based network consisting of two service categories, the QoS objectives of the end users are achieved while allowing the network to maximize backbone link utilization. The ER-ABR flow control in the core pushes congestion to the edge of the network and the need for frame discard at the VP level is eliminated. The ER-ABR in the core can also allocate unused bandwidth fairly among the VPs, according to a defined fairness policy (e.g., weighted based on MCR). Fairness at the VC level is enforced at the edge of the network where the ABR loop starts and where most of the congestion occurs. At the edge of the network, the isolation between the non-real-time service categories is achieved via proper service scheduling and sophisticated per-VC traffic management functions. These ensure that the VC QoS objectives for the different service categories are achieved. Any unused bandwidth from real-time VPs is made available to the

ABR VP to fully utilize the network capacity. ABR VPs are able to adapt dynamically to the available bandwidth in the network core. Core switches can ultimately be simplified to support only CBR and ABR service categories, thus significantly simplifying the scheduling algorithms and congestion control functionality.

References

[Ros98] Rosenberg, S., Aissaoui, M., Galway, K., and Giroux, N. "Functionality at the Edge: Designing a Scalable Multi-service ATM Network," *IEEE Communications Magazine*, vol. 36, no. 5 (May 1998), 88–90, 95–99.

CHAPTER 11

Summary

Efficient support of multiple services with differing Quality of Service requirements and traffic characteristics requires a networking infrastructure that implements a comprehensive set of traffic management functions.

Quality of service defines among other things the minimum acceptable level of delay and loss performance objectives that the network must meet for each connection.

The ATM networking technology standardizes a complete set of traffic management functions that can be implemented with various levels of complexity to achieve different levels of efficiency. Since it is standardized by the ATM Forum and the ITU-T, ATM networks can interoperate with equipment from multiple vendors.

In a practical network, simply increasing the link bandwidth and providing large amounts of buffering cannot provide for QoS guarantees and differentiation between services. Bandwidth allocation, isolation, scheduling, and congestion control are functions required to achieve this goal. Further efficiency can be achieved by applying flow control.

Because of its fixed-length cells and its set of traffic management capabilities, ATM can guarantee very stringent delay and loss requirements at the cell or frame level while achieving statistical multiplexing gains (Chap. 4). Initially, ATM was intended to support only a basic level of traffic management complexity (e.g., two queues, simple exhaustive scheduler, and small buffers with cell-level priority discard). It was quickly understood, however, that in order to achieve reasonable efficiency *and* stringent QoS guarantees, more sophisticated capabilities were required (e.g., packet-level discard, weighted fair queuing, traffic shaping, per-VC accounting, and explicit-rate calculations for flow control). This complexity is not intrinsic only to ATM; it is required of any technology that aspires to carry traffic efficiently while meeting QoS guarantees. In fact, the implementation of most of the traffic management functions is simplified in ATM because of the short fixed-size cells.

The traffic management capabilities of ATM are applied according to different time scales. The traffic contract (Chap. 3) is established between the user and the network at connection-provisioning time (for permanent connections) or at connection setup (for switched connections).

The *traffic contract* (Chap. 2) defines the type of service, the QoS objectives, and the traffic characteristics of the connection (Chap. 3). The traffic contract is used by the *connection admission control* function (CAC) on a node-by-node basis to allocate sufficient resources to ensure that the QoS objectives are met (Chap. 4).

Once the connection is admitted, the source performs *traffic shaping* in order to ensure that the cell flow conforms to the negotiated traffic contract. This function is important because the network is likely to *police* the cell flow of each connection and discard cells or lower their priority if they do not conform to the traffic contract. The policing function helps ensure that a connection cannot keep other connections from achieving their QoS objectives. Instead of applying a strict policing function, the network can *reshape* the traffic at any point to ensure that accumulated jitter does not affect the QoS of any connections (Chap. 3).

Once a cell is admitted into the network, it passes through multiple contention points prior to reaching its destination. A contention point occurs wherever the short-term demand for a resource (e.g., bandwidth) exceeds its capacity. The contention point needs to *buffer* the contending cells into a queuing structure that preserves the QoS requirements of the different types of connections (Chap. 5). The queuing structure may consist of multiple queues that store the cells and maintain cell ordering. A queue may store cells from one or more connections. A *scheduling* function determines which cell can next acquire the resource. The scheduling function is also designed to ensure that the QoS objectives are achieved, while it divides the dynamically available bandwidth fairly among the queues.

Even if enough bandwidth is allocated by the CAC and proper scheduling is applied among the queues, the buffering may not be sufficient to handle transient congestion. In this situation, congestion control techniques such as priority discard and packet discard (Chap. 7) are utilized in order to handle the transient congestion. Some level of intelligence, such as per-VC accounting, can be applied to the congestion control to increase the fairness. For AAL-5 traffic, it is more efficient to apply frame-level discard than to carry cells that are to be discarded by the reassembly function. Priority discard may also be useful for video or voice applications.

When the ABR service is used (Chap. 6), the ATM network provides feedback information to the traffic source (or virtual source) in order to control the flow of the traffic into the network and prevent cell loss within the ATM network.

The ITU-T and ATM Forum define the behavior of the traffic management mechanisms without mandating a specific implementation [TM4.0, I.371]. The implementation has to comply with the behavioral restrictions (e.g., to meet the delay requirements of the CBR traffic) in order to ensure interoperability. However, the flexibility allowed by the standards gives equipment manufacturers a lot of latitude when implementing the various traffic management functions. This book discusses a spectrum of implementations related to each TM function. The complexity and accuracy of the implementation directly impacts the cost of the equipment and the efficiency of the network, and can serve as criteria for distinguishing among manufacturers. A careful balance needs to be established in designing equipment and networks.

Networks do not need to provide all the services defined in Chap. 2. At one extreme, a network could support only the CBR service and map all the connections to that service. Such a network generally does not allow for statistical gains (other than through overbooking) and leads to low link efficiency. Another extreme might be a network that offers multiple classes for each of the service categories. Such a network can achieve higher statistical gains but also added cost and greater complexity. A network needs to offer a set of services sufficient to support the QoS requirements of the targeted applications while allowing the network to achieve reasonable "goodput." The goodput represents the ability of the network to maximize link utilization while carrying only data that is useful at the destination and needs not be retransmitted. For example, a network which mainly supports IP traffic and voice traffic could offer only CBR and GFR, without supporting VBR. Marketing, tarrifing, and billing issues are important factors in the decision which services to deploy.

Evolution of ATM Traffic Management

ATM traffic management has evolved considerably over the last decade. It now offers a comprehensive set of functions that can be combined to design efficient networks. The standards organization and the ATM Forum are currently focusing on the issues that require immediate consideration (e.g., GFR and alignment between ITU-T and ATM Forum), so no new services or functionality are expected in the near future.

However, there is still a lot of research related to more cost-effective, feasible, and efficient implementations of the various TM functions. The new implementations should provide flexible and fair allocation of buffers and bandwidth. Increased flexibility permits support of varied policies and might allow logical grouping of VCs for bandwidth and buffer allocation (e.g., all the VCs of a customer obtain some percentage of the bandwidth).

Finally, network-level issues such as network design, end-to-end performance, and QoS-based routing for the P-NNI protocol [PNNI1.0], as well as load-based routing and rerouting, are also being researched.

Meanwhile, technological advances will allow manufacturers to increase the complexity and flexibility of the systems cost effectively without sacrificing scalability.

References

[I.371] ITU-Telecommunication Standardization Sector. *Traffic Control and Congestion Control in B-ISDN*, recommendation I.371 (May 1996).

[PNNI1.0] The ATM Forum Technical Committee. *Private Network-Network Interface Specification*, version 1.0 (1996).

[TM4.0] The ATM Forum Technical Committee. *Traffic Management Specification*, version 4.0, af-tm-0056.000 (April 1996).

ITU-T Traffic Management Standard

This book focuses on the TM4.0 specification and uses its terminology. The [I.371] combined with [I.173.1] and [I.356] are the ITU-T standards covering material similar to the TM4.0 specification. Both documents cover a common set of features and each one has some unique functions. For the set of common features, the requirements are compatible although the terminology may be different. As with the ATM Forum, the ITU-T does not standardize the CAC, queuing, and scheduling functions. This appendix attempts to identify the main differences between the two specifications.

Traffic Contract

An ATM Forum traffic contract is defined in terms of a service category, a conformance definition, and negotiated QoS parameters, while an ITU-T traffic contract is defined in terms of an ATM transfer capability (ATC) [I.371] and an appropriate QoS class [I.356].

The ATC specifies a combination of traffic parameters and the accompanying conformance definitions along with other potential behaviors (e.g., flow control). The service category specifies which QoS parameters are applicable, and the minimum acceptable value of these parameters are requested at call set-up. The ATC does not specify related QoS parameters. The QoS class defines the subset of ATM performance parameters that apply to the connection [I.356]. Therefore, any QoS class can theoretically be used with any ATC, although some combinations do not make sense. An ATM Forum service category, together with a conformance definition and the negotiated QoS objectives, is loosely speaking the equivalent of an ATC associated with a QoS class.

The ITU-T and ATM Forum traffic contracts that can be specified at a UNI and NNI can be compared as sketched in Table A.1.

Table A.1 identifies that, for the time being, the ITU-T does not support the equivalent of the VBR.2 and VBR.3 conformance definitions for the rt-VBR, nor the UBR.2 conformance definition. The UBR service is mapped as the DBR ATC because they both describe the PCR of

Table A.1. Relationship between [I.371] and [TM4.0] traffic contracts.

TM4.0 service category	Conformance definition	ATM transfer capability	QoS class
Constant bit rate (CBR)	CBR	Deterministic bit rate (DBR)	1
real-time variable bit rate (VBR)	VBR.1	Statistical bit rate1 (SBR1)	1
	VBR.2	Statistical bit rate2 (SBR2)	4 (under study)
	VBR.3	Statistical bit rate3 (SBR3)	4 (under study)
non-real-time variable bit rate (VBR)	VBR.1	Statistical bit rate1 (SBR1)	2
	VBR.2	Statistical bit rate2 (SBR2)	3
	VBR.3	Statistical bit rate3 (SBR3)	3
Available bit rate (ABR)	ABR	Available bit rate (ABR)	3 or Unspecified
Unspecified bit rate (UBR)	UBR.1	Deterministic bit rate (DBR)	Unspecified
	UBR.2	Not included	
Not included		ATM block transfer (ABT)	1
Generic frame rate (GFR)	GFR.1	Generic frame rate (GFR)	3 or Unspecified
	GFR.2	Generic frame rate (GFR)	3 or Unspecified

the aggregate cells as the traffic descriptors. The combination of DBR with an unspecified QoS class is equivalent to the UBR.1 service.

In the ATM Forum, the ABR conformance definition is network specific, and example implementations of a dynamic GCRA (D-GCRA) are provided. In ITU-T, the ABR conformance definition is standardized to a D-GCRA for the explicit-rate mode; there is no conformance definition for the binary mode.

The guaranteed frame rate (GFR) service is being developed in parallel by both organizations and should be included in the next versions of both documents.

Traffic Descriptors

The [I.371] uses the same traffic descriptors as [TM4.0] and the same terminology.

QoS Parameters

The ITU-T does not currently support the capability of signaling individual QoS parameters. Furthermore, the [I.356] currently defines the CTD as the average of the cell transfer delay, as opposed to the maximum CTD, as described in Chap. 2.

The CDV in [I.356] is not expressed in terms of the peak-to-peak CDV but uses a two-point CDV measurement as described in Chap. 2. This difference may have an impact on the completion of a call set-up message, since the definition of the QoS objective is different in the case of a network that mixes network elements, some compliant with the ATM Forum, others with ITU-T.

Conformance

The conformance definitions are equivalent for the same services supported, except for rt-VBR and UBR, as discussed in the traffic contract section. However, the CDVT is defined separately for PCR and SCR in the ITU-T. Additionally, the ITU-T allows for explicit signaling of the CDVT parameters.

Policing

The policing functionality is the same in both [TM4.0] and [I.371]. However, the ITU-T also recommends accuracy requirements for the policing function [I.371, Appendix IV].

Traffic Shaping

Traffic shaping is optional in both [TM4.0] and [I.371].

ABR Flow Control

The [I.371] specifies an ABR flow control mechanism that is equivalent to [TM4.0]. The [I.371] does not include the same level of implementation details, but the requirements are compatible. That is, an implementation based on [TM4.0] is also compliant with the [I.371] requirements. The level of details provided by the ATM Forum includes specific actions that the source, destination, and network must do. The ITU-T provides a high-level description of the required behavior and is currently working on a formal conformance definition. Therefore [TM4.0] specifies many ABR operating parameters, as defined in Chap. 6, that are not considered by [I.371].

ABT Transfer Capability

The [I.371] standardizes the ATM block transfer (ABT). The ABT is an ATC that is not supported by the ATM Forum [TM4.0]. The ABT is a protocol based on the concept of fast reservation of bandwidth.

The ABT uses resource management cells (RM) with a protocol ID different from that of ABR. A connection using the ABT protocol transfers the information by *block of a given number of cells*. The block is delineated by a leading RM cell and a trailing RM cell. The block of cells is sent to the network at a particular block cell rate (BCR). The leading RM cell is used to specify the BCR. The BCR is the rate at which cells are shaped for the duration of the block.

The traffic descriptors for an ABT connection include a PCR and, optionally, SCR and MBS. Additionally, the maximum rate of renegotiation of the rate is also provided in terms of the PCR of the RM cells (PCR_{RM}). There is no tagging option supported with the service.

The ABT protocol supports two modes of operation:

Delayed Transmission (ABT-DT). Under this mode of operation, the source cannot transmit the block of cells at a BCR higher than the previous BCR until the RM cell has returned from the network (i.e., the egress UNI) with an acknowledgment that the requested BCR, or some acceptable value, has been allocated. Once the acknowledgment is received, the cells are shaped into the network at the BCR rate, and the network is guaranteed a CLR equivalent to the CBR service. If the acknowledgment is negative, the source can retry, but not earlier than $1/PCR_{RM}$ units of time. It takes at least one round-trip delay before the source can transmit a block of cells at a rate higher than the rate previously allocated.

Immediate Transmission (ABT-IT). With immediate transmission, the source sends the RM cell and immediately follows it with the data cells shaped at the requested BCR. If one node in the path cannot support the block, all the cells from the block are dropped by that node. The resources used by the previous nodes are wasted, but the entire block is discarded. This behavior is similar in GFR and UBR; however, ABT-IT drops an entire group of cells (e.g., a frame) without having to look at the AAL information. The source can send continuous blocks of cells (i.e., within the limits imposed by PCR_{RM}) without any reception of an acknowledgment from the network.

The ABT is currently not defined for use with point-to-multipoint connections. The ABT protocol cannot guarantee access to the required cell rate when the RM cell is received. If sufficient bandwidth is pre-allocated, the bandwidth may be available within a bounded time. When more bandwidth is pre-allocated to the connection, it is likelier that the negotiation will succeed within a short time frame. To ensure that the negotiation is not rejected or does not result in a reduction of bandwidth, the PCR needs to be allocated, in which case the overhead required by the protocol is not necessary (i.e., CBR achieves a better performance).

In the case of ABT, the performance is measured at the block level. Some performance considerations, similar to the ones discussed for ABR (Chap. 6), include:

- Level of fairness achieved when allocating bandwidth to different blocks.
- Block blocking (ABT-DT) or block loss (ABT-IT) probability (or probability of denying a request for transmission or reducing the rate) as a function of the amount of bandwidth allocated.
- Capacity for handling requests for block transfer (maximum request rate) and complexity of the mechanisms for allocating the PCR_{RM} to prevent overflow of the RM processors.

It is also unclear how the ABT and ABR protocols can efficiently coexist at the same contention point.

Congestion Control

Both [TM4.0] and [I.371] include the optional use of the concept of *priority discard*. The [I.371] is in the process of including the *frame discard* concept. Other congestion control mechanisms are not included in either specification and are implementation specific.

References

[I.356] ITU-Telecommunication Standardization Sector. *B-ATM Layer Cell Transfer Performance*, recommendation I.356 (October 1996).

[I.371] ITU-Telecommunication Standardization Sector. *Traffic Control and Congestion Control in B-ISDN*, recommendation I.371 (May 1996).

[I.371.1] ITU-Telecommunication Standardization Sector. *Traffic Control and Congestion Control in B-ISDN-ABR and ABT Conformance Definitions*, recommendation I.371.1 (June 1997).

[TM4.0] The ATM Forum Technical Committee. *Traffic Management Specification*, version 4.0, af-tm-0056.000 (April 1996).

ABR Implementation Comparisons

This appendix illustrates the performance of different ABR implementations. As discussed in Chap. 6, the ABR flow control mechanism involves the cooperation of the source, the switch, and the destination. There are many parameters associated with the ABR flow control. Some of these parameters are signaled, while others are various engineering parameters. The performance of a chosen configuration depends on the setting of these parameters. Although there are many possible enumerations with various parameter settings, this appendix shows only a few examples illustrative of the expected performance of ABR flow control schemes. Note that the presented performance results can also be tweaked by using a different set of parameters.

In the following sections, both binary ABR and explicit rate ABR performance are presented. First, a binary ABR simulation model is discussed, followed by an explicit rate ABR model. For the binary ABR, a single-node network is considered, and for the explicit rate ABR, a network of ABR switches is used.

Binary ABR

In this section, the binary ABR (BABR) and Relative Rate ABR (RRABR) flow control mechanisms are simulated and studied. The network under test is illustrated in Fig. B.1. Here, D_1 through D_4 represent the link delays between the various sources and the switch. The application modeled is an FTP application. In particular, the source models represent greedy FTP sources, which always send traffic to the destination. The greedy FTP source provides a worst-case scenario for the study.

The following parameters are assumed for the simulation:

- All delays D_i are assumed to be uniform and equal to 12 msec (milli-seconds).
- The link speed is assumed to be about 149.6 Mbits/s (OC-3).
- The TCP maximum window size is assumed to be 900 Kbytes, equal to the bandwidth delay product for OC-3 with a round trip delay of 48 msec ($2 \times (D_1 + D_5)$).

Figure B.1. Test network BABR, RRABR.

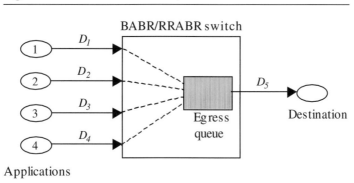

- PDU size is 1536 bytes.
- The buffer sizes at the egress queue is assumed to be 4000 cells and the EFCI threshold is assumed to be 25 percent of the buffer size.
- Other parameters are set as: RIF = 0.03125, RDF = CDF = 0.0625, and TBE = 32.

Simple EFCI

Figure B.2 demonstrates the behavior of ACR under the simple EFCI scheme. Under the simulation assumptions, the problems noted in this algorithm include rate oscillations and slow

Figure B.2. ACR trace for EFCI—5 sec.

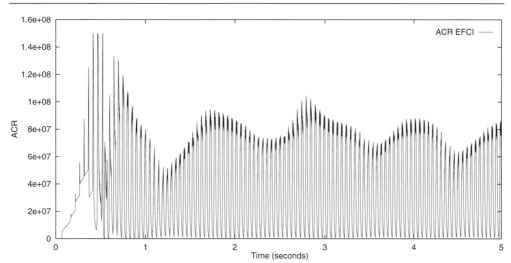

convergence, explained in detail below. Note that, ideally, with all four sources equally utilizing the OC-3 link at the destination, each source would have an ACR of (OC-3)/4 = 37.4 Mbps.

Figure B.2 shows the ACR of a VC over a period of 5 seconds. It shows that ACR is very periodic. Figure B.3 shows ACR of a VC over a period of approximately 1.00 second. Congestion is detected at 0.48 seconds. Consequently, the EFCI bit is set in data, and the RM cell in the forward direction. The RM cells ahead of this congestion cause ACR to increase at approximately 0.52 seconds. After the ACR increase and before the ensuing congestion-induced decrease in ACR, CRM causes a slight decrease in ACR as defined in source behavior #6 (see Chapter 6). A good example of CRM decrease is seen from 0.60 to 0.62 seconds. It takes approximately 3/4 RTT (0.036 seconds) before the congestion indicator returns to the source. It can be seen that under this simulation setup, the EFCI algorithm causes the ACR to oscillate. The following pattern can be observed for the duration of the simulation:

1. Congestion occurs in the switch. Cells have their EFCI bits marked.
2. ACR increases due to RM cells with CI = 0 already in the backward direction.
3. CRM decreases ACR to a moderate value.
4. ACR decreases to a very low value due to congestion indication.

Rate oscillations lead to slow convergence, which in turn affects the network utilization. Further, it may cause cell/packet loss when a sudden burst arrives at a high rate. The "goodput" for simple EFCI under the simulation assumptions is about 89 percent.

Figure B.3.   ACR trace for EFCI—1 sec.

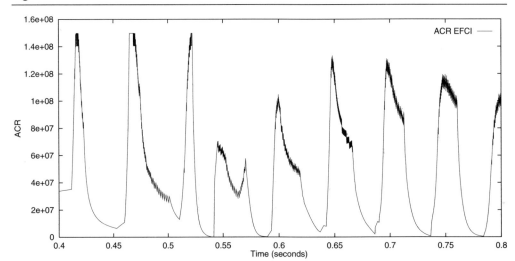

Backward Marking of the CI Bit

Figure B.4 and Fig. B.5 demonstrate the behavior of ACR when this algorithm is used. Under the simulation assumptions, the problems noted in this algorithm include a low TCP goodput, explained in detail below.

Figure B.4. ACR trace for backward marking of the CI bit—5 sec.

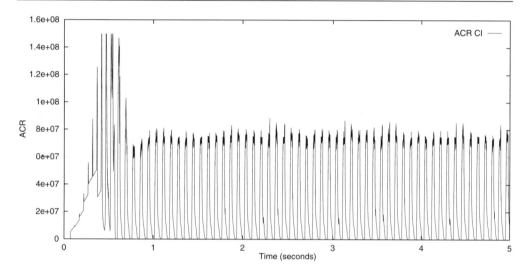

Figure B.5. ACR detailed trace for backward marking of the CI bit.

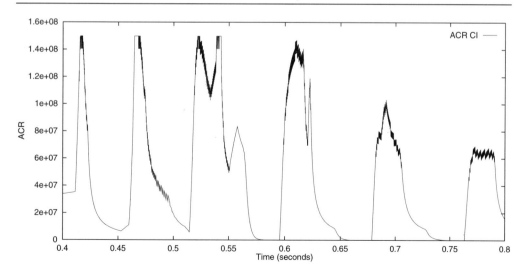

This algorithm results in a lower goodput of (69 percent) than the simple EFCI algorithm due to the following behavior: Congestion is first detected at the 0.50 second mark. The algorithm settles into a pattern after 0.60 seconds. At about 0.67 seconds, ACR increases due to a no-congestion indication from the RM cells. After reaching the peak ACR, the CRM mechanism reduces the ACR to a low value (less than 30 Mbps) at approximately 0.71 seconds. At that time, congestion occurs in the switch. ACR is at a low value already, plus it only takes 1/4 RTT before the congestion notification is relayed to the source, causing a further ACR reduction. The ACR stays at a lower value for a longer time when compared to EFCI. Consequently, a lower average ACR is observed, which causes lower goodput than simple EFCI.

EFCI and Backward Marking of the CI Bit

Figure B.6 and Figure B.7 illustrate the behavior of ACR under this algorithm. Under the simulation assumptions, the problems noted in this algorithm include cell loss, low TCP goodput, and slow reaction to switch congestion, as explained in detail below.

Cell loss occurred at the 2-second mark in Fig. B.6. All VCs lost back-to-back packets. As a result, all TCP sources were forced to time out. No data was transmitted between 2.0 to 4.5 seconds. Implementing EFCI and setting the CI bit in the backward direction causes a double reduction of ACR for each congestion period. The pattern observed above shows that the double reduction of ACR extends over a much longer period of time (approximately 4 times greater) than EFCI alone. Due to this ACR double reduction, the occupancy of the output buffer is very

Figure B.6. ACR trace for EFCI and backward marking of the CI bit—5 sec.

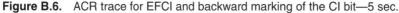

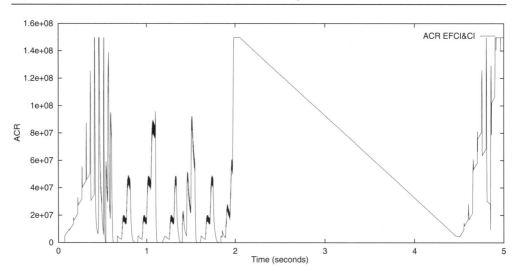

Figure B.7. ACR trace for EFCI and backward marking of the CI bit.

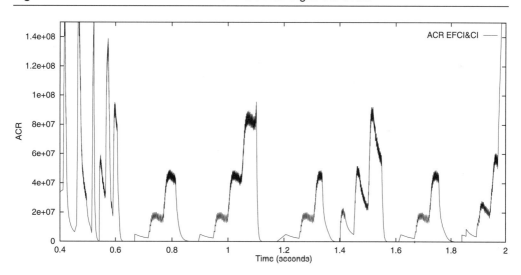

low, which allows ACR to increase in steps (1.40 to 1.55 seconds). The ACR is allowed to increase for a longer period before congestion is detected than with simple EFCI. Because of the large link delays and the ACR increase over a long period, the output buffer of the switch becomes overwhelmed by the number of cells received. It takes too long to slow the sources through backward marking of the CI bit. Therefore, cell loss occurs. Goodput is lower (45 percent) than EFCI because cell loss occurred.

EFCI and Backward Marking of the NI Bit

Figure B.8 illustrates the behavior of ACR under this algorithm. Under the simulation assumptions, the problems noted with this algorithm include cell loss, low TCP goodput, and slow reaction to switch congestion, as explained in detail below.

In Figure B.8, cell loss occurred at the 1-second mark. All VCs lost back-to-back packets. As a result, all TCP sources were forced to time out. No data was transmitted between 1.0 to 3.5 seconds. It can be seen from Fig. B.9 that ACR has a large period of growth of 0.1 seconds, from 0.7 to 0.8 seconds. Similar to the EFCI-with-CI-backward-marking case, ACR is allowed to increase for a larger period of time before the source reacts to congestion at the switch. Consequently, cell loss occurs because it takes too long to signal the source to decrease ACR. Goodput is lower (47 percent) than EFCI because of cell loss.

Figure B.8.   ACR trace for EFCI and backward marking of the NI bit—5 sec.

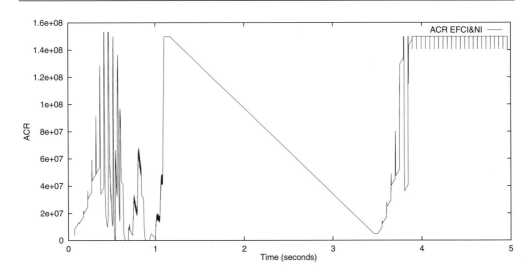

Figure B.9.   ACR trace for EFCI and backward marking of the NI bit.

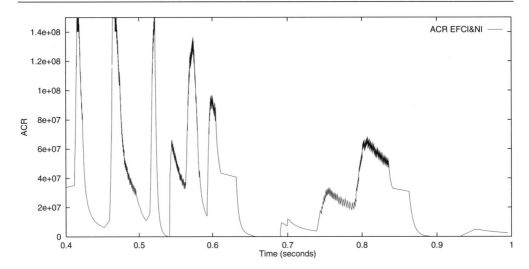

Explicit Rate ABR

The network under test is chosen so that the benefits of achieving global fairness can be illustrated. Specifically, the goal is to attain network-wide max-min fairness by allocating an equal share of bandwidth for each connection traversing a contention point. Figure B.10 illustrates the test network. The test network exhibits both upstream and downstream congestion. The transmission rate for links 1, 2, and 3 is represented by *LR* and is set to the OC-3 rate. The following inequalities must hold:

$$BW_1 + \ldots + BW_{16} \leq LR,$$

$$BW_{15} + \ldots + BW_{19} \leq LR,$$

$$BW_{19} + \ldots + BW_{26} \leq LR.$$

Under equal-share allocation policy (i.e., max-min global fairness), with all sources active, the sources get the following bandwidth allocation:

- Sources 1 through 16 each allocated *LR*/16.
- Sources 17 and 18 each allocated 3*LR*/8.
- Sources 19 through 26 each allocated *LR*/8.

Max-Min Computation Details

Link 1 is utilized by S1 through S16, thus each gets equal share of *LR*/16 at link 1. Link 2 is utilized by S15 through S19. Equal share gives each source a bandwidth of *LR*/5. However, S15 and S16 were only allocated *LR*/16 at link 1 and therefore bottlenecked at link 1. Thus, available bandwidth at link 2 for S17 through S19 is *LR*–2 × *LR*/16 = 7*LR*/8, so that each of S17 through S19 is allocated 7*LR*/24 at link 2. Link 3 is utilized by S19 through S26. Equal share gives each source a bandwidth of *LR*/8. Taking into account the previous allocation for S19, the link 3 allocation for S19 is the minimum of (7*LR*/24, *LR*/8) = LR/8. The available

Figure B.10. Test network.

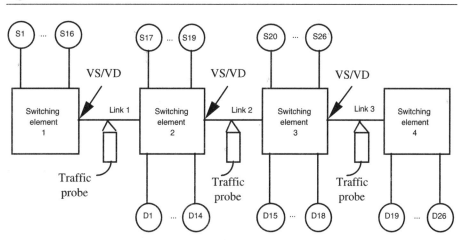

bandwidth for S17 and S18 at link 2 would therefore be $7LR/8 - LR/8 = 6LR/8$, so that each of S17 and S18 are allocated $3LR/8$.

An ER algorithm that does not respond to source utilization measures (i.e., does not achieve global fairness) but allocates equal share for each link achieves the following allocation:

- Sources 1 through 16 each allocated $LR/16$.
- Sources 17, 18, and 19 each allocated $LR/5$.
- Sources 20 through 26 each allocated $LR/8$.

It is clear from this simple example that a network employing switches without global (or network-wide) fairness capability will exhibit high under-utilization in certain scenarios. In this example, link 2 would be underutilized by $7LR/20$ ($= 2 \times 3LR/8 - 2 \times LR/5$); that is, link 2 is utilized only to up to 65 percent.

All simulations are conducted using the equal-share for local fair-share calculation. That is, each source is assigned the same bandwidth at a contention point. Sources 1 through 26 are modeled as greedy sources, taking up all the bandwidth given by the network. Performance is analyzed both with and without VSVD points, as explained below. Frame (i.e., AAL5-type) simulations are not performed here. Three traffic probes are placed on the links connecting the switching elements, which monitor the attained per-VC rates.

Under max-min fairness, with all sources active, sources obtain the following bandwidth allocation for a link rate of OC3. Sources 1 to 16 are each allocated $LR/16$ ($= 22076$ cells/s at OC3); sources 17 and 18 are each allocated $3LR/8$ ($= 132453$ cells/s at OC3) and sources 19 to 26 are each allocated $LR/8$ ($= 44150$ cells/s at OC3). For this evaluation, the network is simulated under the following assumptions:

1. No link delays in the network. This gives us how fast the algorithm converges in a network scenario. Link delays are considered in later parts of the simulations.
2. Sources are greedy and take whatever the network allocates to them.
3. Per-VC queuing is implemented, with a round-robin scheduling implemented among the contending VCs. A per-VC buffer of 100 cells is used.
4. The four algorithms considered are BT-1, BT-2, DRA, and CB.
5. The other parameters used are RIF = 0.03125, RDF = CDF = 0.0625

With these assumptions in mind, the four algorithms are compared below for the ACR achieved by three cell sources. Source 1 with a max-min allocation of 22076 cells/s, source 17 with a max-min allocation of 132453 cells/s and source 26 with a max-min allocation of 44150 cells/s in Fig. B.11, Fig. B.12, and Fig. B.13, respectively.

Figure B.11. ER comparison for source 1 (BW = 22076 cells/s).

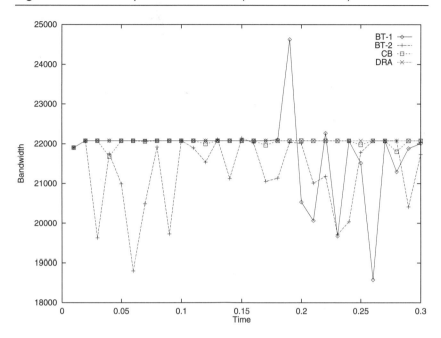

Figure B.12. ER comparison for source 17 (BW = 132453 cells/s).

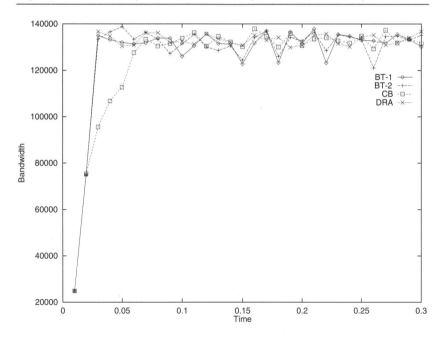

Figure B.13.   ER comparison for source 26 (BW = 44150 cells/s).

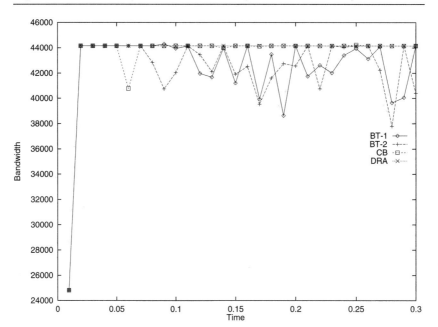

- At a cell buffer size of 100 for each VC, some cell loss is observed for both BT-1 and BT-2, with BT-1 having a much higher cell loss. No cell loss occurred for DRA and CB. Figure B.14 compares CB and DRA for source 26.
- When the buffer size is increased to 1000, no cell loss occurred for BT-2, but a small cell loss occurred in BT-1. Figures B.15 and B.16 illustrate this behavior of BT-1 and BT-2 with various buffer sizes. It can be observed that there is a marginal improvement in the bandwidth achieved due to decrease in cell loss. Otherwise, they perform similarly in both cases.

VS/VD Coupling

For the VS/VD simulation, three VS/VD points shown in Fig. B.10 are used. The simulation model incorporates the source and destination behavior at the VS/VD. The VS points include shapers that shape the traffic to ECR. In this simulation, only the link delays on links 1, 2, and 3 interconnecting the switching elements 1, 2, 3, and 4 are considered. In additoin to the general simulation assumptions described earlier, a one-way link delay of 10 ms on each link direction is also considered.

Figure B.14. CB & DRA comparison for source 26 (BW = 44150 cells/s).

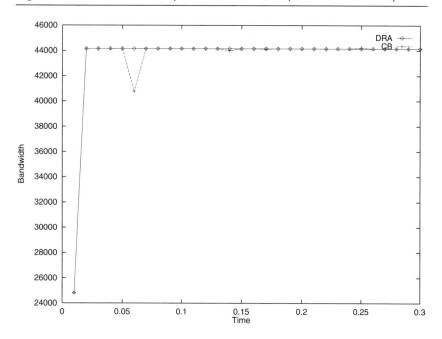

Figure B.15. BT-2 performance for variable per-VC buffer size for source 26.

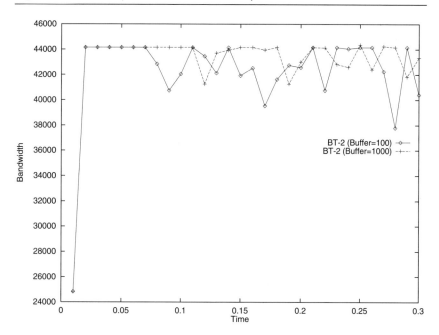

Figure B.16. BT-1 performance for variable per-VC buffer size for source 26.

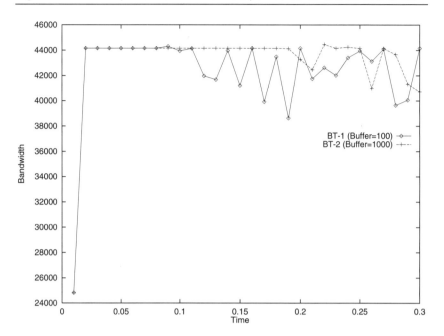

The ATM Forum source rules do not explicitly specify how to take care of the local congestion at a VS point. The local congestion can be taken care of by setting the shaping rate to *min* (*BER*, *ACR*, *OCR*). This way, if the OCR is the max-min (bottleneck) rate, the shaping rate will be immediately set to this rate (tight coupling). The results presented in this appendix employ just such a technique, where it can be observed that the shaping rate immediately adjusts to the local bottleneck rate under congestion. For CB, such local information cannot be coupled in the shaping rate. Otherwise, the incoming rates match the outgoing rates and the CB may not be able to achieve global fairness, as the queue length lies in the dead-band region, where the OBW calculation is not modified. Such modification is included for CB in these simulations. Due to this, there is a possibility that some of the connections may be shaped at a much higher rate.

Figure B.17 does an ER comparison for source 1 with 10ms delay. Since this VC is originating on the first switch, which is also a bottleneck node for this VC, a very normal behavior is noted for this VC. Figure B.18 compares source 17 with 10ms delay. This source is originated and bottlenecked at switch 2. With larger delays, this VC gets its max-min bandwidth after some time. Initially all the VCs passing through switch 2 get equal share. Figure B.19 compares source 26, which is originated and bottlenecked at switch 3. For large delays, both BT-1 and BT-2 give lower

Figure B.17.   ER comparison for source 1 with VS/VD and delay = 10 ms.

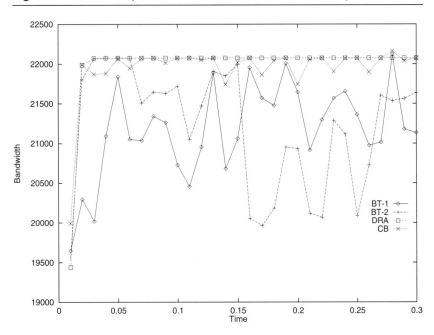

Figure B.18.   ER comparison for source 17 with VS/VD and delay = 10 ms.

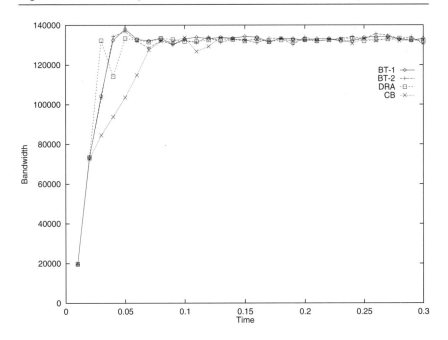

Figure B.19. ER comparison for source 26 with VS/VD and delay = 10 ms.

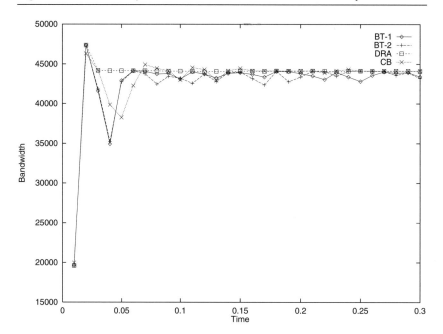

than max-min due to source 19. Source 19 is originating on switch 2 but terminating on Switch 4 and passes through switch 3. For this source, switch 3 is the bottleneck node. However, due to long propagation delay, the backward coupling takes a while to reach. This causes switch 2 to give equal share bandwidth of about 100K cells/s to this connection, whereas its max-min bandwidth is 44150 cells/s. This can be seen in Fig. B.20 at probe 2. From these simulations it can be concluded that:

* DRA outperforms the remaining three algorithms in the large network delay scenario. In this case, the DRA does not bear down other connections if one connection is transmitting at more than its share.
* With delays, VS/VD points, and shaping BT-1, BT-2, and CB perform alike.

Figure B.20. ER comparison for source 19 at probe 2 with VS/VD and delay = 10 ms.

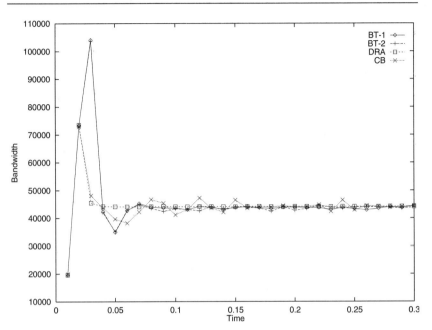

AAL   The ATM Adapation Layer allows multiple applications to have data converted to and from the ATM cell. A protocol used that translates higher-layer services into the size and format of an ATM cell.

AAL-1 The ATM Adaptation Layer Type 1 provides functions in support of constant-bit-rate, time-dependent traffic such as voice and video.

AAL-5 The ATM Adaptation Layer Type 5 provides functions in support of variable-bit-rate, delay-tolerant connection-oriented data traffic requiring minimal sequencing or error detection support.

ABR   The Available Bit Rate is an ATM-layer service category that specifies a flow control mechanism to react to the load feedback provided by the network.

ABT   The ATM Block Transfer is an ITU-T ATM transfer capability. A connection using the ABT protocol transfers the information by *block of a given number of cells* delineated by resource management cells.

ACK   The Acknowledgments sent by the receiver of a transmission control protocol session.

ACR   The Allowed Cell Rate is an ABR service parameter; ACR is the current rate in cells/sec at which a source is allowed to send.

ADTF The ACR Decrease Time Factor is the time permitted between sending RM cells before the rate is decreased to ICR (initial cell rate). The ADTF range is 0.01 to 10.23 sec with granularity of 10 ms.

AINI The ATM Inter-Network Interface (AINI) is the interface between two networks (private or public) implementing the P-NNI protocol.

AIR   The Additive Increase Rate is an ABR service parameter. The AIR controls the rate at which the cell transmission rate increases. It is signaled as AIRF, where AIRF = AIR $\times$ Nrm/PCR.

AIRF The Additive Increase Rate Factor: Refer to AIR.

ATC   The ATM Transfer Capability is the ITU-T term that specifies a combination of traffic parameters and the accompanying conformance definitions, along with potential other behaviors (e.g., flow control). Contrary to the service categories, the ATC does not include the QoS class.

ATM   A switching/transmission technology that employs 53-byte cells as a basic unit of transfer. The ATM cell is divided into 5 bytes of ATM-layer overhead and 48 bytes of ATM payload. ATM is fundamentally statistical in nature, with many "virtual circuits" sharing bandwidth.

AUU   ATM-layer-user-to-ATM-layer-user (AUU) bit is the end-of-packet (refer to EOP) indicator set in AAL5 packets.

Bc   Frame Relay Committed Burst. Size of the burst that the frame relay network commits to carry with low loss probability.

Be   Frame Relay Excess Burst. Amount of excess traffic that the network may carry on a best-effort basis.

BECN   The ATM Backward Explicit Congestion Notification is a resource management (RM) cell type, generated by the network or the destination, indicating congestion or approaching congestion for traffic flowing in the direction opposite that of the BECN cell. In frame relay, the BECN is a bit in the frame header, that indicates congestion has occurred in the forward direction of the connection.

B-ICI   The B-ISDN Inter-Carrier Interface is an ATM-Forum-defined specification for the interface between public ATM networks to support user services across multiple public carriers.

B-ISSI   The Broadband Inter-Switching System Interface is the interface between two switches.

BN   The BN bit of the ABR resource management (RM) cell indicates whether the cell has been generated by the network or the destination (BN = 1) or whether it is an RM cell generated by the source (refer to BECN).

BRM Cell   Backward RM cell. Refer to RM cell.

BT   The Burst Tolerance applies to ATM connections supporting VBR services and is a limit parameter of the GCRA that relates to the maximum burst size (MBS).

CAC The Connection Admission Control is defined as the set of actions taken by the network during the call setup phase (or during call renegotiation phase) in order to determine whether a connection request can be accepted or should be rejected (or whether a request for reallocation can be accommodated).

CBR The Constant Bit Rate service category provides a constant or guaranteed rate to transport services such as video or voice, as well as to circuit emulation, which requires rigorous timing control and performance levels.

CCR The Current Cell Rate is a field in the ABR RM cell that is set by the source to indicate its current ACR when it generates a forward RM cell. This field may be used to facilitate the calculation of ER and may not be changed by network elements. CCR is formatted as a rate.

CDF The Cutoff Decrease Factor is an ABR parameter that is used as part of the function to control the decrease in ACR (allowed cell rate). This parameter applies to the binary mode of ABR.

CDV The Cell Delay Variation is a component of the cell transfer delay induced by buffering and cell scheduling that introduces variations in the traffic characteristics. When cells from two or more ATM connections are multiplexed, cells of a given ATM connection may be delayed while cells of another ATM connection are being inserted at the output of the multiplexer. Similarly, some cells may be delayed while physical-layer-overhead or OAM cells are inserted. Consequently, some randomness may affect the interarrival time between consecutive cells of a connection (refer to P2P-CDV).

CDVT The Cell Delay Variation Tolerance represents the limit on the cell clumping tolerated by the policing function in the network. The CDVT is not a parameter that represents the behavior of the traffic when it is generated. It is used to account for jitter (CDV) that may have accumulated upstream from the policing function.

CER The Cell Error Ratio represents the ratio of errored cells in a transmission in relation to the total cells sent in a transmission. The measurement is taken over a time interval and is best measured on an in-service circuit.

CET The Cell Emission Time represents the departure time of a cell at a shaping function.

CI The Congestion Indicator is a field in an ABR RM cell used to cause the source to decrease its ACR. The source sets CI = 0 when it sends an RM cell; the destination sets

CI to one in the return RM cells to indicate that one or many forward data cells were received with the EFCI bit set to one.

CIR   The Committed Information Rate is the bandwidth that a frame relay network commits to carry for a given connection. CIR is defined as Bc measured over a given time period.

CLP   The Cell Loss Priority bit is located in the ATM cell header and indicates two levels of discard priority. CLP = 0 cells are higher priority than CLP = 1 cells. CLP = 1 cells may be discarded during periods of congestion to preserve the CLR of CLP = 0 cells.

CLR   The Cell Loss Ratio is a negotiated QoS parameter. The Cell Loss Ratio is defined for a connection as (lost cells)(total transmitted cells). The CLR parameter is the value of CLR that the network commits not to exceed as an objective measured over the lifetime of the connection. It is expressed as an order of magnitude, having a range of 10^{-1} to 10^{-15} and unspecified.

CMR   The Cell Misinsertion Rate is the ratio of cells received at an endpoint that were not originally transmitted by the source or were not destined for the endpoint in relation to the total number of cells properly transmitted.

CRC   The Cyclic Redundancy Check is a mathematical algorithm that computes a numerical value based on the bits in a block of data. This number is transmitted with the data, and the receiver uses this information with the same algorithm to verify the accurate delivery of data by comparing the results of the algorithm and the number received. If a mismatch occurs, an error in transmission is presumed.

CRM   The Missing RM-Cell Count (CRM) is an ABR parameter that limits the number of forward RM cells that may be sent in the absence of received backward RM cells.

CTD   The Cell Transfer Delay is defined as the time elapsed between the departure of a cell at a given point in the network and the arrival of the cell at another point in the network for a particular connection.

DBR   The Deterministic Bit Rate is an ITU-T ATM transfer capability that can correspond to the CBR or UBR service, depending on the QoS class.

D-GCRA   The Dynamic Generic Cell Rate Algorithm is used to define the conformance of ABR traffic, taking into account the network feedback and appropriate reaction delays.

DE   The Discard Eligibility bit is located in the header of a frame relay frame. It indicates the frame discard priority. Frames with DE = 0 have higher priority than frames with DE = 1. The network can discard frames with DE = 1 in order to maintain a low frame loss ratio for frames with DE = 0.

DIFF-SERV   The Differentiated Services is the terminology to describe the current QoS model in IP.

DIR   This is a field in the ABR RM cell that indicates the direction of the RM cell with respect to the data flow with which it is associated. The source sets DIR = 0 (forward RM cell) and the destination sets DIR = 1 (backward RM cell).

DS-3   Digital Signal, Level 3 is the North American Digital Hierarchy signaling standard for transmission at 44.736 Mbps that is used by T3 carrier. The DS-3 supports 28 DS-1s plus overhead.

EBW   An Effective BandWidth is the amount of bandwidth allocated by the connection admission control (CAC) for a given connection.

EFCI   The Explicit Forward Congestion Indication is a bit in the ATM cell header. The EFCI bit can be set by a network element to indicate impending congestion. When used with the ABR service, the end-system uses this indication to adaptively lower the cell rate of the connection to prevent congestion from occuring.

EIR   The Excess Information Rate is the excess bandwidth that a frame relay network attempts to carry for a given connection. The EIR is defined as Be measured over a given time period.

EOM   The End of Message is an indicator used in the AAL that identifies the last ATM cell containing information from a data packet that has been segmented. Also referred to as End-of-Packet (EOP).

EOP   End-of-Packet. Refer to EOM.

EPD   Early Packet Discard is a congestion control method that discards complete AAL-5 packets.

ER   The Explicit Rate is a field in the ABR RM cell used to limit the source transmission rate to a specific value. It is initially set by the source to a requested rate (such as PCR).

It may be subsequently reduced by any network element in the path to a value that the element can sustain.

FCFS First-Come-First-Serve is the service discipline that serves the cells in the order of their arrival. This is also called First-In-First-Out (FIFO).

FECN The Forward Explicit Congestion Notification is a bit in the frame relay frame header to indicate that the frame has encountered impending congestion. This information can be used by proprietary protocols to implement flow control mechanisms.

F-GCRA The Frame-based Generic Cell Rate algorithm is used to evaluate service eligibility in the GFR service category.

FIFO First-In-First-Out service discipline. Refer to FCFS.

FR Frame Relay is a transfer protocol used for variable-length frame sizes.

FRM Cell Forward RM cell. Refer to RM cell.

FRTT The Fixed Round-Trip Time is an ABR parameter and represents the sum of the fixed and propagation delays from the source to the furthest destination and back.

FTP File Transfer Protocol is an application that generally runs over TCP or UDP and is designed to transfer files between two end stations.

GCRA The Generic Cell Rate Algorithm is used to define conformance with respect to the traffic contract of a connection. The GCRA defines conformance to either the PCR or a combination of the PCR and the SCR.

GFC The Generic Flow Control is a field in the ATM header that can be used to provide local flow control. It has local significance only and the value encoded in the field is not carried end to end.

GFR The Generic Frame Rate service category provides a bandwidth-on-demand service that treats the traffic at the AAL-5 frame level when evaluating service eligibility and applying congestion control actions. GFR offers a minimum guaranteed bandwidth.

GPS Generalized Processor Sharing is a scheduling technique that divides the link capacity in proportion to a given weight.

HOL Head-Of-Line blocking occurs in input-buffered ATM switches when multiple inputs have cells destined for a given output port and only one cell gets a chance, causing remaining cells to be blocked although these cells may have different destinations.

ICR The Initial Cell Rate is the cell rate a source starts sending when the source is up or after a long idle period.

IETF Internet Engineering Task Force: The organization that provides the coordination of standards and specification development for IP networking and related protocols.

IP The Internet Protocol is a connectionless switching protocol that allows for variable-size packets.

ITU-T International Telecommunications Union Telecommunications: ITU-T is an international body of member countries whose task is to define recommendations and standards relating to the international telecommunications industry. The fundamental standards for ATM have been defined and published by the ITU-T (previously CCITT).

IW An InterWorking unit generally converts traffic from one protocol to another (e.g., IP to ATM, FR to ATM).

LANs A Local Area Network is designed to interconnect computing devices over a restricted geographical area (usually a mile or so).

LCT The Last Conformance Time is used in the leaky bucket implementation of the GCRA to indicate the time at which the last conforming cell arrived.

Max-CDV The Maximum Cell Delay Variance is the absolute value of the maximum one-point CDV measured.

Max-CTD The Maximum Cell Transfer Delay is the $(1 - \alpha)$ quantile of the CTD that could be experienced by any delivered cell on a connection during the entire connection holding time. The parameter α is the probability of a cell arriving late.

MBS The Maximum Burst Size indicates the number of cells that can be sent at PCR before having to conform to the SCR.

MCR The Minimum Cell Rate is a service traffic descriptor, in cells/sec, that is the rate at which the source is always allowed to send. The MCR is defined for ABR and GFR. It can also be understood as a QoS parameter, it represents the minimum bandwidth the network commits to maintain for a connection.

MFS The Maximum Frame Size is part of the GFR traffic contract and defines the maximum allowed frame size. Frames longer than MFS are considered non-conforming.

Mrm The Minimum RM cells is an ABR service parameter that controls allocation of bandwidth between forward RM cells, backward RM cells, and data cells.

NI The No-increase Indicator is a field in an ABR RM cell used to cause the source not to increase its ACR. The congested node sets the NI bit in the BRM cell and the EFCI bit in the FRM cell.

NNI The Network-to-Network Interface is a generic interface between two networks.

NPC The Network Parameter Control refers to the set of actions taken by the network to monitor and control traffic from the NNI. Its main purpose is to protect network resources from malicious as well as unintentional misbehavior that can affect the QoS of other already established connections by detecting violations of negotiated parameters and taking appropriate actions.

Nrm The Number of data cell per RM cell is an ABR service parameter. The Nrm is the maximum number of cells a source may send for each forward RM cell.

nrt-VBR Non-Real-Time Variable-Bit Rate is a service category that allows statistical multiplexing gains using the traffic descriptors (PCR and SCR). The nrt-VBR does not provide delay commitments.

OAM Operations Administration and Maintenance refers to a group of network management functions that provide network fault indication, performance information, and data and diagnosis functions.

P2P-CDV The Peak-to-Peak CDV is a QoS delay parameter associated with CBR and real-time VBR services. The peak-to-peak CDV is the ($(1 - \alpha)$ quantile of the CTD) minus the fixed CTD that could be experienced by any delivered cell on a connection during the entire connection holding time. The parameter α is the probability of a cell arriving late.

PCR The Peak Cell Rate is the cell rate that the source may never exceed (cells/sec). That is, the time between two consecutive cells cannot be smaller than 1/PCR.

PDU   A Protocol Data Unit is a message of a given protocol comprising payload and protocol-specific control information, typically contained in a header. The PDUs pass over the protocol interfaces that exist between the layers of protocols (per OSI model).

PNNI The Private Network-Network Interface includes routing information protocol that enables extremely scalable, full-function, dynamic multivendor ATM switches to be integrated in the same network.

POTS Plain Ordinary Telephone System.

PPD   Partial Packet Discard is a congestion control method that discards the remainder of AAL-5 packets once a cell of the packet is discarded. The last cell of the packet is kept to allow delineation with the next packet. Also referred to as tail dropping (TD).

PS   Processor Sharing is the bandwidth allocation approach that divides the link capacity equally among the contending connections.

PT   The Payload Type is a three-bit field in the ATM cell header that discriminates between a cell carrying management information and one carrying user information.

PTI   The Payload Type Indicator is the value of the payload type field distinguishing the various management cells and user cells. Example: Resource management cell has PTI = 110; end-to-end OAM F5 Flow cell has PTI = 101.

PVC   A Permanent Virtual-Channel connection is an ATM connection where switching is performed on the VPI/VCI fields of each cell. A permanent VCC is one that is provisioned through some network management function and left up indefinitely.

PVP   A Permanent Virtual Path connection is an ATM connection where switching is performed on the VPI field only of each cell. A permanent VPC is one that is provisioned through some network management function and left up indefinitely.

QoS   Quality of Service is defined for each connection on an end-to-end basis in terms of the following attributes of the end-to-end ATM connection: cell loss ratio, maximum cell transfer delay, and peak-to-peak cell delay variation.

RDF   The Rate Decrease Factor is an ABR service parameter; RDF controls the decrease in the cell transmission rate and is a power of 2 from 1/32,768 to 1.

RED Random Early Discard is a congestion control method that randomly discards complete AAL-5 packets. The probability of discarding a packet increases as a function of the queue occupancy or loading.

REM Rate Envelope Multiplexing is a connection admission method that admits connections such that total aggregate arrival rate (rate envelope) is less than the link capacity.

RIF The Rate Increase Factor is an ABR service parameter that controls the amount by which the cell transmission rate may increase upon receipt of an RM cell. The additive increase rate AIR = PCR $\times$ RIF. RIF is a power of 2, ranging from 1/32768 to 1.

RM cell A Resource Management cell is used by different flow control protocols (e.g., ABR and ABT) to carry control information across nodes and networks. The RM cells in the forward direction of an ABR loop are referred to as FRM cells, and the RM cells in the backward direction are referred to as BRM cells.

RR Round-Robin is the scheme that serves a set of queues one after another in a round-robin fashion.

RS Rate Sharing is the connection admission method that assumes sufficient buffer is available at a contention point to absorb momentary rate mismatch between the arrivals and the service.

rt-VBR Real-Time Variable Bit Rate is a service category that allows statistical multiplexing gains using the traffic descriptors (PCR and SCR). The rt-VBR service provides delay commitments.

RTT The Round-Trip Time represents the sum of all the delays encountered by a cell from the source to the destination and back.

SBR The Statistical Bit Rate is an ITU-T ATM transfer capability that corresponds to the VBR service category.

SCR The Sustained Cell Rate is the average cell rate of the source measured over a never-exceed (cells/sec). The relationship between the SCR, MBS, and PCR parameters is defined by the GCRA algorithm.

SECBR The Severely Errored Cell Block Ratio: The SECB occurs when more than M errored cells, lost cells, or misinserted cell are observed in a received block of cells. The Ratio is the number of Severely Errored Cell Blocks over the total transmitted blocks.

SVC   A Switched Virtual Circuit is a connection established via the ATM signaling protocol.

TAT   The Theoretical Arrival Time is the earliest time at which a nonjittered cell can arrive in order to conform to a contracted rate. This parameter is used by the virtual scheduling implementation of the GCRA.

TBE   The Transient Buffer Exposure is a negotiated ABR parameter. It represents the number of cells that the network would like to limit the source to sending during startup periods, before the first RM cell returns.

TCP   The Transmission Control Protocol is a protocol that provides end-to-end, connection-oriented, reliable-transport-layer (OSI layer 4) functions over IP-based networks. TCP performs flow control between two end systems through acknowledgments of packets received.

TCR   The Tagged Cell Rate is an ABR service parameter that limits the rate at which a source may send out-of-rate forward RM cells. The TCR is a constant fixed at 10 cells/second.

TD   Tail Dropping. Refer to PPD.

TDF   The Timeout Decrease Factor is an ABR service parameter that controls the decrease in ACR associated with TOF. The TDF is signaled as TDFF, where TDF = TDFF/RDF times the smallest power of 2 greater than or equal to PCR. The TDF is in units of 1/seconds.

TDFF   Refer to TDF. The TDFF is either zero or a power of two in the range 1/64 to 1 in units of 1/cells.

TDM   Time Division Multiplexing is a method by which a transmission facility is multiplexed among a number of channels by allocating the facility to the channels on the basis of time slots.

TM   Traffic Management is the set of functions required to manage the quality-of-service of connections.

TS   Traffic Shaping is the scheduling function at a queue; it outputs the cells as per the connection's traffic conformance definition.

UBR   Unspecified Bit Rate is a service category that does not provide any commitments in terms of quality of service.

UDP   User Datagram Protocol generally uses IP as the underlying protocol. The UDP allows applications to send messages or files to other applications with minimum protocol mechanism (e.g., no flow control). The protocol is transaction oriented (as opposed to connection oriented), and delivery or protection against duplicate packets is not guaranteed to the application.

UNI   The User-to-Network Interface is the interface between a user or private network and a public network.

UPC   The UPC function refers to implementation of the GCRA algorithm or an equivalent at the UNI in order to police the traffic and ensure conformance.

VBR   Variable Bit Rate is a service category that allows statistical multiplexing gains, using the traffic descriptors (PCR and SCR). The VBR service can provide real-time commitment (rt-VBR) or not (nrt-VBR).

VC   Virtual Channel connection extends between the points where the ATM service users access the ATM layer. The points at which the ATM cell payload is passed to, or received from, the users of the ATM layer (i.e., a higher layer or ATM entity) for processing to signify the endpoints of a VC. VCs are unidirectional.

VCI   A Virtual Channel Identifier is a unique numerical tag as defined by a 16-bit field in the ATM cell header that identifies a virtual channel over which the cell is to travel.

VD   A Virtual Destination replicates the behavior of an ABR destination endpoint. Forward RM cells received by a virtual destination are turned around and not forwarded to the next segment of the connection. Virtual Destinations can be located at any point in the network.

VP   Virtual Path: A unidirectional logical association or bundle of VCs.

VPI   Virtual Path Identifier: An eight-bit field in the ATM cell header that indicates the virtual path over which the cell should be routed.

VS   A Virtual Source implements the behavior of an ABR source endpoint. Backwards RM-cells received by a virtual source are removed from the connection.

VS/VD   Virtual Source/Virtual Destination: An ABR connection may be divided into two or more separately controlled ABR segments. Each ABR control segment, except the first, is sourced by a virtual source (VS). Each ABR control segment, except the last, is terminated by a virtual destination (VD).

WAN A Wide Area Network spans a large geographic area relative to the office and campus environments of LAN (Local Area Network). The WAN is characterized by having much greater transfer delays due to laws of physics.

WFQ Weighted Fair Queueing is the general scheduling technique for serving queues using time-stamps. The flows are assigned a time-stamp as per a fictitious fluid-flow. The time-stamp is determined from the weight of the connection. The flows are then served in the increasing order of the time-stamps.

WRR Weighted Round-Robin is a scheduling scheme that serves a set of queues in round-robin fashion and in proportion to the weights set on each queue.

WWW The World Wide Web refers to the interconnection of computers and servers across the world.

A

AAL-5 frames, discarding, in congestion control, 173–77

ABT transfer capability, 215–16

Additive property, 70

Asynchronous Transfer Mode (ATM)
adaptation layer, 6
basic principles, 6–9
cell header, 6–7
internetwork interface, 8
managing Frame Relay traffic on, 180–90
managing Internet Protocol traffic on, 191–99
selecting service categories, 182–83, 194–99
switch architectures, 86–91

Asynchronous Transfer Mode Forum Traffic Management working group, 3–4, 211, 213

Asynchronous Transfer Mode traffic management
challenges, 1–9
components of, 4–6
evolution of, 212
standardization of, 3–4

Available bit rate (ABR), 14
binary, 218–24
cell conformance for, 46–47
conformance definition, 36
connection admission control for traffic, 76–77
explicit rate, 224–28
Frame Relay (FR) over, 187
Internet Protocol over, 196, 198–99
policing connections, 50
shaping, 56–57
using virtual paths to carry non-real time virtual connections, 206–8

Available bit rate (ABR) flow control, 122–63, 215
accelerating BRM information, 152–534
available bit rate services, 122–26
binary mode available bit rate, 134–36
control loop parameters, 124–25
control loop performance metrics, 126–29
destination behavior, 131

efficiency, 128–29
fairness, 127–28
robustness, 129
source behavior, 130
stability, 129

engineering available bit rate parameters, 156–62

explicit rate mode available bit rate, 136–52
bandwidth-sharing strategy, 142–43
bandwidth tracking, 149
congestion bias algorithm, 148–49
detailed rate accounting, 150–51
explicit-rate algorithms, 147–48
fair share policy, 140–41
generic types of ER algorithms, 144–47
system measurements, 139–40

point to multipoint available bit rate, 155–56

resource management cell format, 125

switch behavior, 133

virtual source and destination behavior, 130–33

virtual source and destination (VS/VD) coupling, 154–55

B

Backpressure, 87

Backward marking of the CI bit, 221–22

Bandwidth-on-demand services, 12, 15

Bandwidth redistribution, 142–43

Bandwidth-sharing strategy, 142–43

Bandwidth tracking, 149

Bandwidth conservation, 142

Beat-down phenomenon, 134–35

Best-effort network, 1

Binary available bit rate (ABR), 218–24

Binary mode, 123

Binary mode available bit rate (ABR), 134–36

BRM information, accelerating, 152–53

Broadband intercarrier interface (BICI), 8

Bufferless approximation, 67

Buffer partitioning in congestion control, 166, 167–70